# THE HISTORY OF
# ARCHITECTURE
## ICONIC BUILDINGS THROUGHOUT THE AGES

## GAYNOR AALTONEN

ARCTURUS

*With great thanks to Graham Vickers and William Aaltonen for their support and advice,*
*and to all at Arcturus, especially Nigel Matheson, Peter Ridley, Anya Martin and Tilly Sklair.*

ARCTURUS

This edition published in 2014 by Arcturus Publishing Limited
26/27 Bickels Yard, 151–153 Bermondsey Street,
London SE1 3HA

Editor: Nigel Matheson
Designer: Zoë Mellors
Cover design: Peter Ridley

ISBN: 978-1-78404-185-4
AD000244UK

Printed in China

# CONTENTS

# THE STORY BEGINS

Step back nearly 4,700 years. The very first architect we know by name was the ancient Egyptian priest Imhotep, who built a vast monumental pyramid for his pharaoh king, Djoser. At a stroke, the inspired and cultured Imhotep had created the profession of architect. In his own lifetime this extraordinary man was revered as a god, so it's somehow typical that our shock-horror culture transformed him into the worst of stage villains. In the 1999 film *The Mummy*, the priest-demon Imhotep isn't just scary – he's a psychopathic killer. Our modern culture turned someone who was arguably the most important architect in history – the man who invented the whole idea of building to last and of 'statement' architecture – into a freak show sorcerer. And one whose body is slowly decomposing, to boot.

This is no accident. Until very recently, architects were seen as Public Enemy Number One: elitist, remote and rich. The real horror movie was taking place out on the world's streets: everywhere was covered with samey concrete towers and faceless office blocks, totally devoid of imagination.

Paradoxically, given architecture's elitist reputation, a British prince would be the first to ride to war to defend 'ordinary' people. Prince Charles opened his famous attack on modern British architecture by denouncing a proposed extension to the National Gallery as 'a monstrous carbuncle'. 'For far too long,' he argued, champagne glass in hand, 'planners and architects have consistently ignored the feelings of the mass of ordinary people.'

In some ways he was right. The dominance of the road, along with the coming of large urban shopping centres, has been a disaster for cities, a disaster for architecture. Cities became monotonous; faceless. Yet this was not entirely the fault of architects. The majority of the flat-faced, featureless blocks that increasingly squat across the urban landscape are 'design-and-build' projects. A developer puts up a steel frame. Flat panels are fixed on, and there: you have a bland building, put up in the space of a month or so. This is 'nothing' architecture and it has very little to do with architects.

In reality, by the time Prince Charles sent forth his arrows, real architects were already rejecting the straitjacket of 'Brutalist' Modernism: the Lloyd's Building showed the

**ABOVE** The mosque of Sultan Hassan, Cairo, 1356–1363. This example of early Marmluk architecture is laid out according to a classical cruciform plan

way. What the prince had done, though, was valuable. He reminded us all that architecture should be *about* something. And that the 'something' involved real people.

Architecture, real architecture, is not just the art of making places function. It affects our moods, our feelings and our way of looking at the world. On an often unconscious level, buildings speak to us. They tell us volumes about our society and its aspirations, as well as its past. Like a story or a piece of music, great architecture can take us on a journey, influencing our moods along the way.

This book takes the form of a story, a personal journey during which I will try to demystify this sometimes complicated subject. Why would a country invent an architect who didn't really exist? What does 'Palladian' mean? Who was 'Le Corbusier', and why does

he matter? Where do minarets come from? You will find the answers to all of these questions, and many more besides, in the following pages.

Like studying music or literature, 'reading' architecture is a reward in its own right. The more you understand, the more you enjoy. Most of all, at a time when architecture has become vital, exciting and – finally – approachable, this book tries to shed a little light on the great, heroic human struggle to create not just built space, but beautiful buildings.

## Why Does Architecture Matter and What Do Buildings Mean?

Architecture matters because it can unite or divide society. It is able to do that because it defines our values. Take the Palace of Westminster in Great Britain – it is a consciously class-ridden statement of history and tradition. The United States' Capitol, by contrast, symbolizes a kind of nascent democratic idealism by basing itself on a centuries-old foreign culture: that of Rome.

In New York, the 'city that never sleeps', the culture of turbocharged capitalism is

**ABOVE LEFT** Comfortable, relaxed and peculiarly English, Chartwell was home to one of Britain's greatest-ever leaders, Sir Winston Churchill. He and wife 'Clemmie' loved it with a passion

**LEFT** At ground level Raymond Hood's Rockefeller Center of 1929 has lots of loving Art Deco detail. Lee Lawrie's statue of Atlas looks out over 5th Avenue. The centre is famous for its sunken ice rink

**RIGHT** The cliff-dwelling Native Americans of Mesa Verde, Colorado built under the overhangs of the canyons. By AD1200 Cliff Palace had 150 rooms, 23 ritual chambers and elegant round defensive towers

documented in mind-boggling skyscrapers – and people like it that way. The much-loved Art Deco Rockefeller Center is one example among many. Built in the teeth of the Great Depression, it's both a monument to out-and-out individualism – a deification of Rockefeller, the self-made millionaire – and to the defiant, pioneer spirit that made America great.

Having given us a sense of cultural identity, architecture then goes on to condition how we behave. As the wartime leader Sir Winston Churchill said: 'We shape our buildings; thereafter, they shape us.'

As a lonely young boy, Churchill grew up in the grand and overbearing Blenheim Palace in Oxfordshire. One of Britain's few Baroque buildings – born out of misery, frustrated ambition and pride – Blenheim was not a happy place. Its vast formal rooms and echoing corridors couldn't have been more different from the straightforward simplicity of Churchill's later, married home.

The cheerful, red brick Chartwell is a far from conventional house for a seriously upper-class Englishman – it's far too lowly. But it makes sense that the mercurial

Churchill understood his own emotional need for quiet, classless normality.

Churchill spent hours, days and weeks here chasing away the 'black dog' of depression and looking out over the rolling Kent countryside. Chartwell healed him.

## Home is Where the Heart Is

This is the point: we bond with buildings. To some families, especially those lucky enough to be able to keep their houses over generations, their home is a companion, a friend and a memory bank: a diary over time.

The English have this disease-cum-compulsion particularly badly. Lady Cynthia Asquith wrote about Stanway, her family's Jacobean mansion in the Cotswolds: 'I loved my home precisely as one loves a human being; loved it as I have loved very few human beings.'

The search for the ideal home is a constant of human nature, although what we see as beautiful or desirable changes radically through time. The Anasazi Indians of Mesa Verde, Colorado built spectacular dwellings in the recesses of the canyon walls. In the Yemeni city of Shibam people used plain unadorned mud to create houses that chimed with the mountains behind (see p.247). Both civilizations were at one with their environment.

We've only got to look at each society's idea of the perfect home to be able to read social patterns through history. English manorial halls tell us about the basic need for armed protection in medieval society. The comfortable canal-side dwellings of the 18th century Dutch trading bourgeoisie are about combining comfort and convenience with a lifetime of on-the-spot barter. The ship-like clapboard homes of New England, settler communities that cared deeply about their class and lineage, are a poignant tale of social one-upmanship, each house fighting to be more 'English' than the next.

Tellingly, by the time we'd reached the health-conscious 20th century, pared-down Modernism rejected nature, just as it rejected history, utterly. It took the clean, calm hospital aesthetic of the Swiss sanatorium – straight lines, clean surfaces, no corners, no dirt, no memories – as its model for the domestic house. Once, the rich had been flamboyantly fat. Now, to be rich, you had to be thin. The rich, as ever, defined the architectural agenda. In an era when the ultimate measure of wealth

was the number of highly trained scientists/beauticians you had at your beck and call, their houses were anti-nature.

Later Modernists, such as the heroic Alvar Aalto, were to break this down gradually. The Finn Aalto adopted a more laid-back, romantic stance, advising his students to design windows as if the girls they loved were sitting in them.

Today, at the newly-built Mountain Dwellings in Copenhagen, the wheel has travelled full circle. The architects, BIG, return to the basic inspiration behind Shibam. If you have to have dense urban housing, why not make it look like a terraced mountain planted with vines?

## Scalping the Architect

As the designer of the Louvre Pyramid, I.M. Pei, once pointed out, architects suffer from a chronic case of 'shoot the messenger' syndrome. You can only build what someone pays you to build. Architects, in short, are only as powerful as their clients allow them to be.

In the past, dense, high-rise housing and the appallingly-named 'Brutalism' destroyed public trust in architecture. 'The Bull Ring (in Birmingham, UK) is perfectly all right – if you want an army fortification in the city centre,' complained one Conservative councillor.

**BELOW** Ziggurats. William Pereira is best known for the later Transamerica Building, but his 'Brutalist' Geisel Library for the University of San Diego was aesthetically groundbreaking

**RIGHT** Making up for past mistakes: it's 2003 and technology has marched on. A cathedral for a nation of retail worshippers, Birmingham's Bull Ring is now wrapped in a sinuous dress decorated with 15,000 spun aluminium discs

The narrow functionalism of many Modernists also created a dangerous void between architects and society, an attitude of 'them' versus 'us'. People hated not having any say in the quality, or otherwise, of the often dreadful civic buildings being thrown up around them. The cartoon historicism of Postmodernism seemed empty, an insult, while the public was still dealing with crushing and dispiriting places like Portsmouth's much-loathed Tricorn Centre in southern England.

Now the Tricorn is demolished and architecture is everybody's best friend. We've understood that the old doesn't have to be swept away for the relentlessly 'new'. In this new mood, a Giles Gilbert Scott power station – a temple to energy – can be successfully transformed into a shrine to art, the Tate Modern. This is an era where we are all cheering on the experiment, and even Brutalist buildings seem less oppressive. The sci-fi looks of the Geisel Library at the University of California, San Diego now seem friendly, rather than threatening (see p.11). Named after the children's author Theodor Seuss Geisel (Dr Seuss), William Pereira's building is more *ET* than *Alien*.

Even in conservative Britain, campaigning figures like Richard Rogers have challenged lacklustre bureaucratic taste by trying to get government to see the point of urban planning. Time and again, we find that hospital design itself can cure us, that schools can be exciting, that a street can be designed to be welcoming and safe. No-one wants to

**ABOVE** Architecture has traditionally focused on geometry when it comes to planning structures: circles, half circles, rectangles and squares. The lounge at Abu Dhabi airport mixes decorative hexagonal shapes with a circular raised walkway

**ABOVE RIGHT** Georgian symmetry: Bath's famed Royal Crescent as seen from the air; a grand semi-circle amidst a sea of green

**RIGHT** Zaha Hadid's computer-rendered design for a new Performing Arts Centre in Abu Dhabi that looks out over the Persian Gulf

face the charge of creating 'carbuncles' while cities from Abu Dhabi to Taipei are vying for some of the stardust that sticks to exciting new architecture.

They know what we all know: that certain buildings, great buildings, share something. They have heart. At its best, architecture can be bold and noble, inspiring and uplifting. At

one end of the spectrum you get the precise, Enlightenment rationalism of the Royal Crescent in Bath. At the other you find the free expression of Frank Gehry's Guggenheim Bilbao (see p.241). Somehow these buildings reach across the centuries. They feel 'right'. Far from turning in his grave, Imhotep would have been proud.

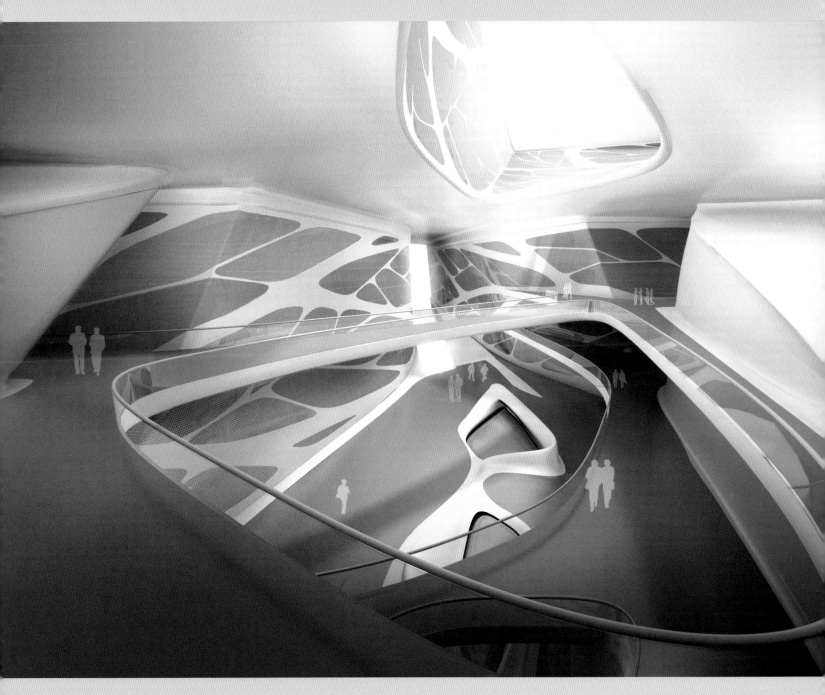

**ABOVE** Hadid's interior is reminiscent of the cell structures of a leaf, or of a bone. But is it functional?

**Author's note:** *Even in a book of this size it is not possible to discuss every intriguing building in every age. We have concentrated on Europe in the main, barely touching on the extraordinary architecture of Japan, China or India. Stories were* *included only if they fitted into the general narrative. For instance, two greats who fall on the cusp of the Victorian and Edwardian ages, Edwin Lutyens and Norman Shaw are mentioned, but not in the great detail they deserve. For those who find that they want to get more of the 'story', there is a short bibliography at the back of the book. Look out in particular for Leland M. Roth, whose book* *Understanding Architecture is detailed and scholarly, but direct. I would also recommend anyone who wants to take their interest in buildings further to search out the work of the sniffy but always incisive Nikolaus Pevsner, who founded what is probably the most informative series of guides ever written on this demanding and inexhaustible subject.*

# THE ANCIENTS

Stone exerts a strange hold over the human imagination. Man must have a primal need to build artificial mountains; monuments that take him closer to the heavens. Entire communities devoted great ingenuity and effort to the building of the highly sophisticated pyramids of Egypt, the ziggurats of Mexico and Peru, and the strange megalithic constructions in Neolithic Europe, dragging and levering mysterious pieces of stone into special sites of mystical significance we no longer fully understand. There are no towers or defences in abandoned Teotihuacan, once a major religious centre. But sacrifice, both animal and human, took place in front of thousands of spectators.

The magnificent ziggurats of Teotihuacan, Mexico. Here we see the Avenue of the Dead from the Pyramid of the Moon, scene of live burials. The Pyramid of the Sun, AD100, looms in the background

# THE FIRST CITY DWELLERS

The northern end of the Great Rift Valley was home to two of the world's earliest settlements. Jericho existed as early as 9000BC and 'Ain Ghazal dates back to around 7500BC.

The citizens of Jericho built a fortified wall around the city as early as 8000BC and the small settlement gradually evolved into a town covering ten acres. Most of the houses excavated at Jericho consist of a single room, but a few have as many as three, suggesting that social and economic distinctions – keeping up with the Jones's – were already a feature of communal life. And the builders of Jericho had a new technology – bricks, shaped from mud and baked hard in the sun. Houses were circular, so each brick was curved on its outer edge. 'Ain Ghazal, near Amman, covered a 30-acre site and was advanced enough to create works of art and use its own form of money.

One of the first (c.7500BC) and best preserved Neolithic settlements, Çatal Hüyük, in southern Turkey, was also built from mud bricks. Here came the first move towards straight walls. Rectangular houses with windows but no doors adjoin, like cells in a honeycomb, and the inhabitants entered through the roof.

But the world's first recognizably fully developed civilizations emerged in Mesopotamia and Egypt. The two regions share two natural resources ideal for creating relatively small buildings in a warm climate: reeds and mud. Reeds can be shaped, bound together and stiffened with mud to form pillars and beams. Their tops can even be bent inwards and tied to form a flexible arch or a dome. And the spaces in the frame can be filled with smaller branches and mud, to complete a weather-proof shelter.

As cities developed and wealth grew, so did the citizens' need to defend their way of life. Gradually, societies began to have leaders who built fortifications and palaces. However, the two most important impulses driving architecture were those fundamentals in human nature: the desire to inspire and the urge to defeat death. The most exciting early building forms are temples and tombs.

In this, the ancient Egyptians, with their deification of the dead, were the first real pioneers. Their architecture, driven by their worship of the divine, towered above that of others. The remains at Sakkara (Saqqara), some of which date to at least 3250BC, suggest that this North African civilization was building sophisticated temple complexes 1,000 years before the construction of the famous Ziggurat at Ur and 750 years before the ancient Britons dragged the first stones to Stonehenge. This leaves civilizations like those of Mycenae and the Persian city of Persepolis looking like relative newcomers.

**LEFT** Nine thousand years ago, a visitor to Çatal Hüyük would have seen hundreds of stacked mud-brick dwellings rising out of the marshy Konya Plain, a settlement of several thousand people. Visitors today see a reconstruction

**RIGHT** The ancient city of Jericho is about 2km from the modern one. In the Bible, the fleeing Israelites destroyed the ancient city, whose walls came tumbling down

# Key Dates

**8000BC** Wall built at Jericho.

**8000BC** Çatal Hüyük settlement in Turkey: multi-level dwellings.

**7250BC** 'Ain Ghazal, Jordan.

**4000BC** Walled city of Hamoukar. City of Ur founded; Chinese start using silk.

**3800BC** Civilization in Malta.

**3300–1000BC** The Minoan and Mycenaean civilizations rise and fall.

**3,200BC** Karnak, Thebes (Luxor).

**3,200–2,200BC** The Orkney Islands village of Skara Brae is established.

**3,200–1,600BC** Pakistan's Indus Valley has city-wide plumbing.

**3100BC** Menes, the first pharaoh of Egypt, rules upper Egypt.

**3100BC** Cuneiform writing emerges in Mesopotamia.

**3000BC** 'Bison Hunter' villages around Middle Lake in California.

**3000BC** Minoans trade with Egypt.

**2950BC** Stonehenge ditch is dug.

**2850BC** Writing on papyrus.

**2668–49BC** Djoser (Dzoser, Zoser), the 2nd ruler of Egypt's 3rd Dynasty.

**2400BC** Large stones are erected at Stonehenge.

**2348BC** Nov 25: Biblical scholars assert this was the day of the Great Flood.

**2300BC** Mesopotamian maps.

**2100BC** Stonehenge 'Bluestones' are erected.

**2013BC** Sumerians built the Ziggurat at Ur (later in Iraq) to draw attention to the god of the moon.

**2000BC** The largest prehistoric mound in Europe, the 130ft (41m) Silbury Hill, near Avebury.

**c.2000BC** The Egyptians domesticate the cat.

**2000–1000BC** Early preclassic period of the Maya.

**1750–1540BC** The Hyksos from Syria and Palestine occupy Egypt using a *blitzkrieg* weapon: the horse and chariot.

**1595BC** Babylon sacked by Hittites.

**1570–1070BC** Egypt's New Kingdom Period. Thebes is the chief city and Pharaohs began to abandon pyramids in favour of hidden tombs in Thebes' Valley of the Kings.

**c.1500BC** A ball court is built in Chiapas, Mexico.

**1340BC** Akhnaton founds new Egyptian capital.

**1300BC** Treasury of Atreus, tomb of Agamemnon is built, Beehive tomb (no arch).

**900BC** Homer writes *Iliad* and *Odyssey*.

**800–700BC** The first hill forts of Britain.

**700–500BC** Ironworking becomes widespread.

**200BC** Earliest buildings, Teotihuacan, Mexico.

**54BC** Julius Caesar launches a full-scale invasion of Britain.

# EGYPT

Ancient Egypt stands very much on its own in the history of architecture. The pyramids, rock tombs and temples of this extraordinary culture were the world's earliest buildings in dressed stone, enriched with faïence, gold inlay and painted stucco.

**H**undreds of Egypt's ancient buildings have survived in exceptional condition. Because the poorer citizens lived in homes made of more perishable mud brick and wood, only the stone monuments, funerary palaces and temples of the elite have survived: but many of these structures are breathtaking. Ancient Egyptian society was both unified and largely at peace with the outside world: a situation enjoyed by few other societies before or since. This harmony was based on the annual cycle of the River Nile's fertility, to which the pharaoh's perceived divinity was inexorably linked. Architecture was the key element in expressing the Egyptians' unparalleled unity of purpose and belief.

Almost everything we can still see today celebrated the life, death and supposed immortality of the pharaohs. Death, and the life the Egyptians believed followed after death, was held in the highest fascination. For a period of more than 3,000 years, from c.3150BC until the Roman occupation of AD31, this fascination fuelled a complex and compelling religious and artistic culture.

At death, the ancient Egyptians believed that the deceased person's heart would be weighed in the balance against the feather of Ma'at, the goddess of truth and justice. If the heart tipped the scales the wrong way then Ammit (or Ammut), the ferocious crocodile-headed monster god, devoured it. This meant eternal oblivion. If the heart was judged pure, then the person began a new life, much like the one that had come to an end. To make sure this could happen, the body and heart of important or rich individuals were mummified to preserve them, placed inside one or more sarcophagi and then sealed in a tomb. Tools, personal possessions and all manner of things that might help in the dead person's new life were placed with the body.

When it came to the pharaohs, the most important people of all in a ferociously hierarchical society, there was no question of oblivion. Egypt's rulers were considered god-kings, at once earthly and divine. The preservation of their earthly form was therefore essential, not just for their own immortal being but for the continued wellbeing of life on earth.

To make sure the mummies and the grave goods placed in them survived, the Egyptians built increasingly large and elaborate tombs. These began in the Old Kingdom

**BELOW** The enigmatic Sphinx, with the body of a lion and human head, faces East, towards the rising sun. Carved out of a single piece of stone weighing hundreds of tons, it is over 200 feet long (60m), about the length of an entire city block

(c.2650BC–c.2158BC) as *mastabas* – ugly, low structures no more than a few metres high. Early examples were made of wood and mud bricks strengthened with reeds. The biggest problem for the ancient Egyptians was tomb robbery, which was rife, and which often appears to have been carried out by the very people entrusted to seal the tomb and keep its location and means of access a secret. Jackals – in both animal and human form – made short work of robbing the early *mastabas*.

In an effort to thwart this, the *mastabas* grew in strength, complexity and size. Often, they were built over subterranean tombs or chambers constructed beforehand. The *mastaba's* development into the true pyramid is arguably the work of an architectural genius – the world's first recorded architect, Imhotep.

Shortly after his accession, the Third Dynasty king Djoser commissioned Imhotep to build a new, more impressive and hopefully impregnable tomb at Sakkara, the cemetery of ancient Memphis. The Old Kingdom capital of ancient Egypt is near modern-day Cairo.

Imhotep did not fail him. Using fine limestone instead of mud brick, he first built a 90-foot-deep (28 metres) complex of royal tomb chambers and then placed a *mastaba* over the underground structure. The tomb could now only be reached through a vertical shaft, which was then sealed with a three-ton granite block. Some of the tomb's subterranean corridors and chambers are faced with blue tiles – perhaps because in ancient Egypt, as now, many believed the colour blue had the power to ward off evil spirits. A number of walls were covered in etched or painted scenes of daily life and ritual spells.

Here, in the desert, rise the first ashlar walls known to man, the earliest columns topped with a capital. Here is where formal architecture – a building that stands for something other than pure practicality – begins. What also makes Djoser's *mastaba* so important is its six-tier, stepped stone construction. Most scholars think Imhotep built a two-tier structure to begin with: the second, smaller tier made of stone blocks piled on top of the first might have been added later, as a tomb for a member of Djoser's family. Four more tiers were eventually added, each smaller than the last, creating the recognizably pyramidal structure – the Step Pyramid – that still survives.

As well as helping protect the contents of the different layers, these steps were a metaphor in stone: a stairway to heaven for the king. Certain spells in *The Book of the Dead* – that huge collection of magical formulae and lore that informed ancient Egyptian life, afterlife and mortuary practice – make this clear.

Until this point, nearly all *mastabas* had been rectangular. Imhotep built to a square plan. The Djoser family remains and possessions were safe inside for posterity – or so they believed – and the art of pyramid building was born.

The Fourth Dynasty (2575–2467BC) architects who built the three pyramids of Chepren, Mykerinos and Cheops (or Khufu), at Giza near Cairo picked up Imhotep's ideas and ran with them. Much bigger and of much finer construction, these were true, flat-sided monumental pyramids of the type that still wows us today. These three pyramids and others like them were dazzling: they were faced in polished limestone and capped with

## Stone flowers

Djoser's mortuary complex holds the first stone capital in the world. It is shaped like a papyrus flower. Later column capitals were carved and painted to look like lotus flowers, palm leaves and papyrus buds. Although the lotus was the emblem of Upper Egypt, and the papyrus that of Lower Egypt, the symbolism of these flower motifs runs deep. The papyrus, with its sweeping flower umbels, was associated with the River Nile and therefore became the symbol of fertility and life itself. The lotus flower, a form of water lily, opens in the morning and closes again at night. The ancient Egyptians saw in it an image of rebirth and regeneration. The young boy Atum, who shed the first tears from which all mankind emerged, had been born from the head of a lotus flower.

**LEFT** Columns at Beni Hasan (see left) prefigure those of the ancient Greeks, as does the idea of a portico. The ceiling is patterned with painted reeds; the walls feature scenes of wrestling and dancing. At Beni Hasan, columns of earlier tombs (see below) are topped with a lotus bud, an ancient motif. A series of 39 tombs is spread across the cliffs here

River Nile from Aswan and Tura, the stone was most likely not, as once thought, moved into position by gangs of slaves, but by willing workers employed in the summer season when they could not farm. These later pyramid-builders were astonishing master masons: the block walls and ceilings of the burial chambers are cut and fitted so exactly that even today it is not possible to slip a piece of paper edgewise between them.

The first subterranean burial chamber intended as Cheops' tomb was abandoned in favour of one that was placed at the heart of the pyramid. Some 35 feet (10.5 metres) by 18 feet (5.5 metres) in plan, the chamber is 20 feet (6 metres) high. Worried about the immense weight of stone bearing down on its roof, the pyramid-builders laid five layers of massive stone slabs across it, with nine slabs in each layer – a total of 400 tons. Above this, they constructed a basic A-shaped relieving arch to deflect some of the weight. The idea was that if the arch gave way the stone slab layers would save the king and his tomb from destruction.

A secret passageway started from a nearby satellite temple complex. It ran up into the pyramid, along a section that had originally led to the subterranean tomb, then back up and on into the spectacular ceremonial space known as the Grand Gallery. Just over 7 feet (2 metres) wide at floor level, this inclined gallery was around 160 feet (48 metres) long, narrowing in stepped corbelling to a ceiling roughly half the width of the base. It was meant to be accessed only once, when the king was immured in his sepulchre. Once this was done, a gargantuan stone portcullis weighing more than 50 tons was lowered to block the entrance, possibly by letting sand out of pre-positioned bags.

All this had been done to keep the royal tombs secure, but thwarting the tomb robbers wasn't the only thing the pyramid-builders cared about. Some of the shafts that pierced the structure might have been aligned with individual stars or constellations in the night sky. Many believe that the northern shaft of the red granite King's Chamber points to the

gold. The gold and the limestone facings have long since been stolen – the limestone was used in the construction of medieval Cairo. Like Imhotep's prototype, the majority of these later pyramids were built over subterranean tombs excavated beforehand. Most of the larger ones have cunning systems of access shafts, with blind corridors designed to confuse robbers.

Few of the subterfuges worked: in case after case, thieves stripped the pyramid tombs of

their valuables, often within weeks of the burial.

The Great Pyramid of Cheops is the largest of the Giza pyramids. It was also named one of the Seven Wonders of the Ancient World: the only one still standing. More than 480 feet (146 metres) high and with a base 756 feet (230.6 metres) square, the structure is truly massive. It took more than 2,300,000 blocks of limestone, each weighing an average of 2.5 tons, to build this monument to Cheops and his queen. Rafted down the

northern polar stars, while the southern King's Chamber shaft points directly to the position of Orion's Belt in the ancient sky. The theory is that these azimuth shafts helped the spirit of the dead pharaoh find its way among the stars.

The Giza pyramids mark the high water mark of pyramid building, which declined as the Old Kingdom fizzled out into economic and political decline.

Middle Kingdom (c.2134–c.1786BC) architects began constructing less ostentatious tombs in cliffs or hillsides, in an effort to preserve the pharaoh's treasures from thieves.

The best early examples of these are at Beni Hasan on the east bank of the Nile, 124 miles (200 km) south of Giza. Mostly constructed between c.2133–c.1786BC, in the Eleventh and Twelfth Dynasties, the 'grotto' or rock-cut tombs here had three elements: an outer colonnaded space for public worship; a shrine/effigy chamber behind that in the form of a columned hall; and a burial chamber, which was cut right back into the cliff.

Some of the 39 tombs have portico columns with bevelled circular uprights and square capitals, which bear a strong resemblance to the first known Greek Doric equivalents. For this reason, the Beni Hasan columns are known as 'Proto-Doric'. The internal columns in the hall take the form of lotus plants, with stone 'buds' serving as capitals to support the roof. These tombs have painted interior decorations which are justifiably famous for their vivid depictions of contemporary Egyptian life.

Despite all attempts to conceal them, almost none of the 'grotto' tombs known to modern archaeologists escaped robbery. The royal attendants, perhaps with the connivance of priests, tunnelled straight back into the carefully sealed chambers and stole everything, from gold to expensive cosmetics. The later pharaohs turned in desperation to 'shaft' tombs – the plain, usually linear complexes that were cut into the cliffs of the Valley of the Kings near Thebes (modern Luxor).

The most famous shaft tomb ever uncovered is that of the Eighteenth Dynasty boy king Tutankhamun, who ruled c.1333–c.1324BC. The English artist and archaeologist Howard Carter discovered it in 1922, after many hot and exhausting years of long, expensive and relatively fruitless exploration in the Valley of the Kings. The solid gold funeral mask, mummy, sarcophagi and lavish, jewelled artefacts found inside are uniquely important, but the shaft tombs themselves hold mainly decorative interest.

The next great step – or leap – in the cult worship of the pharaoh-god was the monumental temple. Some of these are astonishing, like the one built by Queen Hatshepsut (c.1508–1458BC) at the base of a cliff face at Deir el-Bahari. Hatshepsut was extraordinary. She was married off to her half-brother Tuthmosis II, who already had an heir by a prior liaison. When her husband died, Hatshepsut took power as regent: then, when the prince reached maturity, she refused to step down. Because tradition demanded a male ruler, Hatshepsut is often depicted dressed as a man, in some cases complete with a ceremonial beard.

Once in power, Hatshepsut was determined to leave her architectural mark. Using the temple of Mentuhotep II built some 500 years before as a model, she and her architect Senmut improved on the previous design. They also demolished most of it to re-use the stone. No one was less respectful of a pharaoh's built legacy than a later pharaoh.

Built in the 15th century BC, the temple is laid out in the form of three elegant flat-roofed terraced sanctuaries, built on an east–west axis at 90 degrees to the soaring cliff. The first sanctuary, reached through a great open rectangular walled courtyard, at once puts approaching worshippers in their place. Now, instead of merely wondering at a pyramid tomb, they have to make a worshipful progress towards the mysteries and shrines beyond. A long, steep ramp guarded by sphinxes leads them up to the next level, a two-storey terraced building whose upper storey, acknowledging the early *mastabas*, is smaller in plan than the lower. It can only be reached by a second ramp.

All three terraces have a double row of Proto-Doric supporting pillars surmounted by plain lintels and a cornice. The square columns wonderfully echo the vertical formations of the natural cliff: the whole complex is a brilliant dramatic use of the naturally majestic site. This exploitation of setting, along with the structure's size, openness and its finely calculated proportions, prefigures the great works of Classical Greece more than any other of ancient Egypt's remarkable buildings.

**LEFT** Dramatic but stately, Hatshepsut's colonnaded temple looks almost modernist. Djeser-Djeseru – 'the sublime of sublimes' – was the first building in the Valley of the Kings

# The First Architect?

Imhotep (2667–2648BC) was one of the most important architects who has ever lived and the first we know by name. He more or less invented monumental architecture. From humble origins, this mysterious figure rose to be Chief Architect and Grand Vizier of the Third Dynasty king Djoser (reigned c.2630–c.2611BC). He was also the first recorded engineer and the world's first known physician.

Djoser commissioned Imhotep to build him a royal tomb. Until then, early Old Kingdom tombs had been built in the form of *mastabas* – low, rectangular mounds of mud and reed brick, often grouped together like the squares of a chocolate bar. These *mastabas* were not only ugly and unimpressive, they were a useless defence against tomb robbery.

Imhotep's great genius was to realize that one *mastaba* could be built on top of the other, using stone instead of mud brick, with the tombs diminishing in size each time. In one imaginative leap he had created the world's first pyramid – the Step Pyramid of Sakkara. Not only did it look more impressive, it was also stronger, longer-lasting and more resistant to thieves.

Djoser was so pleased that he appointed Imhotep 'First after the King of Upper Egypt, Chancellor of the King of Lower Egypt, Administrator of the Great Palace, Hereditary Nobleman, The Great One of the Ibis, Builder, Chief Carpenter, Chief Sculptor and Maker of Vases in Chief'. Imhotep was later given the title 'High Priest of Heliopolis'. As a plain old architect, he may also have designed the Temple of Edfu. But Imhotep was much more than that. An accomplished physician, he was also a seer, a sorcerer, a priest, a writer and a philosopher.

About 100 years after his death, Imhotep was raised to the status of demigod. People prayed for his intercession in illness or injury. In 525BC, the doctor-architect became one of only a handful of mortals ever to be made a god.

Given his status as one of the world's first historical figures, archaeologists have spent many years searching for Imhotep's tomb. In 1962 the American Walter Emery thought he had found a clue – a trail of pottery fragments of the right date strewn across the desert near Sakkara. Emery believed that these shards had been left by pilgrims worshipping at Imhotep's tomb. Digging down, he discovered a burial shaft containing the bodies of sacrificial bulls – the sign of a senior official. From this he broke through into a series of underground galleries lined with mummified ibises packed in earthenware jars.

Emery remembered two things. Firstly, Imhotep had been known as 'The Great One of the Ibis'. Secondly, when Napoleon's expedition had tried to find Imhotep's tomb in the early 19th century, his archaeologists described finding 'The Tomb of Birds'.

To the astonishment of his colleagues, Emery brought in a bulldozer and used it to shove aside the tons of sand dumped on the site from adjacent digs. Then to his delight he uncovered more linked passages lined with mummified baboons, a symbol of wisdom and knowledge in ancient Egypt. Others followed, this time lined with mummified hawks.

Finally, Emery came upon a wooden box placed in a small niche. Inside was a piece of stone about eight inches (20cm) long. Inscribed on it, in ancient demotic text, were the words: 'Imhotep the Great. The Son of Ptah the Great God and other Gods Who Rest Here'. Had Emery found Imhotep's tomb? If so, there were no other goods to confirm it. Some fellow archaeologists were certainly unconvinced: the search for Imhotep's final resting place goes on.

**ABOVE** A thousand years before Karnak, Imhotep began monumental architecture with this Step Pyramid.

**RIGHT** Located on the west bank of the Nile, the Temple of Edfu was built in honour of the falcon god Horus over a 180-year period

# KARNAK

The New Kingdom temple of Karnak is near the modern town of Luxor, which in turn sits on the ruins of ancient Thebes. If Hatshepsut's temple was daunting, the scale and complexity of Karnak, begun c.1530BC, is almost overwhelming. Now, instead of crossing an open courtyard, the faithful had to negotiate a ceremonial trio of monumental stone pylons, or gateways.

T he first gateway is 50 feet (15 metres) thick at the base, 376 feet (114 metres) wide and almost 150 feet (45.5 metres) high. These pylons are 'battered', which means that they slope inwards from the ground up. Twin granite obelisks commemorating Tuthmosis I and Hatshepsut tower to either side, and the soaring, cliff-like façade leaves you in no doubt about the importance of what lies beyond. There, rising before you, is the prodigious Great Temple of Amun, probably the greatest temple in all Egypt.

Once through the third pylon via an initial courtyard and an associated hall, the worshipper continues through a narrower hall and on into a maze-like sanctuary that seems intentionally designed to disorientate. At the heart of the Great Temple is one of the world's great architectural masterpieces, Amun's Hypostyle Hall. This is a dense forest raised up in stone, whose mighty, close-packed trunks leave the modern-day visitor staring in wonder.

We can only guess at its effect on someone seeing it in all its glory for the first time. Two rows of matching 'papyrus' columns 69 feet (21 metres) in height and 12 feet (3.6 metres) in diameter provided the central support for the monolithic stone slab roof (now missing). Seven rows of smaller 'lotus' columns 42 feet (12.75 metres) high

## A good read

Elaborate low-relief carvings are crucial to the aesthetic appeal – and the mystery – of Egyptian structures. No other architecture tells us so much about the minutiae of lives long lost to the world. When in 1822 the extraordinary linguist Jean-François Champollion began to decipher the Rosetta Stone, the world could finally 'read' these buildings like a book.

and 9 feet (2.7 metres) thick flanked these central uprights, making 134 columns in all set in 16 parallel rows. The difference in height between the central columns and those supporting the sides created a clerestory that would have admitted a shadowy, suffused and mysterious light. Even without its roof, the space is still magnificent.

As if their sheer towering presence were not already enough to inspire shock and awe, the columns are densely incised with pictograms, hieroglyphs and symbols of all kinds. Originally, they were painted.

Next to the Great Temple of Amun was a sacred lake. To the west, but still inside the greater walled compound lay the much smaller Temple of Ptah, with the Temple of Khons, a medium-sized wonder in its own right, sited in the southwest corner. Khons is architecturally important in that it served as a template both for the overall Karnak complex that eventually engulfed it and later

**ABOVE** The Hypostyle Hall was begun by Seti I and completed by Ramesses II. Beautifully carved hieroglyphics and designs cover the columns in an area large enough to hold Notre Dame cathedral

New Kingdom temples of the same type.

Although it is sometimes called a necropolis, or city of the dead, Karnak was as much devoted to the daily worship of the living pharaoh as it was to his spiritual power after death. A vast army of priests, artists, artisans, scribes, scholars, labourers and slaves worked to this common goal.

In effect, these devotional sites were some of the world's first cities. It is the architecture's monumental scale as well as its sheer ambition that have captured the world's imagination. This temple has stood for three and a half millennia, an astounding achievement that has made Karnak a top tourist destination, and star of many films and even operas. Above all, Egyptian architects knew how to inspire a lasting sense of wonder.

# ZIGGURATS

The simple ziggurat or stepped pyramid at Ur, built to the moon god Nanna between 2250 and 2233BC, is the best preserved Sumerian monument. Ur was then the capital of an empire, and it was in Ur's Third Dynasty that the idea of a monumental ziggurat, like an artificial mountain, came along. Like the minarets of today, or the spires of the great medieval cathedrals, the ziggurat would have been seen by all around, a sign to the people that their priests were praying to their gods and interceding on their behalf. Made of baked brick reinforced with reeds and measuring 210 by 150 feet (64 by 46 metres) at its base, it rose to some 76 feet (23 metres) through a series of three massive staircases, each with 100 steps. All three staircases led to a staggered entrance between the first and second terraces. The Sumerians angled the walls at carefully judged heights to draw the eye upwards. They might have planned an even more exotic sight to greet the eye: the levels were perhaps planted with trees.

**BELOW** When the ziggurat was completed, King Shulgi declared himself a living god. He reigned for 48 years, a time when Ur (now in Iraq) flourished

**RIGHT** The ceremonial stairway of the Ziggurat at Ur, which was dedicated to the moon god and thought to be his dwelling place on Earth. The bedchamber of the god is said to have been at the top

The first civilizations of the Americas – the Olmecs in the highlands of central Mexico and the Peruvian Chavín – both built vast, dressed stone temples that have been compared to the Sumerian ziggurats. But the Olmec temples were not built until some time after 1200BC, while Chavín de Huantar did not evolve until after 900BC.

The architecture of the city of Teotihuacan was much influenced by the Olmecs. Although the identity of its builders is still the subject of debate, at its height it was larger than any European city of the 1st Millennium, including Rome.

But the most famous ziggurat in history was the so-called Tower of Babel, which is described in the Book of Genesis. According

**LEFT** Reproduction of the Ishtar Gate, Iraq; the original was removed lock, stock and barrel just before World War I and relocated to Berlin

**ABOVE** The guardian figures or lamassu from Khorsabad: the Assyrians' figures had five legs, to the later Persians' four-legged lamassu

to the Bible, this was the first city built after the Great Flood and a home to all peoples. Jewish versions of the tale add that there was a stone idol at the top of the great spiral tower.

The term Babel is the Hebrew word for Babylon, as the Greeks knew it. Here were the world-celebrated Hanging Gardens. Babylon, which came to prominence around 1800BC, was not the only great city in the area between the Euphrates and the Tigris that is known as the Fertile Crescent. Ur was thriving in 2600BC – some theorize that its ziggurat was in fact the Tower of Babel – and Nineveh is mentioned from around 1800BC. The palace and town of Khorsabad, another great city, were built in 713BC. Nineteenth-century excavations of the Assyrian Nineveh yielded the remains of sumptuous palaces built on a vast scale, their principal gateways 'guarded' by sculpted stone human-headed bulls or lions.

After the fall of Nineveh in 612BC, a new dynasty of kings in southern Mesopotamia revived the glories of early Babylon. Nebuchadnezzar lived up to his impressive name with a much extended 'New City' approached by a great marble-paved Procession Street that led through the famous Ishtar Gate. The gateway was faced with blue-glazed bricks and ornamented with heraldic animals. In the early 1900s a number of German excavations took place in Babylon, Uruk, Miletus, Priene and Egypt. German excavators removed the ruins of the gate in 1913 and reconstructed it in the Pergamon Museum in Berlin.

# EUROPEAN NEOLITHIC

As societies in Syria and Iraq settled, giving up hunter-gathering and the nomadic lifestyle for farming as early as 9000BC, the new ideas spread rapidly across the south. However, the Neolithic revolution did not reach northern Europe until 5000–4500BC. So at a time when some other cultures were developing complex civilizations, and an architecture to match, northern Europeans were still erecting structures from hewn stone: megaliths.

**M**any communities expended great ingenuity and years of effort dragging and levering massive, found boulders on to naturally impressive sites. You find them in the most unexpected of places, mysterious and unexplained. The function of these so-called menhirs, from the Breton word 'men' for stone and 'hir', meaning long, has provoked more debate than practically any other issue in European prehistory.

Are they way-maps, or sun markers? Were they used by Druids? Were they points of sacrifice? The Roc Branlant near Saint-Estèphe in France sits in deep country, in the middle of a broad stream. Why? One intriguing stone, the Björketorp Runestone in Blekinge, Sweden, carries a gloomy message: 'I foresee perdition.'

The tallest one we know of, the Menhir Brisé at Locmariaquer in Brittany, once stood at 67 feet (20.3 metres) and weighed 330 tons.

Carnac in northwestern France is one of the greatest open sites for megaliths. It is home to just under 3,000 stones in local granite. Even on the ground they are an impressive sight. But to see them from above is to realize that they form a long path through the landscape, creating a form of map or marker. Unlike tombs or temples, menhirs do not enclose space; a conspicuously human design imposed on the landscape, they seem to encourage movement, if not direct action.

Some menhirs were broken up and incorporated into later passage graves – a type of Neolithic tomb where the burial chamber is at the end of a long stone entry way. We don't know if this re-use of the sometimes carved and decorated stones was deliberate, or if the passage grave builders simply saw menhirs as a convenient source of stone.

As in Egypt, some of the greatest architectural innovations have come about through honouring the dead. The dome makes a dramatic appearance in a famous early example of a stone passage grave of about 4000BC on the Île Longue, off the coast of Brittany. It is formed by corbelling, where each ring of stone juts slightly inwards from the one below.

**BELOW** At Carnac, on a peninsula near the medieval town of Vannes, are more than 3,000 prehistoric standing stones. Legend has it that they are Roman legionaries, turned to stone by the magician Merlin

# Stonehenge

Stonehenge is one of the world's special places, a panoramic window on to a Neolithic landscape. Stand on any nearby hilltop, the breeze in your face, and let your gaze sweep the landscape: cursi; ceremonial henges; round barrows; processional avenues – the ribs and vertebrae of Britain's prehistory lie scattered all around. When they were first built, the mounds of dug chalk around the monument gleamed white in the sunset.

But Stonehenge the sacred ruin – the sublime and sophisticated religious complex that archaeologists are only just beginning to understand – is a giant laid low. Road noise and pollution blight the dignity and spirit of the place. In effect, it is a traffic island, its silent poise destroyed by the roar of surrounding roads.

Stonehenge is an enigma. It has been a place of great spiritual significance for at least 4,500 years. Built in concentric rings, the monument is set within a great ditch that separates it from the rest of the landscape. The ditch was first begun in 2750BC; the last (fourth) phase of building took place around 1500BC.

The first stones to be brought to the site, in c.2550BC, were bluestones. Around 1500BC these stones were rearranged to form the inner circle. It is thought they were transported from the Preseli Mountains in Wales, 240 miles away: if so, it was an extraordinary feat by any standards. The sarsen stones, which form the main structure, were perhaps dragged to the site over the following one or two centuries: these stones came from the nearby Avebury Hills.

Construction was first begun at the end of the Neolithic period, by what seems to have been a structured and organized society. What is almost certain is that the early Britons who built Stonehenge over a period of 1,000 years or so were communing not with the dead, as in Egypt, but with the sun and the moon. American astronomer Gerald Hawkins argued that Stonehenge's trilithons are aligned to predict the times of sunrise and sunset over the seasons, as well as lunar and solar eclipses – a calendar in stone.

Durrington Walls, or 'Woodhenge', is an enormous enclosure just to the northeast of the stone ring, with a 17-foot-deep (5 metres) ditch. It may well have been a companion monument to the stone 'henge': evidence shows that people feasted here at midwinter.

There is little to see at Durrington now. Its 3-foot-thick (1 metre) timber posts have long since rotted away. The once-great circle simply looks like a lot of marks in the ground and the vast ditch around it is

**ABOVE** The mysteries of Stonehenge have yet to be unravelled. Many believe its stones were placed to predict the rising and setting of the sun

obscured by bushes and undergrowth. But experts now realize that this was in fact Britain's largest henge. Some 1,320 feet (400 metres) across, it was bigger even than Avebury. The timber circle seems to be aligned directly on the winter solstice sunrise. Was Woodhenge about midwinter, in the same way that Stonehenge's ceremonial highpoint was midsummer?

The latest theory is that these two magnificent monuments were part of a vast planned landscape linked together by the River Avon and the Avenue. Was it a funeral complex, where the dead were given a wake, laid out at Woodhenge, carried in ceremony down a double-ditched processional route and then along the river to Stonehenge itself? Crest the hill from the A303 and the magnificent stones still take your breath away. The ceaseless din of the surrounding roads and the modern villages nearby confuse our understanding of this ancient ceremonial landscape. But it is still there, waiting patiently for rescue.

**BELOW** A fake forest? The nearby Woodhenge, here marked by modern cut-off stumps indicating what would once have been a forest of tall tree-trunk pillars at the site

# KNOSSOS

Even in translation, Homer's description of Crete is wonderful: 'A rich and lovely island, set in the wine-dark sea...' Founded c.2000BC on the ruins of a prior Neolithic settlement, the palace of Knossos on Crete was discovered in 1878 and then bought up, lock, stock and barrel by a rich English archaeologist, Sir Arthur Evans. Evans spent the next 40 years of his life uncovering and restoring the site. What he found was extraordinary by any standards: a warren of interlocking courtyards, apartments, storage chambers and rooms built over several stories on a wooded hillside. Its flat roofs and multi-storey layout remind us of modern apartment blocks, but in terms of its proportions, its aesthetic brilliance and its sheer liveability, the design of this labyrinthine palace puts many modern buildings to shame.

Arthur Evans has been criticized for over-restoration, but if he was right then the use of colour at Knossos was brilliant: plain stone walls and floors contrast with black and red-painted support pillars to winning effect, while superbly painted and brightly coloured frescoes depicting the hedonistic everyday life of the court adorn the walls.

The state rooms and administrative offices were on the upper floors, while west of the central courtyard lay the rooms used for ritual: shrines, temples and a great throne room. But whereas contemporary Egyptian civilization was obsessed with the cult of death and its fearsome attendants, the lively Knossos frescoes give us the impression of a culture based on music, dancing and sports: one that included a spectacular form of acrobatic bull-jumping – and joy. All this is documented by lyrical and colourful frescoes on the walls. The Minoans – named for their fabled or perhaps real King Minos – also excelled at metalwork, jewellery and sculpture: dozens of artisans and craft workers had their workshops on the northern side of the palace.

Clever light wells, bays and deep colonnades combine to keep the palace shady, cool and well illuminated. Timber frames and support beams probably allowed the construction to flex, making it better able to withstand the earthquakes that plagued – and still threaten – the region. As for the plumbing, fed in a very environmentally-friendly way by springs and rainwater collected from gutters and special roof channels, it would take most European countries the best part of another 4,000 years

**LEFT** 'King Minos" apartments are also known as the Hall of the Double Axes, from the symbols on the walls. The rooms are notably well-built, of stones without mortar

before they attained the same levels of sophistication. The citizens of the later Knossos enjoyed running water, flushing toilets, a working sewerage system and multiple bathrooms. The ruler's symbol, found throughout the palace, is a double-headed axe: *labyros* in Greek. Walls and partitions are of unbaked brick. Shaded sub-basements kept wine and olive oil cool in huge, decorated terracotta amphorae while grain stocks and other perishables were preserved in deep pits.

The remains of a number of villas lie outside the palace complex, along with an ancient road, but there is little other surviving evidence of the estimated 100,000 ordinary citizens thought to have lived here when the Minoan civilization was at its height. As at the palace, there is no sign that people used either kitchens or hearths when it came to cooking: instead, archaeologists think they grilled the fish and game they caught on portable charcoal braziers.

A barbecue culture, then. When you view the architectural evidence you can't help feeling that the Minoans could teach us a few things about living the good life in peace, harmony and some contentment. The only sad thing is that in the end the warlike Myceneans came along to spoil it.

**BELOW** Fresco from the Queen's Chamber: dolphins could often be seen playing in the sea around Crete

**LEFT** Thousands of years ago, visitors arriving by sea entered Knossos by the North Propylaeum. Evans rebuilt it, identifying the colours by tiny pigment scrapings

# The Minotaur

No one has yet discovered any evidence that the Minotaur, a giant, terrifying monster that demanded yearly human sacrifices lurked below ground, or that the legendary Greek hero Theseus might have slain it with the help of Ariadne and a ball of twine. But then, we probably shouldn't let the facts get in the way of a good story.

# MYCENAE

Homer sang the fame of the great fortress palace of Mycenae in the *Iliad*. At the age of eight a young boy named Heinrich Schliemann was so fired up by the epic that he declared that he would one day discover the ruins of Troy.

Mycenae was a citadel: an exercise in projecting power in the form of built stone. Perched high on a rock spur in the Eastern Peloponnesus, and with a panoramic view, its builders clearly understood the military advantages of an elevated location.

Like Knossos before it, Mycenae concentrated all the important functions of its culture and administration inside massive walls. Most of the walls and monuments seen today were erected in the Late Bronze Age, between 1350 and 1200BC, when the city's influence was at its peak.

The city-state's domineering architectural presence owes much to the Myceneans' understanding of geometry and proportion, both in terms of the size and form of the buildings and the individual dressed stone blocks used in their construction. These stone blocks are so big that later Greeks believed they could only have been placed in position by the fabled giants, the Cyclopes. The remarkable Lion Gate was the citadel's main entrance. It was built at roughly the same time as the first fortifications, in c.1350BC, and the same 'Cyclopean' masonry was used.

Mycenae's profoundly hierarchical society is reflected in the size and location of the royal palace, the biggest structure, which was placed at the citadel's heart. Though much robbed and ruined, the palace seems to have had a megaron, or throne room, very like the one at Knossos, only on a much smaller scale. There was a raised central hearth or altar, possibly surrounded by pillars, with the throne being set against the wall behind it, so that the ruler could be seen from the entrance. Stepped shelving may have served as a place for votive offerings.

All of these factors convinced Schliemann that he had found the fabled Troy. The houses of lesser nobles, rich merchants and what may have been a priest class sprawl south from the royal court in a kind of extended teardrop

**RIGHT** The impressive Lion Gate is approached via a long, monumental stone causeway. Two lionesses guard a column that represents a deity

**LEFT** The Treasury of Atreus, or Tomb of Agamemnon as Schliemann called it, is an impressive *tholos* tomb dating from around 1250BC. The lintel stone above the doorway weighs 120 tons

**BELOW** Built around 400 years before the alleged time of the Trojan War, the *tholos* is remarkable for its size. Technically, it was way ahead of its time

**ABOVE** Not the face of Agamemnon: but who is he? One of five masks discovered in shaft graves, including two of children, covered in gold leaf. It is possible they date from 1550BC

shape that follows the natural contours of the site. Outside the walls lay hamlets, farms and estates, whose inhabitants could retreat inside the citadel in time of war.

Today, no one is entirely sure why the towering conical *tholos*, or 'beehive' tombs – named by Schliemann after mythological Greek figures – were built. We do know they were approached by open walled passageways that gave access to the tombs proper. It is in these tombs that we find the first domes of ancient Greece. Some doorways have gigantic limestone lintels: the one marking the threshold to the *tholos* Schliemann called the Treasury of Atreus weighs more than 100 tons.

It was here the adventurer archaeologist discovered a mummified body, its face covered with a golden death mask.

A dazed Schliemann reportedly said: 'Today I gazed on the face of Agamemnon.' He later named his two children Andromache and Agamemnon. In fact, the *tholos* tombs, like the shaft graves inside the citadel, date from a good four centuries before the end of the Trojan War. The real Troy is in Anatolia, modern-day Turkey.

Constructing conical stone-lined barrows of this size and ingenuity at this site would tax many modern engineers today. Some 50 feet (15 metres) in diameter and slightly less than that in height, the beehive tombs have beautifully constructed circular corbelled walls that taper to an apex. These were built by placing successively smaller rings of brick or stone one on top of the other. The fact that the Myceneans were able to do it repeatedly pays testament to their architectural and engineering ability. Like the ancient Roman and Greek tourists who admired the site before us, we can only wonder how this Bronze Age culture managed to lift and manoeuvre these enormous monoliths. One thing is for certain: they helped inspire the architecture, as well as the literature, of Classical Greece and Rome.

# PERSEPOLIS

The world's first great empire was the Achaemenid Persian Empire. Founded by Cyrus II, who lived c.600–530BC, its profound political and cultural influence would last for 300 years. At its height the Persian Empire stretched from Greece and Libya in the west to the Indus River in present-day Pakistan. The Delian League, an association of Greek city-states under the leadership of Athens, was formed with the sole purpose of opposing the warlike Persians. And the invasions of Greece by Darius and Xerxes form the background to the most celebrated Greek and Latin literature. Herodotus' *Histories,* for example, contrasted the despotic character of the Persian kingdom with that of the democratic Greeks. The greatest of Greek monuments, the Parthenon, was built to celebrate the defeat of the Persians.

The ancient cultures of Egypt, Mesopotamia and Anatolia were absorbed into this cosmopolitan new empire. Persepolis, now a magical series of ruin sites, lies some 43 miles (70km) northeast of the modern city of Shiraz in modern Iran. This ceremonial capital of Darius and Xerxes is the world's first example of a creative fusion of aesthetic styles. Craftsmen from across the empire were brought in to create a new, decorative form of lasting stone architecture.

Here, Assyrians, Babylonians, Egyptians and Ionian Greeks, famed for their skills, joined forces to glorify a new sophisticated imperialist civilization. The earliest remains here date from around 515BC.

The great Palace of Persepolis was built at three different levels on an enormous terrace cut out of the mountain of Kuh-e Rahmet, the 'Mountain of Mercy'. Darius I's cosmopolitan new capital was approached via a magnificent double-reversing stairway and a main ceremonial gateway munificently called 'The Gate of All Nations'.

The palace was on a magnificent scale. One can imagine the war-leaders' regal horses being ridden up the ceremonial stairways – which had especially shallow steps – flanked on either side by rich relief carvings. The 646-square-foot (60 square metres) *apadana*, or audience hall, had verandas to three sides. Its heavy oak and cedarwood ceiling was supported by 72 columns rising over 66 feet (19 metres) high, 13 of which are still standing.

We in the West are used to abstracted designs on decorative columns; at this time in

the East they were groundbreaking. The square-plinthed columns are topped by elaborate sculpture: lions, hawkish eagles, double-headed bulls. The cultural mix is evident: the bulls, for instance, are supported on Ionic-type scrolls.

The palace walls were covered with a layer of mud and stucco. Darius ordered his name and the details of his empire to be written on plates in gold and silver, before being placed in covered stone boxes in the foundations of the Four Corners of the palace.

Because the east staircase lay buried beneath ashes and rubble for centuries, its delicately carved relief sculptures remain in excellent condition. The nearby Throne Hall, the second largest building at Persepolis, was where the king received nobles, dignitaries and subject rulers. An enormous throne room, 230 by 230 feet (70 by 70 metres), occupied the central portion of the Throne Hall. It is also known as the Hundred-Column Hall after the 100 columns that supported its roof. Made of wood, only their stone bases survive.

The enormous Treasury next to the Throne Hall served as an armoury and a storehouse for the sumptuous tribute brought by the Persians' subject nations at the New Year's feast: carved reliefs show the ruler receiving long lines of envoys bearing tribute. According to Plutarch, when Alexander The Great plundered Persepolis in 330BC, he needed 20,000 mules and 5,000 camels to carry away the two centuries-worth of loot.

**ABOVE** Persepolis, in what is now Iran, was a cultural melting pot. Its highpoint was the Hall of a Hundred Columns, a forest of multi-coloured double bull-headed columns and an amazing sight

**FAR LEFT** Awed citizens and those bringing tribute approached through the Gate of All Nations. Its giant figures, lamassu, guard against evil spirits. Their human faces and wings are similar to earlier Assyrian prototypes – see p.25. Inscriptions declare: 'I (am) Xerxes, the Great King, King of Kings'

**RIGHT** A sculpted griffin from the *apadana*. The warlike griffin has a special place in Persian art and architecture

# THE CLASSICAL WORLD

The shadow cast by classical antiquity is vast. Each new empire has claimed to be the heir of Rome: but if giants on the scale of ancient Greece and Rome can fall into decay, then why not London or New York? The ruins inspire us, yes. But they also frighten us, by showing us just how fragile civilization can be.

Greek temples celebrated gods like Apollo, the ideal of manly beauty and the god of light and of the sun. The fluted but simple Doric column is a symbol of masculinity, beauty and truth

# DIVINE HARMONY

The critic Nikolaus Pevsner described the Greek temple thus:

*'... the most perfect example of architecture finding its fulfilment in bodily beauty... placed before us with a physical presence more intense, more alive, than that of any later building.'*

**T**he ancient Greeks believed that everything in nature was controlled by a god. The gods were immortal, and people believed they could shift shape, become invisible and travel anywhere instantaneously. The gods all too often had very human frailties. One weakness was

beauty: Pluto carried away Persephone; Aphrodite fell in love with the handsome human, Adonis. For the Greeks, as with other civilizations, monumental architecture began

**LEFT** The ancient Greeks are famed for their detailed and subtle approach to ceremonial architecture. Here it is possible to make out the triglyphs channelled into the marble (see box right for info), along with the *guttae*

**ABOVE** One of the finest Greek temples outside Greece, this was built at Agrigento, Sicily in the 6th century BC. It was used as a Christian church in later years: continued use would often guarantee survival

in the service of their gods. So as homes to the deities, Greek temples were a conscious exercise in the pursuit of beauty.

Temples were designed to convey a sense of the divine and to look other-worldly, by virtue of their harmonious proportions. The Greeks also believed in the mystical power of mathematics: the careful emphasis they put upon ratio and proportion was part

# Key Dates

**1300BC** China first introduces books.

**1300–1200BC** A major administrative centre dating from this time was discovered by Dutch archaeologists in 1977 in Rakka, Syria. The site included a 15-foot-high (4.5m), two-storey building with two bathrooms and a tiled floor.

**1292BC** An Egyptian document describes a construction worker who went off on a beer binge. His brother-in-law was chief engineer on the job and did not sack him.

**1250BC** Lion Gate at Mycenae, Greece.

**1150BC** Troy falls; *The Aeneid* is begun.

**814–44BC** Carthage rises from a Phoenician trading nation to rival Rome.

**900–317BC** Sparta, with its elected council, holds supreme power in Greece.

**700–500BC** The Etruscans build an independent culture in Italy.

**550BC** The temple of Apollo by Ictinus at Corinth.

**525–406BC** First use of tragedy in literature.

**510BC** Athenian Treasury, Delphi, Greece.

**500–480BC** The temple of Aphaia at Aegina.

**490BC** The Battle of Marathon; Phidippides set outs on a 26-mile run, inspiring the Olympic event.

**480BC** The Acropolis temples are destroyed by the Persians; Battle of Thermopylae.

**447–432BC** The wealth Athens gained after the Persian Wars enables Pericles to embark on a vast building programme, which includes the Parthenon and other monuments on the Acropolis.

**427BC** Temple of Athena Nike by Callicrates, Athens.

**425BC** Herodotus writes his history.

**421–405BC** The Erectheion by Mnesicles, Athens.

**410BC** Battle of Cyzicus; democracy restored in Athens.

**404BC** Athens surrenders to Sparta. This marks the beginning of the end for classical Greek culture.

**384–322BC** Founding father of philosophy, Aristotle, is teacher to Alexander the Great.

**333BC** Alexander the Great defeats Darius III.

**315BC** The Arch of Constantine, Rome.

**300BC** Theatre at Epidauros is designed and built by Polykleitos.

**218BC** Hannibal crosses the Alps.

**205BC** Arch of Severus.

**120–135BC** Hadrian's Villa, Tivoli, Italy.

**117–120BC** Library at Ephesus, Turkey.

**81BC** The Arch of Titus, Rome.

**80BC** Vitruvius, Roman writer and engineer, is born.

**64BC** Domus Aurea by Severus and Celer, Rome.

**AD16** Maison Carrée is built at Nîmes, France.

**AD20** The rise of the last Arabian empires, the Hadhramaut Kingdom. Capital city: Shabaw.

**AD43** The second Roman invasion of Britain.

**AD70** The first Jewish revolt is crushed by the Emperor Titus.

**AD70–82** The Colosseum, Rome satisfies the Romans' desire for 'bread and circuses'.

**AD118–126** The Pantheon, Rome.

**AD312** Constantine the Great guarantees religious freedom with the Edict of Milan. AD330, Constantinople, the new seat of empire, is founded. After his death, Rome's empire gets split between West and East.

## Turned to Stone?

Before stone took over from wood in Greek temples, any beams that projected beyond the walls were cut off (unlike those in Japan and China, where they were sculpted to turn upwards). The beam ends were ornamented with boards painted with blue wax. When temples began to be built out of stone, a form of decoration called the 'triglyph' was added. This is the vertically channelled tablet in the Doric frieze. *Guttae,* or tears, were small drop-like projections that were frequently carved under the triglyphs. Scholars speculate that triglyphs represented the bars of wooden joists and *guttae* the wooden pegs that held them in place. This is often described as Greek 'conservatism', but perhaps this piece of architectural symbolism is something more – a conscious celebration of history. If so, that history has had a long and fruitful life. You can see the decoration adapted freely in Victorian, and more especially the Georgian architecture of the USA and UK. The stucco buildings of John Nash, in particular, bring a drop of Arcadia to old London town.

of this search for the architectural ideal.

The earliest known ancient Greek temple appeared on the beautiful island of Samos some time around the 9th century BC. It had a timber colonnade and the roof was supported by a long row of single columns placed along a central axis.

A set of almost universally applied proportions evolved by the end of the 6th century BC, as stone replaced wood. What was developed was an architecture of power, presence and rigorous simplicity that has influenced us for over 2,500 years. The very word 'style' is thought to come from *stylos*, the Greek word for a column.

In most earlier cultures, the column was a secondary feature of small importance. By contrast the ancient Greeks' sophisticated system of construction was completely based on the column and the dramatic superstructure it carried. That graceful system was immensely flexible: human figures known as caryatids or atlantes could even stand in for the columns. Columns, made up of a shaft, a base and a capital, were often waxed to make them gleam in the light.

Temples now had internal colonnades composed of two orders of columns, one on top of the other to support the roof. A cult room, or *cella*, created a tunnel view to the statue of the god at the far end. The peristyle, or open arcade of columns, emphasized the approachability of the temples.

The ancient Greeks of the period 750BC to 350BC learned much from ancient Egypt, adopting the idea of monumentality as well as the post and lintel stone construction system. The original, plain Greek Doric column follows most Egyptian columns by tapering towards the top. The Temple of Zeus at Olympia, c.470BC, was a prime example of a temple of the Doric order. However, the Greeks took the idea a stage further when they developed a system of the Orders.

Pediments were an important feature of ancient Greek temples. Not every temple's pediments were sculpted: the Temple of Hera Argiva at Paestum in Italy (c.460BC), better known as the Temple of Neptune, does well enough without. But strong and lively colour schemes were probably a common feature to all.

# The Orders

There are five main 'orders' of classical architecture. Both the Greeks and the Romans used the Doric, Ionic and Corinthian orders, while the Tuscan and the Composite orders were usually only featured on Roman buildings.

The plain, unadorned **Doric** order is thought to have been the first of the classical orders, mainly because the earliest known temples were built in this style. A Doric column is shorter than those of the other orders: its height is between five and six times its diameter. In the 6th century BC a simpler form of Doric evolved in northwestern Asia Minor: the 'Aeolic'.

The Greeks tapered the shafts of their columns and made them bulge slightly at the centre: this corrects the visual illusion that the columns curve inwards. In the same way, the base platform, known as the *stylobate,* billowed upwards at the centre. This counteracted the impression of a concave dip in its surface. This 'entasis' – from the Greek *'en'* (in) and *'tasis'* (stretch) – emphasizes how important the concept of a 'view' was to the Greeks. Their temples were designed to be admired from a long way off.

Developed on the Ionian islands of eastern Greece, the Ionic order was perhaps inspired by contact with the Middle East. The Ionians had a treaty port on the Nile Delta and temples at Ephesus, Samos and Didyma. They were colossal, suggesting an understanding of the scale of Egyptian monuments.

The columns of the **Ionic** order have fluted shafts and elaborately moulded disc bases – with capitals that gradually came to resemble the curled horns of a ram. The Roman writer and engineer Vitruvius tells us that the height of an Ionic column should be eight or nine times its diameter. He wrote that the order was developed in honour of the goddess Diana. The delicate tapered shape of the column echoed her figure, clad in deep folds of fine cloth, with the hair delicately tucked beneath the ears.

From the 4th century BC onwards the Ionic capital was beginning to give way to a new style: the **Corinthian**. Callimachus, a Greek sculptor of the 5th century BC, was inspired by the grave of a young girl from Corinth. Her nurse had left a wicker basket on her tomb; an acanthus plant was growing through it. An architect using the order – the height ten times the diameter of its base – is knowingly or unknowingly alluding to the fate of the young girl from Corinth, and the fleeting nature of life.

In ancient Greece the order was often used decoratively inside buildings that were externally Doric. Perhaps it was seen as too ostentatious for the outdoors. The Romans, by contrast, loved it. In Roman hands the column became taller, which meant designing taller capitals: it was easy to add another row of acanthus leaves.

The plainest order by far is the **Tuscan**. Columns are unfluted, sometimes without a base, and the entablature has no triglyphs. At the other end of the scale, the most complicated was the **Composite**. In this lavish order Ionic scrolls are combined with Corinthian acanthus leaves. After Composite was used on the Arch of Titus in Rome in the 70s AD, it became associated with military campaigns. The 'giant order', spanning two storeys of a building, is a Renaissance invention.

The idea of combining orders came about in the 4th century BC, when two-storeyed buildings became more common in the Hellenistic period. Much later, the construction of the Colosseum, which began in c.AD72–3, provided the world's most famous example of the orders working together within a single building.

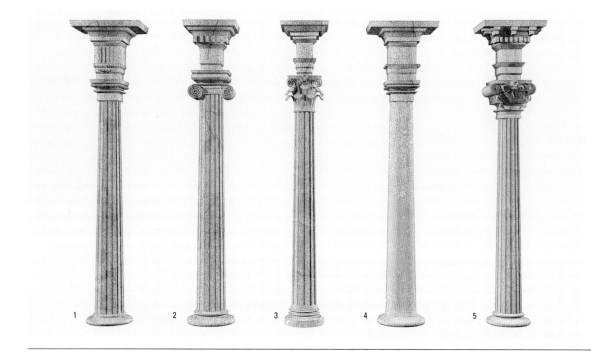

1. Doric
2. Ionic
3. Corinthian
4. Tuscan
5. Composite

# STORIES IN STONE

In 480BC the mighty Persian empire invaded Athens and razed the Acropolis, including a temple on the site of the Parthenon. At the 'hot gates' of one of the most famous battles in history, Thermopylae, a tiny army of 300 Spartans and 700 Thespians, aided by a small cluster of Greek allies, stood at the mountain pass and fought the vast Persian army of Xerxes I. Shortly afterwards, the victorious admiral Pericles commissioned Pheidias, universally regarded as the greatest of all classical sculptors, to rebuild the Acropolis.

The largest temple to be rebuilt was the majestic Parthenon, which was commissioned in honour of Athena, virgin goddess of war and wisdom. Pheidias designed the statues of the goddess Athena and may have sculpted much of the Parthenon frieze, but he turned to the architects Ictinus and Callicrates to perfect the remainder of the great Doric temple we see today.

Two other fine structures crowned the Acropolis complex: the Propylaea or ceremonial gateway and the Erechtheion.

Also known as the temple of Athena Polias, the Erechtheion was built by the architect Mnesikles to house the city's original, wooden statue of Athena. It was also a shrine to Poseidon: a large golden lamp at the centre of the temple served as a beacon for ships at sea.

The Erechtheion has three main sections: the main temple, the northern extension and the Porch of the Maidens. Here caryatids – beautifully carved female figures whose drapery echoes fluted Ionic columns – support the main structure.

Each of the caryatids of the Erechtheion is different. It's as if they have the faces of real women, immortalized in stone. Unlike the famous 300 of Sparta, the nearby city of Caryae joined the Persians in the fight against mainland Greece. The Caryan men were slaughtered wholesale in revenge for the treachery. The women were taken into slavery. The Caryatids of the Porch of Maidens are a memorial, and a warning to posterity. For the sake of their menfolk, they suffer under the burden of a huge, overbearing weight – and for all time.

Every ancient Greek city had at least one temple. But over time, Hellenistic cities began to develop public fountains, gymnasia, schools and libraries. Alexandria and Corinth even had a limited form of street lighting. Town planning became important as Alexander the Great founded new colonies across Asia. Trading centres like Ephesus or Pergamon began to have exceptional civic, as well as religious architecture. Pergamon was home to a world-famous library – Antony reputedly gave the entire contents to Cleopatra.

The ancient Greeks left many works of art that help us understand their inquisitiveness, their love of geometry and astronomy, and their quest for truth through the study of philosophy. Democracy began with the free citizens of Athens, so elitist symbols such as palaces or grand tombs were rare. Theatres, on the other hand, were not just popular: they were an essential part of life, built in honour of Dionysus, the god of sexuality, fertility and wine.

Remarkably, the theatre at Epidauros, constructed c.350–300BC, is still in use today.

Built into the side of a hill in a semicircle, this extraordinary 13,000-seater auditorium in the Peleponnese has 55 rows of stone seats in the *theatron*, or 'seeing place'. By this time, the circular *orchestra* or 'dancing place' and the *skene*, the backdrop behind the orchestra, had become standard architectural practice. To the rear of the theatre are open rolling hills, which provide a god-given natural backcloth against which to see the morally uplifting plays of an Aeschylus or a Sophocles.

Epidauros was a famous centre for healing, with mineral springs like 18th century Bath. Its buildings included a ceremonial banqueting hall, baths and a *palaestra*, or wrestling school. Wrestling was one of the most important sports in the ancient world, although it was restricted to free men. Nearby is the stadium, another trend-setting building design. Greek architects later introduced tunnels leading out from under the tiered seating, just as we do in many of our stadia today.

Olympia, just down the coast from Epidauros, is now globally famous for its games, first instituted in 776BC. Yet in ancient Greece the site had much more significance as the home of the Olympians, the deities living on Mount Olympus. The Los Angeles of its day, the cult city was dedicated to Zeus. It was a great show town, with every facility known to civilization. Inside the temple was a famously colossal statue of Zeus, made of ivory and gold. Sculpted on site by Pheidias, it was named one of the Seven Wonders of the Ancient World.

Every four years the Olympic flame is still lit here, before being taken round the world (undimmed, we hope) until it reaches the latest home of the games. Today we expect to create an Olympic complex in the space of a few hurried years. At Olympia, it took more than six centuries. The Classical period (5th to 4th centuries BC) saw the first serious sporting facilities, including the hippodrome for chariot racing. In the Hellenistic period (late 4th century BC) the largest building on the site, the Leonidaion, was constructed to house important visitors. The Palaestra was built in the 3rd century BC and a new Gymnasion subsequently followed in the 2nd century BC.

This was before the Romans took over and the games became a world event. The Romans, being Romans, then began an extensive period of improving the site – particularly, of course, the all-important baths.

## Temple terms

Breathe in. The horizontal structure that is supported on top of the columns, like a beam, is called an 'entablature'. This is made up of the architrave, the frieze and the cornice. The surface of the pediment of most Greek temples contains 'triglyphs' (small vertical bars, in threes) and 'metopes', the flat area between them. They alternate across the frieze below the pediment. The metope is often sculpted.

The 'peristyle' is a court or space enclosed by columns, from the Greek *peristulos*, whereas a colonnade is an architectural screen of columns. The central cult structure of the temple is called the *naos*, which is divided into the main room, the *cella* where the cult statue 'lived' and a porch, the *pronaos*.

# The Parthenon

'For this reason are the works of Pericles all the more to be wondered at; they were created in a short time for all time. Each one of them, in its beauty, was even then and at once antique. Such is the bloom of perpetual newness upon these works of his, which makes them ever to look untouched by time, as though the unfaltering breath of an ageless spirit had been infused into them.'

Plutarch, *Life of Pericles*

Floodlit on the Acropolis, the Parthenon looms spare and white in the night. This temple is Western society's ultimate vision of built perfection; the highest in cultural accomplishment. Yet the Modernist architect Le Corbusier saw it somewhat differently.

'One clear image will stand in my mind for ever: the Parthenon, stark, stripped, economical, violent. A clamorous outcry against a landscape of grace and terror.'

After the battle of Thermopylae in 480BC, the Persian army invaded Athens and burned the Archaic shrines already on the Acropolis to the ground. Unexpectedly, the Greeks hit back against the mighty Persians with a decisive victory at the naval battle of Salamis. Pericles, the victorious general, then ordered the rebuilding of the Acropolis. The first building he decreed was a new temple. It was dedicated to the maiden goddess of wisdom and war, Athena Parthenos.

It was duly called the Parthenon.

Built 447–438BC by the architects Iktinos and Kallikrates, the Parthenon was a defiant statement of Greek power. Made of gleaming white marble, it could be seen from everywhere in the surrounding city. The perfect new temple pointed towards the Bay of Salamis, where the Persian navy had gone to its watery grave, its great beauty asserting Athenian military, cultural and intellectual prowess, or *logos*. The Greeks had defeated the baseness, or *chaos,* of the barbarian (for which read 'the Persian') foe.

The Parthenon is larger than most Greek temples, with eight columns across the ends instead of the more usual six. This gave the sculptors a large space to play out their narrative. With a brilliant handling of depth and perspective, the friezes show the sack of Troy, the battle between the Olympian gods and the earth giants, and a remarkable symbolic battle between men and Amazons.

Over the pediment was a scene showing the birth of Athena, virgin goddess of wisdom and war. She was striding with spear and shield in hand, having been born fully formed from the head of her father Zeus. A vast ivory and gold figure of Athena in full battle array stood inside the large east chamber. It was sculpted by Pheidias, the celebrity sculptor of the day.

Greek temples weren't designed for a congregation to enter – the people simply gathered outside to worship. Inside, the sumptuous new temple was used as a treasury, a home for votive offerings and

valuables as well as the great silver throne from which King Xerxes watched the Greek navy crush his fleet.

The architects marked the Parthenon's importance by lavishing extreme care on its construction. Using a system of mortar-free construction known as *anathyrosis,* the builders cut and squared the marble blocks with Egyptian precision, grinding their surfaces absolutely smooth.

The temple is 45 feet (13.7 metres) high to the top of its cornice and approximately 100 feet (31 metres) wide by 230 feet (69.5 metres) long. This mysterious ratio of 4:9 is found throughout the building. It governs the relationship between the proportions of the columns and the spacing between them: it also dictates the height of the temple's entablature above the columns.

Since the 17th century people have been trying to decipher the mysterious temple's secrets. It seemed to have been constructed according to some ancient mystical understanding of geometry: mathematicians and architects alike were fascinated. Then in 1751 the British travellers James Stuart and Nicholas Revett voyaged to Athens to survey and record its ruins. When they published the first volume of *The Antiquities of Athens* in 1762 the Western world was amazed. Almost overnight, the Parthenon was accepted as the most beautiful building the world had ever seen. It was a miracle

produced by an extraordinary, ancient wisdom, one that gave Western architecture and design a new vocabulary. Yet when the Society of Dilettanti measured the temple, they were horrified to find that this culminating masterpiece of Greek architecture – the embodiment of ordered, classical geometry – didn't have a single straight line.

What on earth were the architects up to? The key to the puzzle can be found in the writings of Vitruvius, a Roman engineer and architect. Greek architecture is designed, says Vitruvius, *'quod oculus fallit'* – as the eyes deceive us. Iktinos and Kallikrates had used cunning and subtle *alexemata*, or 'betterments', to make sure the Parthenon's lines pleased the human eye. The corner columns must be thicker, says Vitruvius, 'since they are set off against the open air and appear to be more slender than they are'. The temple's corner columns are indeed more than 2 inches (5cm) wider, and are set 2 feet (0.61m) closer together than the others. The *stylobate*, or base, has a convex curve towards the building's centre. Logically this should push the columns outwards. Instead, the opposite is true: the columns compensate by leaning slightly inwards, about 6cm from true.

The technique is now known as entasis (from the Greek *'tasis'*, to stretch). Even the columns themselves have a slight curve. This artistry is the key to the Parthenon's structural grace. Iktinos – or was it the consummate sculptor, Pheidias? – put every emphasis on lightness of structure. Even the flutings of the columns diminish as they rise. The whole composition is masterly: a subtly balanced play on contour and line. When we admire the Parthenon as a vision of architectural grace and proportion, we first of all see a building constructed within the rules of the 'Golden Mean'. But then we become aware of a subtle and quite stunning use of eye-pleasing *alexemata*.

The Parthenon's current battered state, however, is due to human behaviour rather than decay. Some time in the 6th century the temple was converted into a Roman Catholic church – Our Lady of Athens. When the Ottoman Turks took Athens in 1456, they converted the Parthenon into a

mosque, adding a minaret. Traces, including its internal staircase, can still be seen.

But it wasn't until 1687 that true disaster struck. A Venetian army attacked the Ottoman forces, who were by now using the grand temple to store gunpowder. On 26 September, a huge mortar round scored a direct hit on the roof and ignited the hoard of gunpowder. A vast explosion at the very centre of the temple sent columns, bits of pediment, roof and sculpture spinning across the Acropolis.

And here begins the great scandal. In 1801, Lord Elgin, Britain's ambassador to Constantinople, obtained permission from the sultan to remove such sculptures as he saw fit. From 1801 to 1812 Elgin peeled about half of the remaining marbles from the Parthenon and shipped them to England. He has been vilified for it ever since.

Transporting the hugely heavy and unwieldy cargo was both dangerous and expensive: Elgin was soon vastly in debt. Desperate, he approached the British Government in a bid to sell the marbles for £74,000. That was about £1,000 less than the whole enterprise had already cost him. In 1816 Parliament offered him £36,000.

Only ten years or so after the last of Elgin's marbles were lifted down to the port in Piraeus, the Acropolis was a war zone once again. Eventually, Western governments intervened in the Greek War of Independence and a new king was found – the young Prince Otto of Bavaria. On the shattered Acropolis, broken pillars,

**ABOVE** The temple, now without most of its famous marble sculptured reliefs, is a bride stripped bare. Vandalism? Perhaps. But it is clear the Parthenon has a potent new enemy: pollution

cannonballs, shell fragments and human skulls and bones littered the ground. Nothing daunted, Leo von Klenze (designer of the Walhalla) set about stripping the site of 'all the remains of barbarity' with glee.

This first major excavation of the site was a disaster, whipping away huge amounts of historical evidence in a frenzy of cultural cleansing. The ancient Greeks walked on a carefully prepared surface, but the Prussian excavations went down deeper and deeper through the soil, until nothing was left but the slippery natural bedrock. All that you can see is what the archaeologists chose to leave, with all later history stripped away.

Le Corbusier may have taken inspiration from the very severity and simplicity of what he saw, but an ancient Greek would have seen the once colourful temple as a mutilated carcass. His reactions highlight the paradox at the heart of the temple's modern, iconic status. We venerate the temple as a noble ruin that speaks of peace and antiquity. But we are far from seeing it as the ancient Greeks did.

Not only that, but the temple's history does not represent peace, but conquest and violence. The intriguing truth is that all of us, from Corbusier to Elgin, from tourist to archaeologist, see in the Parthenon only what we want to see.

# ROME: CROSSING CONTINENTS

According to Livy, when workers began digging the foundations for Rome's first temple they came upon a human head.

*'All the features [were] in perfect condition. There could be no doubt the discovery meant that this place would be at the head of the empire – and the world.'*

Livy was right. In a built history that extended for more than a thousand years, the Romans did not just transform their own 'eternal' city: they forged an empire. Their achievements in engineering and architecture are unparalleled. By the time of Julius Caesar (c.100–44BC) Rome's vast empire stretched from Spain to Syria, from North Africa to Germany, bringing together the people from three continents.

When Caesar conquered Gaul (later France) and then set his sights on Britain, the citizens of this proto-Europe may well have

appreciated many of the innovations the invaders brought with them. Creature comforts such as baths and underfloor heating were unknown before Roman rule, as were other practical innovations like the wine press and the sewer. Civilizing institutions like the rule of law made life easier and safer for most citizens, as did improvements to the infrastructure such as the building of market places *(fora)* and the superb Roman roads.

During the first half of Rome's history – the Republican period – architecture was relatively restrained. After the civil wars it was the great generals – Sulla, Pompey and Julius Caesar – who began to create the architecture of a world capital whose remains we still admire today. A ruler who has unimaginable power and wealth turns to his architects. Julius Caesar was no exception, but it was Augustus, who came to power in 27BC, who had the biggest impact on Rome. Before Augustus, Rome was a jumbled, messy, crowded city made of wood and brick. Augustus left it, as he himself said, 'a city of marble'.

The Romans were the first to use sheets of marble as a wall cladding, which made laboriously cut marble go much further. The trick was to use their new invention, cement, to hold the marble facing in place.

During Augustus' reign marble and marble-clad buildings were going up everywhere, with more than 50 varieties of the stone available. He also built and enlarged Rome's roads, restored its temples and remodelled the Forum. The Forum was at the heart of the central political, administrative, judicial and economic power of the city.

Augustus thought big – the large and richly-decorated Basilica Aemilia was regarded as one of the most beautiful buildings in ancient Rome – but he could also think small. He even commissioned a study on roof tiles, to find out which design best resisted storm damage. Augustus rebuilt public buildings like the Senate House, where his adoptive father Julius Caesar had been assassinated. Across Rome, richly ornamented buildings in precious polychrome marble sprang up, often using the flamboyant

**LEFT** The cool and calm of the Roman baths at Bath, England. Cities across Europe, Africa and the Middle East bear the civilizing stamp of the Romans

Corinthian order, with its implied overtones of purity and rebirth. Augustus reigned for 41 years, for which period of prosperity and development Rome – and the rest of the world – has to be grateful.

Under Trajan and Hadrian, the Roman Empire reached the height of its power. The non-patrician Trajan (c.AD53–117), who ruled from AD98, took control of the immensely wealthy Dacian region in Romania, and a new flood of gold hit the imperial treasury. He then had a new forum built that was more than 300 times the size of Augustus'.

Not content with that, he positioned a freestanding column on its main axis, celebrating (mainly) his ego. Although this was an unusual feature in the Roman architecture of the time, the basic idea has since been emulated all over the world. Originally, a bronze equestrian statue of Trajan himself sat on top.

Taken together, the *fora* of Caesar, Augustus and Trajan occupied a huge area. It's a thoroughly urban composition and one we would recognize today for its thoughtful and public-spirited design. It

allowed people to wander through gracious colonnaded spaces in order to shop and browse.

Hadrian (AD76–138) was a poet, a painter and a military commander all in one, proclaimed emperor by the army in AD117. His effect on architecture would be felt in every corner of the empire, not least when it came to Hadrian's Wall, the spectacular fortification that marches between England and Scotland. He restored ancient Athens. In Rome, he commissioned many fine buildings, none so revered as the Pantheon (c.AD125). Hadrian had spent time in Alexandria and the Hellenistic east and his new building rejected the old model of the *cella*, which deliberately excluded the light. Instead, a special oculus pierced in the summit of the Pantheon's immense dome invites the light to enter with ease.

The building can seem dour from the outside. It has lost its original marble cladding, as well as the broad stepped court that would once have led up to it. All this was long ago sacrificed to the modern deity of the motorcar. But step inside and your perception is transformed: the Pantheon is a hymn to light.

The sun's rays move like a searchlight through the space, slowly illuminating the interior in a moving pattern – from the floor, with its patina of orange, red and white marbles brought from all over the empire, to the alternating rectangular and round niches of the walls. Overhead, the coffering emphasizes the sense of perspective as its rings of sunken panels diminish in size the nearer they get to the oculus. The overall effect is to create the sensation of a roof floating in space, just like the dust motes in the bright shaft of light. Although the coffering was once opulent and gilded, the way it is now, we feel its pared down and severe structural effect much more strongly .

The oculus might have had a more esoteric significance. Here was a temple to all the gods – the meaning of 'pantheon' – and the heavens where they lived. The cultivated Hadrian may well have been initiated into the Eleusinian Mysteries, a Greek cult in which the sun played a an important mystical role. The alternating niches in the walls perhaps contained images of the gods and the planets, each illuminated by the great searchlight of

**BELOW** Crazy paving: marble stone floor in Trajan's Forum which dates from AD106–112; the material used is *pavonazzetto*, a granitic marble mined in Turkey

**FAR LEFT** The Forum Romanum was the centre of political, religious and commercial life in Rome, a natural focal point between the seven hills. In the foreground is the Temple of Saturn

**ABOVE** Trajan's column, an astounding pillar monument and a historic scroll in architectural form, shows the triumphant progress of his Dacian campaign

**LEFT** The Pantheon's dome, the widest in the world, was not bettered until the 19th century. The revolutionary construction comes from a single shell of concrete, made light by a mix of volcanic tufa and pumice

# Marble

Their conquest of the Mediterranean basin gave the Romans access to an extraordinary array of coloured stones: yellow marble *(giallo antico)* from Tunisia, purple and white marble *(pavonazzetto)* from Turkey, and red, green, and a rich green-black from Greece. Egypt was the richest source of coloured rock, providing red, grey and black granite, basalts, sedimentary stones and even shiny black volcanic glass (obsidian). Sardonyx was imported from as far as India. Cippolino, named after the onion, is one of the most famous marbles of Greece because of its sinuous, curving veins. It was used at the Victorian Westminster Cathedral and in the 20th century for pillars in New York's Public Library.

the sun in turn. But the building, with its sculptures of both gods and deified emperors could also have had a political purpose. Here, Hadrian held judicial court. The Pantheon may have been the great emperor's impressive structural metaphor for Rome as the cosmos of the earth.

Hadrian was an enthusiastic architect. He sponsored hundreds of buildings around the empire, travelling with a court of 'geometers, architects and every sort of expert in construction and decoration'. The emperor also built himself one of the most important villas in history, near the modern town of Tivoli. Hadrian's Villa (early 2nd century AD) looks out from the countryside towards Rome. It is important in history because it was not simply a house and not simply a garden: it was designed as a built story – a garden of memories and allusions, full of references to Hadrian's campaigns, victories and unparalleled travels through the empire.

The villa's luxuries included a stadium and a series of baths that ended in the spectacular Canopus: a long lake lined with sculpture, including copies of the caryatids of Athens' Erechtheion. Diners reclined on bench seats near a semicircular pool, where they could float food back and forth to each other.

While Rome had seen some great and popular emperors Nero, who ruled from AD54, was not one of them. A notorious tyrant and profligate, he was nevertheless a great patron of architecture, sport and the arts. He commissioned a number of amphitheatres and gymnasia and his love of games and spectacle didn't stop with sport. Nero was also famous for his parties. The guilty secret of Nero's refulgent pleasure palace was hidden for centuries until, at the end of the 15th century, a young Roman fell through a deep cleft in the Aventine hillside. He landed Alice-like in a magical cave or *grotta* filled with painted figures; it was Nero's Domus Aurea. Soon artists such as Pinturicchio, Raphael and Michelangelo were all crawling undergound to see the remarkable frescoes. The influence of Nero's fantasy house spread as far as Robert Adam's *grotesques* in the 18th century – the very word taken from Nero's cave.

The Domus Aurea, or 'Golden House', was extravagance and ostentation laid out in stone. Set in its own special landscape park, its rooms were clad in polished white marble. Pools and fountains splashed in the salons and corridors, while semi-precious stones and ivory veneer embellished the villa's walls. Mosaics, previously used only on floors, brought the vaulted ceilings to life, the first known use of a technique that would become a crucial feature of early Christian and Byzantine art.

**ABOVE** Statues from Nero's sumptuous Golden House were taken to Hadrian's own countryside villa (see also below). Nero's villa was lost to history, but miraculously rediscovered in the Renaissance

**BELOW** Hadrian's lyrical villa and garden, near Tivoli in Italy, celebrated this scholar/tactician's military campaigns and his travels throughout the Roman Empire

## Concrete

Without the invention of concrete the Romans could not have built on anything like the size and scale that they did. The Colosseum's massive walls and vaults are concrete. The modern substance, developed in England by Joseph Aspdin in 1824, is made of chalk and clay. Its Roman antecedent is based on volcanic ash, which was ground up and mixed with water. The process sets off a chemical reaction that turns the mix into artificial stone. Made solely of concrete, the dome of the Pantheon is an engineering marvel. It would have been layered – it was too thick to pour – against a temporary wooden framework. Because it needed to be seamless, this would have been an immensely complex process, involving gangs of skilled labourers working at top speed. The Pantheon's dome has a span of 142 feet (43 metres), which made it the largest dome of its time. And for some time to come – 1,300 years, in fact.

The historian Tacitus describes an amazing mechanism, cranked by slaves, that made the ceiling underneath the dome revolve like the heavens, while perfume and rose petals descended on to the party animals below. One unlucky guest is said to have suffocated. Tacitus also tells us that Nero personally oversaw the work of the architects Celer and Severus as they engineered a navigable canal through the grounds. In AD72–3 Vespasian began his floodable Flavian Amphitheatre, later called the Colosseum, on the site of the lake of Nero's Golden House (Domus Aurea). Titus later built his Baths (AD81) over the rest of the Golden House.

The Colosseum was a remarkable landmark from its very beginnings. It sits at the heart of a valley between three hills, visible from all sides. The arena's entertainments included mock sea battles *(naumachiae)*, during which the auditorium was flooded, re-enactments of famous historical tales and the all-important gladiator fights. When Titus, Vespasian's son, inaugurated the amphitheatre in AD80, the occasion was marked by 100 orgiastic days of festive games. The arena became a tropical jungle, and gladiators fought panthers, elephants and ostriches. Five thousand animals were killed.

Despite subsequent abuse at the hands of the Romans themselves, this symbol of Rome's might remains one of the best-loved and probably most-studied buildings in the world. Generations of schoolchildren are introduced to the whole idea of architecture, design and indeed history through this one structure. History, though, has been hard on the Colosseum. The great theatre where defenceless Christians were fed to the lions survived earthquake, fire and looting, but was less successful at deflecting the architectural depradations of successive popes. Only two-thirds of the travertine marble exterior remains.

The Colosseum was a highly innovative building. It was the first freestanding theatre – other examples, like the one in Lepcis Magna in North Africa, were partially carved out of the rock. Practically speaking, the remaining shell owes its longevity to its amazing concrete vaults. Aesthetically, the exterior has a unique and rhythmic system of attached columns and arched entrances, divided into Doric, Ionic and Corinthian layers, with a fourth walled storey that is measured in (flatter, Corinthian) pilasters. The columns are severe, stripped down to their basic form. The overall effect is to emphasize the masculine character of the

**ABOVE** The Colosseum, largest amphitheatre in the Roman world and emblem of the might of Rome. Underground, thirty niches had tackle blocks to winch wild beasts and gladiators into the arena

structure. This architectural device was so successful that the Colosseum set the rules for the classical orders – Doric at the bottom, Ionic in the middle and Corinthian at the top – from then on.

The elliptical colossus was welcomed as the 'eighth wonder of the world' by the poet Martial. It could hold up to 70,000 spectators. Barrel-vaulted passages ran round the building, allowing quick access to and from any level. The Colosseum is the ultimate symbol of a society at its mightiest, but also its cruellest. It seems somehow apt that its awful beauty has been plundered. It is the fate of so many great buildings to be ransacked, their treasures stolen and their stones reused: *sic transit gloria mundi.* It happened at Petra, at the Parthenon, at the Pantheon.

Yet the architecture of Rome has been a fount of inspiration to the world's best architects – and has also fed the imagination of tyrants. Rome's buildings express the contradiction faced by even the best builders and architects. Architecture can only be as ambitious as the society it serves.

# Outpost of Empire

The well-ordered city was at the heart of Rome's success. Civilized cities were the prime agents in spreading 'Romanitas': Roman privilege, values and culture across the empire. People who lived in the countryside were *'paganus'* – the origin of the word 'pagan'.

Nîmes in southeastern France was one such outpost, in what was then Gaul. Named Nemausus by the Romans, the city was strategically important as a *mansio* or stopping point on the Via Domitia. Begun in 118BC, this remarkable Roman road connected Italy to Spain. Veterans who had served Julius Caesar in his Nile campaigns were given their own plots of land on the city's surrounding fertile plain.

Nîmes is lucky enough to have one of the world's best-preserved amphitheatres and possibly the world's most revered aqueduct, a technical masterpiece in the shape of the late 1st century AD Pont du Gard. 'I walked along the three stages of this superb construction, with a respect that made me almost shrink from treading on it,' Jean-Jacques Rousseau wrote in awe. 'The echo of my footsteps under the immense arches made me think I could hear the strong voices of the men who had built it. I felt lost like an insect in the immensity of the work.'

The landmark, a three-tier combination bridge and aqueduct whose arches span 900 feet (274 metres), has outlasted everything the years have thrown at it. What the Romans knew was that arches placed end to end (an arcade) cancel out lateral force. Buttressing is needed only at the extremities.

Nîmes is also lucky in having a perfectly-proportioned and virtually untouched Roman temple which has been hugely influential in architecture. The Maison Carrée survived down the centuries because the townsfolk converted it for other uses. It is now flanked by a modern art gallery in steel and glass known as the Carrée d'Art. This rather sterile space echoing the temple's shape was built by British architect Sir Norman Foster – 2,000 years after the original.

Despite being built in the reign of Augustus, the Maison Carrée's design is

**ABOVE** The Pont du Gard's unadorned stone blocks emphasize the beauty and sheer scale of this engineering achievement, the highest aqueduct the Romans ever built. Its third tier provides a footbridge

**RIGHT** Town halls and art galleries across the world have mimicked this best preserved of Roman temples. The Maison Carrée's architrave is decorated with restrained acanthus leaves and rosettes

typical of early Roman temples. Its Corinthian columns are emphasized at the front, while the *cella* (or inner chamber) is protected by a wall with 'engaged' columns that are part of its surface. Roman buildings increasingly exploited the idea of a wall as a standing sculpture, with the column as a first step. This idea would be picked up with enthusiasm by the architects of the Renaissance and later, the Baroque.

Despite its beauty, the 'square' house has a sad story. It was built c.19–16BC by Marcus Vipsanius Agrippa, a brave and ingenious military commander who had fought with Mark Antony and Octavian. A driving force in the improvement of Augustan Rome's sewers, aqueducts and public gardens, Agrippa so impressed Augustus that the emperor adopted his sons, Gaius and Lucius.

In 1758 Jean-François Séguier, a local scholar, realized that bronze lettering had once been fixed to the temple portico. From the order and number of the fixing holes he painstakingly reconstructed the inscription. It read:

*'To Gaius Caesar, son of Augustus, Consul; to Lucius Caesar, son of Augustus, Consul designate. To the princes of youth.'*

Sadly, both sons died long before they could fulfil their father's hopes. The temple at Nîmes was their funerary monument.

# Petra: Becalmed in the Desert

Petra's ethereal, abandoned beauty is testament to an ancient and cosmopolitan culture. High in the Esh Shara mountains, it was capital to the Nabataean Kingdom, which controlled one of the most important trading routes in the world. Arabian myrrh, frankincense and spices moved up the trade route from here to the Mediterranean. In turn copper, iron, sculpture and the purple-dyed cloth of the Phoenicians flooded back through its marketplaces. These goods were ultimately destined for the powerful trading posts of the Red Sea and the Persian Gulf.

Carved out of the cliffs of a remote gorge in Jordan, Petra's temples, homes and warehouses were lost under a shroud of sand until a Swiss explorer, Johann Burckhardt, disguised himself as a Muslim in 1810 and set off across Syria by camel. He came upon a long and winding canyon, with high red sandstone walls and dense vegetation to either side. Burckhardt became convinced that whatever was at the end of it must be of real importance.

*'In continuing along the winding passage of the Syk, I saw in several places small niches cut in the rock, some of which were single; in other places there were three or four together, without any regularity ... they vary in size from ten inches to four or five feet in height; and in some of them the bases of statues are still visible.'*

**RIGHT** The Treasury, or Khazneh. Legend says that the pharaoh pursuing Moses left his treasure in the topmost sandstone urn of its surprising split pediment. No wonder Petra was used as a backdrop for Hollywood's *Raiders of the Lost Ark*

Petra's wealth, remoteness and the impregnability of its chasm home made it a formidable enemy. Before the indomitable Romans, the city was left to develop largely in peace. It had a highly individualistic culture: there were no slaves and women attained high social rank. No-one, not even the king, was exempt from work. The thousands of private houses, inns and stables that would once have greeted visitors and traders were made of mud and brush, but have long since melted back into the desert.

What we have left are the ceremonial buildings, the ruins of the great central temple known as Qasr el-Bint and more than 500 princely grand façades, hewn out of the cliffs. The Nabataean style owes a lot to the ancient architecture of Greece, but its idiosyncratic broad ledges and cut pediments were unprecedented. Scholars believe that the flat plateaux carved out of the surrounding mountain summits were once used as open air sanctuaries for animal sacrifice. Their carved altars would have been covered in beaten gold.

In AD106 Trajan finally won the prize pearl of Petra and it became a Roman province. Next came Arab invaders and Christian crusaders, who finally abandoned the 'city of stone' to the red-veined desert from which it had sprung.

When Burckhardt scrambled out of the dark, forbidding cold of the overgrown gorge, he suddenly found himself facing an extraordinary sight. The majestic Khazneh Firaoun loomed up in front of him. Its colonnade, made up of slightly baroque, curved-top Corinthian columns, was about 35 feet (10.5 metres) high. This was topped by an architrave adorned with sculpted vases, connected together by festoons. He later wrote:

*'It is one of the most elegant remains of antiquity existing. Its state of preservation resembles that of a building recently finished, and on a closer examination I found it to be a work of immense labour.'*

The Khazneh is fancifully named: it translates as 'the Treasury of the Pharaohs'. But Burckhardt got it right on instinct: these grand hand-carved creations were tombs for the Nabataean dead.

# The Roman Arch

Just four of Rome's massive triumphal arches still stand. They deserve a mention here because of their huge architectural influence. The Romans did not invent the arch – the Mesopotamians, Sumerians and Etruscans all used them – but they managed to use it in really inventive ways. It was masterfully employed in structures such as aqueducts, bridges and dams, where it was able to efficiently span space while supporting significant weight.

The triumphal arch, however, was an innovative, even megalomaniacal, flight of fancy. It was architecture as celebration, as story: its surface carried the narrative of military victory in sculptural form. It also relieved architects from the responsibility of having to design a useful building that actually had to 'work'. This enviable freedom from responsibility may be why these arches are so creatively designed.

The Arch of Titus (below right) was built on the Via Sacra in Rome after the sack of Jerusalem in AD70. The capitals are the first known use of the Composite order, in which acanthus leaves are combined with Ionic volutes. Until the creation of the State of Israel, Jews refused to walk under this arch, in protest at the Romans' desecration of Jerusalem's Temple. Now they may pass beneath it – but only in the opposite direction to Rome.

The Arch of Septimius Severus has been much mangled by time and the muddy waters of the river Tiber. It is somehow all the nobler for it. The arch commemorates Septimus' victories over the Parthians in AD197–9. Just under 70 feet (21 metres) high and 76 feet (23 metres) wide, it is made of delicate Proconessian white marble from the Sea of Marmara.

The monumental Arch of Janus is interesting from the point of view of architectural proportion. Its two blocky intersecting arches look ugly solely because the arch is out of kilter. It has lost its attic. Used at one point as a fortress, it was torn down in error by people who thought the top of the arch was a later addition. The niches – now empty – would have once held figurines. It was perhaps built by Constantine I the Great (AD274–337).

The Arch of Constantine stands right beside the Colosseum. It was erected in AD312–15 to celebrate Constantine I's victory over local pagan rival Maxentius. It is highly elaborate and rhetorical, in contrast to Titus' relatively restrained monument, with three arched openings instead of one and imposing sculptural figures gazing out from the attic storey.

**ABOVE** The mighty arch of Septimius Severus is now badly weathered. Dedicated to the Emperor and his sons Caracalla and Geta in AD203 – but Caracalla had his brother murdered, and removed all mentions of his name

**RIGHT** The Ianus Quadrifrons, or Janus arch, may once have been a roofed street crossing in the lively commercial quarter. In Latin, Janus means 'passage'

**ABOVE** The beautiful Arch of Constantine is a magpie monument: by the 4th century, Rome had lost much power, and all of the great sculptors' studios had closed. Most of these reliefs are taken from older buildings

**RIGHT** The oldest surviving example of a Roman arch, the restrained Arch of Titus, was restored in the early 1820s

51

# THE MIDDLE AGES

Mont Saint Michel is an ideal place to begin a journey through the medieval world. Although built as an abbey, it also had to function as a castle, typical in a highly unstable Europe under frequent attack. The colourful life story of its architect, William de Volpiano, tells a similar tale about these lawless times. The son of an Italian count, he was born during an assault on his family's island citadel. The victor, Emperor Otto the Great, adopted the infant. This was a dangerous world, but Otto became the first 'Holy Roman Emperor' and the Christian faith – and Volpiano's church-citadels – his means of control.

Le Mont Saint Michel in Normandy, France: Italian architect and monk William de Volpiano designed the Romanesque abbey in the 11th century, with daring details in the new Gothic style

# IN PURSUIT OF THE DIVINE

Poverty-stricken and persecuted, early Christianity was rooted in simple living and the pious expectation of a Second Coming. The slaves and artisans to whom this religion first appealed looked forward to a heavenly paradise rather than any reward on earth. Forced to worship in secret, at first there was no occasion – and no money – for elaborate earthly shrines.

**B**ut as the Roman Empire converted to the new religion, churches slowly became the buildings into which a community would pour its entire being – mind, body and soul. In AD313 the first Christian emperor of the Roman Empire, Constantine I, made the new religion official. Gradually, the old culture of Rome and the new forms of Christianity began to fuse.

Early churches were deliberately plain. Places of worship were, in a sense, a metaphor for the human body: their souls – the important and interesting bit – were on the inside. So long as it functioned, the shell was unimportant. But human beings have a tendency to confuse spiritual values with temporal ones: architecture is often caught in the middle. So the basic basilica plan was adapted from the palace template – 'basilical' originally meaning royal. In essence, the basilica was a long oblong hall, usually with a semicircular apse.

In AD330 Constantine attempted to strengthen the fragmenting Roman Empire by refounding Byzantium as Constantinople. His new metropolis would become one of the world's greatest capitals, surpassing many in wealth, beauty and ambition. It also moved Roman power decisively east, with far-reaching cultural implications.

Byzantine art and architecture reinforced religious experience by creating an otherworldly atmosphere of mystery and sensual delight. High mosaic-lined domes lit by flickering lamps were flooded with the heady odour of incense. Colourful mosaics brought churches like San Vitale in Ravenna, built by the Emperor Justinian between 532 and 548, to dazzling life.

**LEFT** The abbey of Romanmôtier is the largest and oldest Roman church in Switzerland; it was built between 990 and 1028 by Cluniac monks

**ABOVE** San Vitale's apse, where the enigmatic figure of Christ sits on the sphere of the world, flanked by the martyr San Vitale, two angels and Bishop Ecclesius

**TOP RIGHT** The ravishing Byzantine mosaics and marbles of Ravenna's San Vitale. The view to the north wall (right) shows Justinian, in imperial purple, preparing to hold the bread for Mass

**ABOVE** San Vitale's calm exterior. The unknown architect cared more about the building's interior and the series of intriguing spaces he could create within than he did about a showy exterior

# Key Dates

**532** Hagia Sophia is built.

**705–15** Foundation of the Great Mosque in Damascus.

**800** Pope Leo III crowns Charlemagne at the basilica of St Peter's, Rome.

**802** The Vikings raid Iona.

**862** Magyar raids on Bulgaria, Moravia and the Frankish Empire.

**962** Otto the Great becomes Holy Roman Emperor, ruling Europe.

**976** The Great Mosque of Cordoba.

**c.1000** Gunpowder is invented in China; First Americans build granaries in the cliffs along the Verde River, USA.

**1045** The beginnings of Westminster Abbey under Edward the Confessor.

**1066** After the Battle of Hastings, William the Conqueror is King of England.

**1070** St Albans Cathedral is commenced.

**1090** Durham Cathedral is founded.

**c.1100** The Tower of London welcomes its first prisoners.

**1104–1260** Chartres Cathedral.

**1140–4** The ambulatory of the abbey of Saint-Denis is built, the earliest complete Gothic structure.

**1147** Moscow is founded by Prince Yuri Dolgoruky, who also built the first fortress, or Kremlin, along the banks of the Moscow River.

**1170** Leonardo Fibonacci, the Italian mathematician, is born. He is said to have discovered 'Fibonacci numbers' after studying the Great Pyramid of Giza; Thomas à Becket is murdered in Canterbury Cathedral.

**1175–1490** Wells Cathedral.

**1184** The first Inquisition begins.

**1189** Richard the Lionheart rules the Angevin Empire.

**1215** Magna Carta is signed.

**1265** Dante Alighieri is born.

# Hagia Sophia

Instead of bringing in a master builder to build his new church in Constantinople, the Emperor Justinian turned to some philosophers. The result, a cube covered by a dome, was a metaphor for the universe. Construction work began in AD532 and the building was completed only five years late. Justinian then fell to his knees in the centre of the church, so the tale goes, and declared 'Solomon, I have surpassed thee!'

Anthemios of Tralles and Isidoros of Miletos, the architects, were both experts in theoretical physics, and the church they devised would be called the 'Church of Divine Wisdom' (Sophia being the Goddess of Wisdom). From the outside, the great basilica looks tired and dusty, like a great beetle that has flown into the crowded, densely packed streets of Istanbul and never quite recovered from the trauma. Some have criticized its masons for using too much mortar, others say that the mortar was not given long enough to dry. Whatever the reason, Sophia is sagging at the stays.

The interior, however, is sublime. It is sheathed in incredibly rich white, green, black and orange marbles from throughout the Roman Empire, with screens of arcades on all sides. The dark green marble columns in the aisles are remarkably graceful: the craftsmen have worked with the grain of their material, moulding the form like sculptors. It is no surprise, then, to find that they were taken from the fabled Temple of Artemis at Ephesus, once a seventh wonder of the world. And the stunning dark red porphyry columns in the *exedrae,* or vestibules, were snatched from the exotic Temple of Zeus at Baalbek.

The walls shimmer opulently with gold mosaic. But this is not what moves the visitor. Sophia's astonishing effect on the emotions lies in the interaction of the lovingly-polished natural surfaces as they gleam in the light that floods from 40 high windows piercing the lofty central dome. Anthemios and Isidoros supported their daring shallow saucer – 107 feet (32 metres) wide – with pendentive vaults

broken by windows, an engineering breakthrough that transformed architecture.

When Constantinople was captured by the Ottoman Turks in 1453, Hagia Sophia became a mosque. Despite its Christian origins, the Hagia then became a model for all of Istanbul's major mosques, such as the Süleymaniye, built by the great Mimar Sinan from 1550.

As with the complex history of the Parthenon, Hagia Sophia's double life as both a church and a mosque poses restoration dilemmas. The early Christian mosaics that are being gradually uncovered threaten later works of Islamic art. The restorers have to find a balance. The minarets that apparently support Sophia are aesthetically far from perfect. One of them is made of red brick, while the other three are white marble. That, however, is the least of the restorers' concerns: the mathematical paradise Anthemios and Isidoros built did not include minarets. Now more museum than mosque, Hagia Sophia awaits the next chapter in her long history.

RIGHT The vast, light-filled interior reaches to an extraordinary gallery and four pendentive vaults, an architectural mannerism that was influential in the Eastern Orthodox, Catholic and Muslim worlds

BELOW Hagia Sophia – the Church of Divine Wisdom – was built in Constantinople, now Istanbul, in a world-record five years. The smaller, peripheral domes are mausoleums built by Muslim worshippers in the 16th century

# The Birth of Baghdad

On the afternoon of Saturday 31 July 762 in the Julian calendar, the caliph of the second Abbasid dynasty, al-Mansur, set about building a new capital for his empire. He called it Medina al-Salam, or the City of Peace – a name which in our own time could hardly be less appropriate. Al-Mansur had assembled an army of 100,000 stonemasons, carpenters, artists, workers and craftsmen of every kind for the building of his new city. However, they had to wait until his personal astrologer, Nawbakht the Persian (c.679–777), decreed that the Zodiac was favourable.

Nawbakht's influence did not just extend to astrological portents. He insisted on a defensive ground plan. The new city, Baghdad (the name, derived from Persian, means 'God-given' or 'the Given Garden'), formed a perfect circle some 1.25 miles (2 kilometres) in diameter. Twin concentric stone walls enclosed the whole, with a moat providing further protection. The massive perimeter was pierced by four gates. At the city's very heart was the mosque. This originally adjoined the caliph's personal residence, the Golden Gate Palace. The Golden Gate Palace had a green dome 160 feet (49 metres) high, surmounted by a magical iron statue of a cavalryman holding a lance. It was said that this horseman always pointed to the enemies of Islam.

Nearby were barracks for the city guards, mansions and administrative offices. Broad, tree-lined avenues interspersed with parks and gardens radiated like spokes from this central hub. People called it 'the navel of the universe'.

Built of bricks measuring 18 inches on all sides, or marble for the grander buildings, Baghdad was an immediate and meteoric success. Abbasid architecture is marked by a new monumental scale, the use of structural systems composed of massive brick piers and arches and decoration in brick or carved and moulded stucco. Although the modern city has

obliterated the medieval one, we can assume that the mosque was also on a monumental scale. The Great Mosque of al-Mutawakkil at Samarra might be a parallel. Still the largest mosque in the world, its minaret forms a dramatic spiral that draws on the ancient Near Eastern tradition of the ziggurat.

By 950, Baghdad's population had risen to c.400,000 – the largest in the world. But perhaps the most striking thing about the 'Round City', as it was sometimes known, was its openness to the outside world. Al-Mansur sought out learned texts from all

ages and traditions and had them translated into Arabic in a purpose-built centre he named 'The House of Wisdom'.

Alas, it was not to last. In 1055 the Seljuq Turk leader Tughril Beg invaded and subsequently conquered the City of Peace. Worse was to come. On 10 February 1258 the Mongols took the city by storm. The caliph, al-Mustasim, offered unconditional surrender. Despite this, Ulegu's men embarked on a terrible week-long killing spree that saw men, women and children slaughtered indiscriminately. Most of the city was razed.

**RIGHT** The burnt brick walls of the Great Mosque at Samarra, Iraq, protect a massive arcaded courtyard and the monumental spiral minaret of al-Malwiya. The winding ramp ascends to 55m (180ft)

# ISLAM

Three hundred years after the rich Byzantine style evolved with Christianity, a new religion, Islam, burst into the vacuum in the Middle East left after the Romans' departure. The faith spread rapidly through the Middle East to Africa, Europe, the Indian subcontinent, the Malay Peninsula and China. With its strict laws forbidding representational imagery, Islam would make an enormous impact on architecture. The first Islamic conquests in Syria, Persia and Palestine were made by the Bedouins, who simply modified the buildings they took.

**ABOVE** Damascus' multi-cultural history is expressed perfectly in the magnificent Great Mosque. The shrine in the main prayer hall contains either the head of Zechariah, the father of St John the Baptist or that of Hussein Ali, depending on your faith

**S**o Christian churches became mosques, just as temples had once been converted into churches. The original inspiration behind any new community mosque came from the Prophet's house Al-Masjid al-Nabawi, at Medina. Built with palm trunks and mud

**RIGHT** The 12th century Courtyard of the Dolls, Seville. The name refers to the legend that the Moors demanded 100 virgins every year as tribute from Christian kingdoms

ABOVE Capital to the Umayyad Empire it may have been, but Damascus' Great Mosque has Byzantine and Roman elements. It stands on ancient Aramaean foundations

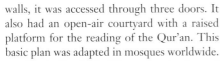

RIGHT Spain's Cordoba Mosque, concealed behind dour stone walls, has a lace-like ceiling and a remarkable, cavernous prayer hall filled with rhythmic granite and jasper columns

walls, it was accessed through three doors. It also had an open-air courtyard with a raised platform for the reading of the Qur'an. This basic plan was adapted in mosques worldwide.

Gradually, the buildings grew in size and splendour. The enormous Umayyad Mosque of Damascus was once part of a 1st century Hellenistic temple to Jupiter. It contains an ornate raised shrine to the head of St John the Baptist, a relic honoured by both Muslims and Christians. Founded in AD705–15 by the Umayyad Caliph al-Walid I, and also known as the 'Great Mosque', the structure was the largest and most impressive in the Islamic world at the time. The three aisles of the prayer hall are supported by truly ancient Corinthian columns.

Under Islam a vast area stretching from the Mediterranean to India was unified for the first time since the days of Alexander the Great. This gave a fresh impetus to urban life, trade and culture. By the 9th century AD Arab merchants were trading as far afield as China and Arab culture was already influencing the Byzantine world of Venice.

Then in AD711 the Muslim leader Tariq ibn Ziyad sailed across the Strait of Gibraltar to what we now call southern Spain. He conquered Baetica (now Andalusia) and Toledo. Arab forces went on to capture Mérida, Saragossa and eventually Seville.

The influence of the Arab conquerors resulted in the Mudéjar style, a fusion of Islamic and Western architectural influences. Originally constructed during the Almohad reign, and rebuilt by Pedro I in 1364, the Alcázar of Seville – particularly the Courtyard of the Dolls – is a striking example of this engagement.

The Great Mosque at Córdoba was retained by popular vote when Córdoba came back under Christian control. In the 16th century Charles V even went on to add a Gothic 'chapel'.

Paradoxically, inventive thinking was stimulated by the Islamic restriction on figurative representation. As mathematicians will attest, Arab designers and architects have given the world many buildings of extraordinary geometrical invention.

## The Minaret

This is the Arabic word for 'beacon', or 'light'. As Islam was a religion of conquest, minarets originally served as watchtowers, illuminated by torches. From these practical origins, minarets gradually evolved into universally-recognized symbols of the Islamic faith. The number of minarets on a mosque can vary from one to six. They often have projecting balconies ascending the tower, or friezes of stalactite vaulting with a distinctive small onion-shaped dome at the top. For centuries *muezzin* took advantage of the minaret's height to cry the call to prayer. In most modern mosques, the *adhan* is called through a loudspeaker. The tallest minarets in the world are currently under construction in Tehran. They will be 750 feet (230 metres) high.

The structures are such a strong symbolic marker of Muslim presence that they are often the object of controversy. Although a minaret was built in Zurich as long ago as 1963 (it's very white, very minimalist and very Swiss), a section of the Swiss population want it to be the last, citing Article 72 of the Swiss constitution.

# The Palace of Symmetry

The Alhambra is a hymn to built perfection. Walk though the courtyards and it seems as if the entire extended complex hovers on water: standing at the end of the pool in the Courtyard of the Myrtles, a flawless mirror image of the Palace reflects into the clear blue sky. Brush the water with a finger and the fleeting symmetry is destroyed – a haunting image of the fragility and transience of human life.

Magnificently sited on a rock outcrop overlooking the city of Granada, the Alhambra, or 'red fortress', was the home of Spain's last Muslim rulers, the Nasrid dynasty. Much of what remains was built between 1350 and 1400, at a time when Christian Spain was pushing the Moors slowly out of *al-andalus,* the south. Tall greenwoods surround the complex, mostly English elm trees planted by the Duke of Wellington. Today the reddish-brown exterior gives little hint of what lies within.

Nature is everywhere used to advantage. The alignment of its courtyards turns the Alhambra into a vast sundial. Light floods through the windows into the Courtyard of the Lions, an intimate private garden for the sultan and his household. As dappled daylight streams through the pillars, the cast shadows act like the hands of a heavenly clock. Water is another essential feature of the Alhambra, as it is in Islamic architectural tradition as a whole. Pools and fountains are valued for their cooling effect and the relaxing sound made by the water's play. But most importantly, water is used for its reflections. It is a foil for the ultimate Moorish architectural weapon: symmetry.

At a smaller, more intricate level of symmetry, the palace is decorated with many-pointed interlocking patterns: a forest of stars, triangles, polygons and diamonds. Covering the ceilings, walls and floors in repeating patterns, they create a rhythm that makes it feel as if the walls have no limits. This artistic suggestion of infinity delighted the Moors, just as it fascinated the Dutch artist Escher, who visited the Alhambra many times.

Throughout the 13th and the early 14th centuries the site was adapted into an

extended citadel, with high ramparts and defensive towers. The slab-sided Alcazaba, or fortress, was reinforced and its watchtower, the Torre de la Vela, was built. But it was during the reigns of Yusuf I (1333–53) and Mohammed V (1353–91) that the beautiful palaces were constructed.

There are three independent areas in the Nasrid Palaces: the Mexuar, the semi-public part; the Comares Palace, the ruler's official residence; and the Palace of the Lions, a strictly private area which housed the harem. Each is different in function, architecture and decoration. Unexpectedly, the Mexuar plays host to a wonderful Renaissance ceiling in the splendid Golden Room.

The interior of the Comares Palace is strikingly Muslim in character. Made of intricately worked cedarwood, the ceiling of the Hall of the Ambassadors, the Alhambra's largest interior space, depicts the seven heavens of the Islamic faith. The cedarwood eaves are beautifully carved, with motifs of pineapples and shells. Fine wooden filigree shutters on the windows below disguise the quarters of the palace concubines. They could peer through the tracery while remaining safe from prying eyes.

Nine adjoining rooms are ornamented with epigraphs from the Qur'an. By

**ABOVE** The Alhambra, a palace-citadel with royal residential quarters, was begun in the 13th century by Ibn al-Ahmar. The Alhambra was an *alcazaba* (fortress), an *alcázar* (palace) and a small *medina* (city), all in one

**RIGHT** The romance of the Lion Court has captured the imagination of centuries of visitors; it is a physical depiction of the Paradise found in Islamic poetry

contrast, the Palace of the Lions shows strong Christian influences, perhaps as a result of the friendship between Mohammed V and his Castilian counterpart Pedro the Cruel. Four dignified great halls enclose the famous Patio de los Leones, or Lions' Court, whose fountain is unusual in that it features sculpted lions. The Qur'an forbids the representation of animal as well as human life.

The most splendid hall is the regal Sala de Dos Hermanas, or Hall of the Two Sisters. It is at the centre of a series of chambers for the sultana and her family. Tiny lateral windows light its amazingly complex ceiling, which is like an infinite honeycomb. Hundreds of tiny, delicate niches are carved like lace into the plasterwork – a highly skilled technique known as *mocárabe*.

The Catholic monarchs Ferdinand and Isabella retook Granada in 1492 and the Alhambra became a Christian court. Later, the Holy Roman Emperor Charles V began another phase of construction.

It is hard to believe, but during the 18th and 19th centuries the Alhambra fell into disuse. Napoleon's troops, who held Granada from 1808 until 1812, converted many of the palaces into barracks. Forced to retreat, Napoleon mined and blew up the Torre de los Siete Suelos and the Torre del Agua, leaving them in ruins.

It wasn't until 1870, when the Alhambra was officially declared a national monument, that any significant restoration began. It is a miracle that the Red Fortress survived. The Alhambra is a stirring reminder that architecture can sometimes aspire to the miraculous.

# Castles

Power and wealth have always attracted marauders, which is why the idea of the fortified emplacement was born. In the 13th century BC the Hittite capital of Hattusha, now in modern Turkey, was one of the first cities to be surrounded by stone fortifications. Later, the ancient Egyptians defended the fluid borders of their empire with mud forts. In a model that would be copied in medieval Europe, pre-Christian Greek city-states sheltered their people and wealth behind high, gated walls.

The Frankish leader Charlemagne did a lot to unify Western Europe. After his death in 814, Magyar and Norse invaders saw their chance to attack. Their murderous raids led to a spate of fortification which is probably without precedent in history. Hamlets, villages, and cities right across Europe set about building defences against the barbarians. High walls, pitched roofs, defensive towers and small windows became the norm. Even churches and cathedrals joined the rush towards self-protection: many, like the Romanesque church of St Michael's Hildesheim, in Germany, sheltered behind massive stone walls pierced with arrow loops, even adding watchtowers, keeps and moats.

The quickest and cheapest way of defending your interests in early Medieval Europe was to build a motte and bailey castle, or a ringwork. The motte was a high mound built of compacted rubble and earth. On top of this went a redoubt, or fort. A bailey attached to the motte let people go about their business when there was no immediate threat. It usually contained a hall, buildings for grain storage and livestock, a forge, an armoury and occasionally a chapel. But the wooden construction of these castles made them vulnerable to fire.

Ringworks were even cheaper to build. In essence these were smaller versions of the Iron Age hill fort, with a concentric ditch and bank construction. Following their conquest of Britain in 1066, the Normans put up dozens of both types of fortification in an effort to assert and maintain power. The architecture didn't always work: in 1075, two years after they had built it, the Normans suffered a

**ABOVE** Rhuddlan Castle in north Wales. Begun in 1277 with concentric rings of stone fortifications, it has a protected river dock with access to the sea, for supplies during sieges

**RIGHT** Built in blood: the fortress towers of Carcassonne, constructed in Languedoc over a period of nine centuries, were long rumoured to be impregnable

resounding defeat at Rhuddlan Castle, Flintshire at the hands of Gruffydd ap Cynan, a local Welsh chieftain. Creative thinking was the enemy of the master masons who designed castles: only a few years later, in 1099, the Crusaders captured Jerusalem by wheeling tall towers up against the walls. The moat was introduced to stop this sort of attack, as well as the undermining of castle walls.

As the feudal system took hold in the 10th century, the tenants-in-chief who leased land from the king (barons in England; shoguns in Japan) felt the need for bigger, stronger castles to protect them from rival lords. Hundreds of stone castles went up across Europe, growing ever more elaborate as the years went on. Carcassonne's 13th-century walls are testament to an extraordinary history of attack and defence. First fortified by the Romans and later by the Visigoths, the city became a Cathar stronghold, with a fearsome reputation for impregnability – until the crusading army of Simon de Montfort, 5th Earl of Leicester, forced a surrender in 1209.

In his bid to conquer Wales, King Edward I of England built some of the world's most impressive castles between 1277 and 1284. Many, including

LEFT AND ABOVE The
ultimate statement of
Edward I's power in Wales,
Caernarfon cost some £22,000
to build – a fortune at the time.
Its linear design is said to have
been influenced by the
defences at Constantinople,
Edward having been a
Crusader himself. The famous
Eagle tower is at the centre

Caernarfon, Conwy, Harlech, and Beaumaris still stand. In Aquitaine, King Richard I 'The Lionheart' (Coeur-de-Lion) built a similar string of fortifications in an attempt to hold the region for the English crown. Richard was killed by a crossbow bolt fired from the ramparts of the castle at Châlus-Chabrol. This is now a ruin. But the nearby Château de Montbrun, built at around the same time as Châlus, in 1179, has survived. Despite being adapted over the many years since its founder Aimery Brun returned from the Second Crusade, it is the perfect Late Medieval castle.

Feudalism began to dissolve as trade routes opened up again, following the absorption of the Scandinavians and Magyars into the European religious and cultural mainstream. The plague hastened this process, putting a premium on labour. As the medieval towns and boroughs found their feet, the age of the castle came to an end. But at Montbrun, with its moat, its fairytale turrets and its forbidding square central keep, the atmosphere and the architectural legacy of the Middle Ages survives.

RIGHT Conwy was built by James of St George. Referred to in the records as an 'ingeniator' or engineer, he was behind at least 12 of the 17 Welsh castles Edward I either built or strengthened

RIGHT Montbrun, in the Dordogne. It is now a private home on a crescent moat lake, its crumbling donjon looking out towards the fortress chateau of Châlus-Chabrol, where Richard the Lionheart died

# Temples to the Stars?

Angkor Wat, the great temple complex in Cambodia, is a vast sculpture in stone. Suryavarman II, king of the Khmer Empire (AD1113–50), built it as his dynastic temple and it is intended to impress. The builders of Angkor Wat made it their business to draw out anticipation, just as the architects of Baroque palaces would do later. The wide stone causeway of the ceremonial approach road crosses a moat 625 feet (190 m) wide. Finally you reach a monumental ceremonial gateway, its three pavilions each crowned with a tower shaped like a lotus bud.

Later used as a Buddhist shrine, the *wat* was originally dedicated to the royal cult of Vishnu, a Hindu god. 'Wat' is the Khmer word for a temple, while Angkor means simply 'city'. The Khmers ran the largest continuous empire in Southeast Asia and Angkor was the largest pre-industrial urban centre in the world.

Angkor's stepped sandstone terraces are topped with five towers that symbolize Mount Mehru, the home of the gods. The causeway leads past formal libraries, and what were once gracious lakes, towards a cruciform platform and a new gateway, beyond which only priests could go. The temple is so exotic and so intriguing that a host of mystical theories has grown up

**ABOVE** At a time when Frederick I reigned and just as the University of Oxford was founded, the high classical style of Cambodia was defined by the vast stepped pyramid of Angkor Wat

**RIGHT** The explorer Mouhot described the temple as 'erected by some ancient Michelangelo', and yet the Khmer masterpiece was nearly lost to the enveloping jungle

about it. Some speculate that its layout reproduces the Constellation of Draco – named for the dragon.

Above all, Angkor Wat is a vast and intricate work of art. Delicate narrative bas-reliefs tell tales from the Indian epic the *Mahabharata* and describe the 37 Heavens and 32 Hells of Indian tradition. The intricate carvings of the 12th century are among the most sophisticated in the world. The 19th-century French explorer Henri Mouhot couldn't believe that the Khmers had built the temple and mistakenly dated it to the same era as ancient Rome.

But Angkor Wat is not the only such stepped temple. The monumental Buddhist Borobudur in Java was also built in a stepped temple ziggurat form. Carved out of a hill in c.AD800, Borobudur was created some 250 years after the Church of San Vitale in Ravenna and 50 years after work began on Japan's Imperial Palace in Kyoto.

When Java converted to Islam, Borobudur was left abandoned to the jungle. It was only rediscovered in 1814 by Sir Thomas Raffles, the British ruler of Java. It must have been an astounding sight.

Both temples ascend according to religious cosmology. At Borobudur, pilgrims journey through a system of stairways and corridors with 1,460 narrative relief panels on the walls. They symbolically pass *Kamadhatu* (the world of feeling); *Rupadhatu* (the world of forms); and *Arupadhatu* (the world of immaterial form).

# ROMANESQUE

The surviving military ruins of Roman buildings were the most powerful architectural model left to the builders of the Middle Ages. A collection of vaguely linked styles developed at this time were later labelled 'Romanesque' by the historian Charles-Alexis-Adrien de Gerville. The style that had been kept alive by the great Emperor Charlemagne was typified by sturdy walls and round arches. Deep-set doorways are usually topped with semi-circular arches; strong geometrical carving often surrounds the windows of more important buildings.

The cathedral group at Pisa (1067–1173), in the Piazza del Duomo, is one of the most celebrated examples of the Romanesque. At the centre of the piazza is the cathedral, or Duomo. Here the architect Buscheta forged the distinctive style now known as Pisan Romanesque. Although black and white marble originally covered the Duomo inside and out, the colours have now faded to delicate shades of grey and russet. The round Baptistery's pointed arches have a distinct Islamic flavour: Pisa was an adventurous trading city, like Venice. The Gothic decoration was added by Nicola Pisano and his son Giovanni.

But it is the drama of the cathedral's 180-foot high (55 metres) campanile or bell tower that catches the imagination. Better known as 'The Leaning Tower' of Pisa, its distinctive colonnaded balconies allowed the town's magnificats to be seen walking up – and up – it during religious processions.

Lacking proper foundations, the tower began to lean in 1173, when it was only 35 feet (10.5 metres) high. But successive architects like Tommaso di Andrea da Pontedera, who completed it in the 14th century, simply compensated for the increasing tilt. The tower's departure from the vertical had its uses – Galileo allegedly used it for his experiments on the velocity of falling bodies. Until recently the tower's inclination was increasing at the rate of 1mm a year. After a restoration costing £200m, you could finally go up the tower without fear of hurtling off the slippery marble surface. Then in 1995, the tower suddenly lurched forward (see p.66)…

One of the earliest interesting remnants

**BELOW** The Leaning Tower of Pisa began to sink in 1178 ,when construction reached the third floor. These days it still leans, despite all efforts, to the southwest. The tilt is nearly 4°

**RIGHT** Speyer Cathedral. Just below the roofline is a colonnaded gallery, a distinctive feature of the Romanesque, as is the symmetry. However, Speyer has begun the medieval stretch skywards, with the help of ribbed vaults

we have of this time is Speyer Cathedral, begun around 1040 although not completed until c.1140. Abandoning the squat compositions of Charlemagne's 'Carolingian' architecture, the nave has a series of wide arches like a Roman aqueduct. Light enters through a band of high windows. Speyer nevertheless marks the end of the true Romanesque style. Driven by the need to accommodate large numbers of the faithful, another style of church was setting an architectural trend – by aiming high.

The pilgrimage was the defining rite of the Middle Ages, equivalent to the Grand Tour, or today's Gap Year. Any villages lucky enough to be near the set route could look forward to greatly increased wealth. Some even found a way of channelling the route to their own advantage. The tiny village of Conques in France sent an undercover brother to live in a monastery in Agen. Ten years later, he returned – with the relics of St Foy under his habit. The axis of the all-important pilgrim route then shifted dramatically and Conques needed a new church to deal with the flood of eager penitents and worshippers.

The design of the new church (c.1050–1120) had to accommodate its new,

## Tilt at the top

In 1934, Benito Mussolini ordered his minions to straighten the Tower of Pisa. They poured concrete into the foundations, but this only made it sink deeper into the ground. In 1993 the angle of tilt of Pisa's world-famous tower had been 'corrected' by restorers at a cost of £200m. Then suddenly, in September 1995, the monument lurched again by 1/16 inch. Instead of concentrating on the subsiding part of the tower, British engineer John Burland, who oversaw the next phase of crisis management, decided to even it out via the stable side – only very, very slowly. Lead weights were placed on the north side, while tonnes of soil were excavated from beneath the structure using corkscrew drills. Gradually, the tower sank back into the new cavity. The lean had been corrected by roughly 16 inches (40 cm). Even so, it is predicted that in 300 years' time the tower will have returned to its former precarious angle.

enlarged function. Pilgrims would circle the interior three times before stopping in front of the golden reliquary. They would then pray for a safe onward journey to Santiago. To deter thieves, the relics were caged behind a fine metal screen supposedly wrought from the melted-down fetters of pilgrims freed from captivity in Muslim-occupied Spain.

Finding it hard to cope with the crowds, the monks copied something devised at Tours: an ambulatory. Essentially, the church interior has a double shell structure. Passages connecting the separate chapels ran around the entire perimeter, so the pilgrims could progress around the building without disturbing the clergy.

But that is not the only innovation in the transitional architecture of St Foy. While other Romanesque churches such as St

Michael's at Hildesheim had flat ceilings fastened to wooden roof trusses, St Foy's 68-foot (20.5 metres) barrel vault soars over the nave. To cope with the extra weight, small buttresses strengthen the external walls while concealed internal arches counteract the vault's pressure. St-Sernin of Toulouse is almost double St Foy's total length, but it still does not match St Foy in height. Christian architecture was heading towards the heavens.

St Foy was amazingly untouched by the calculated vandalism seen everywhere in France after the Revolution. Even the saint's gold statuette survived. The effect of the pilgrim bonanza on this tiny village has been to create one of the most unified medieval towns in Europe, right down to the half-timbered houses whose roofs echo the great pointed towers of the church.

# 'To Be a Pilgrim'

For Christians in the Middle Ages, a pilgrimage to Santiago de Compostela in northern Spain was the journey of a lifetime. Pilgrims flocked from every corner of Europe to the place where the bones of the apostle Saint James were said to be kept. With little in the way of organized law enforcement, the pilgrims risked robbery or worse. But they had their faith to keep them going.

There were four main pilgrim routes through France: Paris–Tours, Vézelay, Le Puy-en-Velay and Arles. Pilgrimage churches were built to house the relics of saints, many of which had been brought back from the Crusades to the Holy Land.

Vézelay shot to fame in the 11th century when a wily monk snaffled the presumed relics of St Mary Magdalene from a rival church in Provence. For two centuries hosts of pilgrims visited Mary's 'tomb'. Because of the money and trade that came with it, pilgrimage became the lifeblood of the town.

As the cult of Mary Magdalene grew, so did Vézelay's importance. Accordingly, Abbot Renaud de Semur, later archbishop of Lyons, raised the new basilica of St Magdalene around 1140. Its huge narthex or entrance area could accommodate large numbers of the faithful – and did. St Thomas à Becket used Vézelay's pulpit to excommunicate some clerics in 1166; St Bernard of Clairvaux preached the Second Crusade there in 1146; and Richard the Lionheart and Philip II of France used it to launch the Third Crusade in July 1190.

What was so special about this particular shrine? The monks who built it must have been truly inspired engineers, because at the heart of the basilica is an experience that is almost mystical. One of the oldest parts of the church, the Romanesque nave, constructed around 1125, has dramatic arches of alternating light and dark stone.

At the time of the summer solstice, light floods in through apertures set high in the walls. Broad bars of light are then suddenly projected from the narthex. They travel down the groin-vaulted nave and towards the choir, creating a 'chemin de la lumière': a miraculous path of

light for our pious pilgrims to follow.

In the 16th century the Huguenots sacked Vézelay and burned the relics. The French Revolution, when thousands of historic buildings were mutilated, saw the ancient monastery buildings destroyed. Only the cloister and dormitory escaped, along with the basilica itself. Although much of the sculpture was either destroyed or looted, some has survived.

Two items in particular are intriguing: the depiction of the Day of Judgment over the main portal and a puzzling relief – a

tympanum – over a portal in the narthex. The tympanum has no precedent in medieval iconography and is a mystery to academics. Here, Christ sits with lines of fire radiating out from his fingertips to his twelve apostles. Perhaps it is a reference to Vézelay's own path of radiant light.

**BELOW** The medieval sculpted tympanum of the new church. Despite the destruction of the French Revolution, it still has its fine Romanesque sculpture

**ABOVE** Vézelay's Romanesque, groin-vaulted nave was world-famous in medieval times

# EARLY GOTHIC

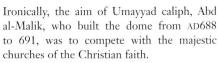

The term 'Gothic' originally evolved as an insult, meaning 'of the Goths'. The single most important factor in the evolution of Gothic architecture was the invention of rib vaults. The Normans initiated the second phase of English Romanesque architecture. While earlier cathedrals like Gloucester had heavy round arches in the arcades, Durham Cathedral's nave vaulting was the first to have diagonal ribs with pointed profiles, moving the ancient Roman groin vault a step on. In fact, the building of Durham Cathedral, which began in 1093, could be said to foreshadow the Gothic revolution.

Whether it is viewed from the west, as it perches perilously high over the river Wear, or from its interior – with its simple, breathtakingly beautiful columns – the cathedral is awe-inspiring. Its high standard of masonry shows a blend of the English decorative tradition with Norman architectural skills. The alternating composite and circular piers of the nave have bold, incised patterns: chevrons, flutes and diagonals. A deep gallery above the aisles houses the first flying buttresses in England. There is also some speculation that Islamic masons were brought in to help with construction. The so-called Galilee Chapel (1153–95), with its long arcaded walls, resembles the arcades of Islamic mosques. It's extraordinary to think that at the furthest northern reaches of the Christian world a building of such originality could have been completed in less than 40 years.

The Gothic style is meant to appeal directly to the emotions, whether those of terror, wonder or religious fervour. It is no coincidence, of course that this began after the first Crusades. The Crusaders saw Constantinople's Hagia Sophia on their way to the Holy Land, followed by the Al-Aqsa Mosque, the headquarters of the Templar knights from 1099. They would come face to face with the rich decorative style of the Dome of the Rock, the oldest Islamic monument in the world, whose gold-topped dome can be seen from all over Jerusalem.

Ironically, the aim of Umayyad caliph, Abd al-Malik, who built the dome from AD688 to 691, was to compete with the majestic churches of the Christian faith.

This was also the time of the Inquisition, and churches were used as an instrument of power. The cathedral at Albi, which looms threateningly over the town, was built in response to a religious rebellion.

Gothic vaults were constructed lightly. Built from carefully dressed stone, they soared upwards. They were also flexible: a cross-vault could cover any bay of any shape, by varying the sharpness of the angle. The fervent Gothic cathedrals literally became stories in stone. They were covered from top to bottom with sculpture that told dramatic stories from the Bible. At the same time, the structural walls of the churches almost began to disappear. Melting into the glorious colours of scriptural glass they became a pictorial Bible for the illiterate. St John had said that the Heavenly Jerusalem:

'... was of jasper: and the City was of pure gold, like unto clear glass. And the foundations were garnished with all manner of precious stones'.

This lavish, jewel-like richness is the effect that the Gothic master masons of the Middle Ages were attempting to achieve.

For centuries the Basilica of Saint-Denis was the burial place of the kings of France and their families. But it was Abbot Suger who put the Parisian church on the architectural map. Suger resolved to create a building suffused with heavenly light. 'Bright is the noble edifice pervaded by the new light,' he wrote.

To achieve his vision of spiritually uplifting walls of heavenly glass he incorporated diagonal arches, slender pillars,

ABOVE The word 'gargoyle' is from *gargouille*, French for throat or gullet. Strictly speaking, a gargoyle is a sculptural waterspout, though they were also intended to ward off dark and evil spirits

BELOW Saint Cecile d'Albi shows the scary side of the medieval Church. Built like a warship, the structure went up during the Inquisition to put the Cathar religion down

and buttresses into his new choir (1144). It was the first appearance of Gothic in a major building. Theologian, crusader and adviser to his childhood friend King Louis VII, Suger was also a skilful administrator. The abbot is a hero in architectural history, not just because of his innovative thinking but also because of the meticulous way in which he recorded events. In his writings, he speculated about the best way to make a religious appeal to 'the dull mind'. The answer, for his money, was through spectacular buildings.

Suger's Saint-Denis has echoes of the Roman Arch of Constantine (AD315) with its three-part division and three large portals (it is not only Renaissance architects who took inspiration from the Romans). The solution eases the problem of congestion at peak times.

The simplest Gothic shape is the narrow window with a pointed arch, known in England as the lancet. As they evolved the windows were grouped together and linked by decorative ribs: tracery. Larger, said Suger, taller, lighter. Strong vertical piers replaced continuous thick walls. Pointed arches replaced the familiar round barrel vault, distributing the downthrust more economically and lending a new delicacy. Gothic was heading to the skies.

Uplifting, delicate, interiors are characteristically Gothic, with rich walls hung with tapestries, carpets, and of course, the disarming glow of stained glass suffusing everything with magical light. And there was always music. Under the Gothic spell, worship became a mystical experience, based on the certain faith that God was very near.

RIGHT The greatest of medieval cathedrals, Chartres, in France. Supporting the walls from outside allowed thinner walls and more height. This opened up the walls for more windows – to allow the uplifting light of God inside

# LUCIDITY

The second phase of Gothic began with a quantum leap made at Chartres Cathedral in France. At a stroke its unknown architect began designing in clearer, simpler lines, elaborating emotional Gothic principles to produce a building of staggering scale. The style is known as Rayonnant in Europe (c.1240–1350) and in England as Decorated Gothic (c.1275–1375). This gradually surged upwards: this dramatic new turn was called 'Perpendicular'.

The most significant innovation of the Rayonnant period was the circular rose window, a distinctive and glorious feature of French cathedrals like Reims, Amiens and Bourges. One of the finest is at Chartres. Although earlier Romanesque round windows do exist, as in the 10th century church of Santa Maria in Pomposa, Italy, it was not until the 12th century that these fantasies in light and colour really caught on. Ever-more flamboyant tracery and colour made the rose window a star of the Gothic show.

The Sainte-Chapelle in Paris, designed by the court architect Thomas de Cormont in 1248, set new standards for ornamentation in the mid-13th century. It was built by Louis IX as a home for yet more relics: Louis had purchased the Crown of Thorns and even parts of the True Cross for an enormous sum.

The overall structure is in fact a unified metaphor: it represents a vast reliquary box, covered with lacy pinnacles and tracery and dedicated to God. The interior decoration actually cost more than the building itself. But the *pièce de résistance* is the astonishing display of stained glass, which almost absorbs the delicate framework of the walls.

The choir of Aachen Cathedral in Germany, with its vast windows, was inspired by the Sainte-Chapelle, but the St James Chapel in Chicago, built in the 1900s, goes one further. It is a near-faithful replica.

Canterbury Cathedral and Westminster Abbey, both constructed over many years, are the earliest large-scale Gothic buildings in England. Parts of the cloister of Westminster Abbey (c.1245–69), a complex building, along with the nave and west front of York Minster (c.1260–1320) are good examples of the Decorated Gothic. A distinct S-shaped curve began to evolve in European tracery, beginning what's known as the 'Flamboyant' style of Gothic. The later Perpendicular (c.1380–1520) English style for which Westminster Abbey is famous is easy to spot, with its larger windows and soaring vertical stonework tracery. The jewel-like splendour of Henry VII's chapel is a particular gem. England is also celebrated for its magnificent carved timber roofs, as at Eltham Palace.

**BELOW** King's College Chapel, Cambridge: a feast for the eyes commissioned during the Wars of the Roses. The actual stained glass was made much later, using Flemish and British craftsmen

## Fan Vaults

The fan vault is one of England's most exciting additions to late Gothic, where a dense cluster of ribs fans out from the top of a column. It first appeared in the cloister at Gloucester Cathedral, and can also be found at Westminster Abbey, but can be seen at its artistic best in King's College Chapel, Cambridge, where the vaults were built by the country's foremost craftsman John Wastell in 1446–1515. The chapel's awe-inspiring ceiling resembles a great canopy of trees.

# HOME AND HEARTH

What of the domestic house? The early medieval home looked inward, and was defensive. Gradually, the ambitious new spiritual style of the Gothic began to have a wider influence.

Architecture documents the changing faces of society. As society became wealthier, the nature of the domestic house was also changing. A new class of entrepreneurs was emerging, and they wanted the world to know exactly who and what they were. The Chipping Camden home of wool merchant William Grevel is a prime example of this architectural hubris. When it came to social aspiration, his Cotswold residence (c.1380) aimed high: as high as the church. Traces of slender stone mullioning in the bow window are identifiably Perpendicular Gothic. Grevel may have been especially religious, but it's more likely that he was particularly ostentatious.

The more successful the family, the more likely the house or hall is to have changed. Penarth Fawr near Criccieth is a mid-15th century stone-built aisle-truss hall house, a typical home for a family of contemporary Welsh gentry. Plainly built in stone with a Romanesque arched doorway, its unchanged history can be seen in the flagstones, worn thin by generations of treading feet.

By contrast, all that's left of the original Great Hall (1460) at the magnificent Knole, in Kent – once owned by Henry VII – are two stone doors. The rest is covered with impressive Jacobean wood and plasterwork, the remarkable oak screen sadly rather obscured by a layer of shellac applied by a Victorian hand.

Cotehele, on the banks of the River Tamar in Cornwall, is another story. It is one of the least-altered Tudor manor houses in existence, a fact largely due to the family moving to a new house 10 miles (16 kilometres) away in 1553, and rarely going back. Ever since, the mellow stone house has only occasionally been occupied. The chapel has a remarkable curiosity – a pre-pendulum clock, powered by two 90 pound weights. And it works.

A very French version of the domestic Gothic ideal can be seen at Bourges in the house of a fabulously rich merchant who became master of the mint, Jacques Coeur. Built in the middle of the 15th century, its highly decorated façade has fretted balustrades decorated with hearts and scallop shells, Coeur's emblems. The wealth of quotations from French cathedral architecture, even down to the gargoyles, was indicative of Coeur's unbounded self-esteem.

**BELOW** William Grevel's House, in the prosperous Cotswolds medieval town of Chipping Camden, England. Grevel was a wool merchant when English wool was desired as far away as Florence

# IN ITALY

San Gimignano is an open museum of dramatic Gothic architecture. Perched high on a hill, the Tuscan city still has its original walls and gates and 14 of its original 72 limestone towers. All is thrown into sharp relief by the surrounding green hills. It is one of the most remarkable views in Italy. The towers that we now find so picturesque were the urban strongholds of competing families. By 998 the residents had built their first set of defensive city walls.

**M**ost of San Gimignano's palazzi were constructed in either the 12th or the 13th centuries. Since the town council dictated building size, the townsfolk turned to architects to distinguish themselves from their neighbours. As a result, San Gimignano is a fascinating mix of graceful Italian building styles. Medieval Sienese Gothic, with its elegant brickwork and pointed windows, mingles with the more robust striped Pisan Romanesque and classical Florentine Early Renaissance. Once the city had imposed a footprint limit to buildings, keeping up with the Jones's meant building high. Those who could afford to build taller towers did so: some built two.

San Gimignano's most important monuments are the crenellated Palazzo del Popolo, the Romanesque Collegiata and the church of Sant'Agostineo, where frescoes outline the life of St Augustine. The town is laid out in a linear form, with a gate at each end and two large piazzas for the marketplace and the public buildings. In the 13th century the town council forbade the destruction of houses 'except to build better ones'. Would that modern-day cities were so enlightened.

The story of Venice, meanwhile, is like a parable for architecture through the Middle Ages, summed up by the four stunning bronze horses that top the basilica of St Mark. St Mark's Basilica is probably the most famous Byzantine building in the world. Legend has it that on a visit to Rome the saint anchored off the floating islands of the Rialto, only to be

**ABOVE** No one ever forgets their first sight of St Mark's, Venice. With its Gothic pinnacles, Byzantine domes and medieval angels, the famous basilica stands at a crossing between East and West

greeted by an angel. The angel told him: 'Peace to you, Mark. Your body will rest here.' Thus St Mark and his symbol, a winged lion, have been an emblem of the city ever since.

Over the centuries, Venetian merchant ships returned bearing columns, capitals and friezes from all points of the globe. Gradually, the exterior of the basilica was covered with a variety of marbles and carvings, some much

**LEFT** The Piazza del Duomo, at the heart of the fortress town of San Gimignano, Italy. The Romanesque interiors of the military-plain *duomo* (left) are lavish

older than the building itself. Reclaimed Roman bas-reliefs mingle with those by 12th-century Byzantine craftsmen, with a later addition of 13th-century Venetian Byzantine Gothic for good measure. The central doorway is Romanesque.

The basilica opens out on to the Piazza San Marco. Napoleon commented that the square was 'the finest drawing room in Europe'. It is true: lined with some of the world's best-loved structures, it functions as a perfect piece of public space. The architect Palladio thought that the Istrian stone Library of St Mark was the most beautiful building since the days of antiquity. It is thanks to its Renaissance architect Sansovino that this square was cleared of a medieval jumble of housing, allowing the remarkable Gothic Doge's Palace to be seen.

The Victorian critic John Ruskin called the city's Palazzo Ducale, most of which was built by master masons around 1422, 'The central building of the world'. Victorian England agreed with him. Gothic Revival imitations include Bradford's Wool Exchange and the Templeton carpet factory in Glasgow, but no imitation can match the Ducale for majesty. The palazzo escaped Renaissance fever, despite a fire which destroyed most of the previous 12th century structure, because the Doges decided to stick with the historic Gothic aesthetic. Its massive walls are

lightened by a delicate patterning of white Istrian and pink Verona marble.

The delicate and poignant 'Bridge of Sighs' connects the Ducal Palace with the grim prisons of the Palazzo delle Prigioni.

Before quitting Venice and the story of its medieval architecture, it is worth stopping briefly at the House of Gold on the Grand Canal (the Ca' D'Oro). It is one of Venice's most lovely sights. As much sculpture as structure, it takes its name from the gilding of its exotic, Islamic-influenced decoration. The exotic ogee arches and the faded red and white colouring – actually once blue and burgundy – have overtones of the Palazzo Ducale. Unsurprising, given the involvement of the architect-masons Giovanni Bon and his son Bartolomeo. The unusual asymmetry reflects the layout of the rooms inside: the entrance hall opens directly on to the canal, but sits behind a recessed loggia for shade and privacy. The quatrefoil windows on the enclosed balcony of the *piano nobile* build into lighter and lighter pierced detail as the flights go higher, making the fairy-cake building appear to float above the water.

Italy is an appropriate place to leave the Gothic adventure, since it was the site of the next great stylistic change to hit the world. If classicism were to be reborn anywhere it would be here, in the land of Dante and Petrarch: the home of humanism.

**ABOVE** Detail of the Doge's Palace, Venice by Filippo Calendario: building began in 1329, but halted when he was executed for treason in 1355

**BELOW** The distinctively Venetian Gothic Ca' D'Oro (centre), 1428, is the most beautiful of the palazzos on the Grand Canal

# THE RENAISSANCE

Renaissance architecture is typified by light, clarity and rationality. Here is our universe, said Renaissance man, and we are at the centre of it. In the literature of the 14th century, humanist writers and intellectuals like Dante and Petrarch had already begun to revive the language and craft of the ancients. After studying the works of Cicero and Virgil they argued that, as in antiquity, the faculty of reason was man's most prized gift from God: and he should use it. From now on the Middle Ages would be regarded as the Dark Ages. A new architecture based on rational – classical – principles would soon be born.

Château de Chambord, largest of the Loire Valley's 300 châteaux, bridges the medieval, with its keep and conical turrets, and the Renaissance, with its carved stone detailing

# NO LIMITS

*'Thou, constrained by no limits, in accordance with thine free will, in whose hand we have placed thee, shall ordain for thyself the limits of thy nature. We have set thee at the world's centre, that thou mayest from thence more easily observe whatever is in the world.'*

Giovanni Pico della Mirandola,
*Oration on the Dignity of Man* (1486)

**LEFT** Designed by Michelangelo's apprentice Bartolomeo Ammanati in 1575, the statue of Neptune above the fountain in Florence's Piazza della Signoria.

**RIGHT** Santa Maria del Fiore, Florence: the cathedral's huge octagonal cupola by architect and sculptor Filippo Brunelleschi (1420-36) was a structural tour de force, the first major architectural feat of the Renaissance

I n 1402, a scruffy young pair of vagabonds arrived in the pestilential, smelly city of Rome and started picking through the ancient ruins. The Temple of Jupiter was now a dunghill; the magnificent Forum had become known as the Campo di Vacchino, the 'Field of Cows'. The glories of ancient Rome were buried under centuries of rubble and detritus, the ancient aqueducts broken and falling down, victim to neglect, earthquakes and successive wars.

The two scavengers, an artist and a craftsman, became known as 'the treasure hunters', because they began digging amongst these vast old ruins before having the soil taken away in carts. This was inexplicable behaviour to the locals, who believed that unearthing the old pagan artefacts of Rome brought bad luck. And what was one of them doing, going about measuring the buildings with a great stick?

A new age was coming. Dominated by the wealthy Medici family, great patrons of the arts and architecture, Florence was 'the new Athens', a city with ambition. Hugely successful in the cloth trade and international banking, the city was run by a communal government that kept jealous control of every aspect of its growth: above all, its architecture. The Medici were determined that the beauty of Florence would reflect the city's image of itself as an ideal republic, inhabited by virtuous and cultured citizens.

In Europe generally there was a huge flowering of interest in ancient knowledge, which gave an unprecedented intellectual stimulus to the Christian world. A new philosophical outlook, later called humanism, re-evaluated the place of mankind in nature. By the mid-15th century humanism described a whole curriculum, the *studia humanitatis*, which embraced the study of classical authors along with rhetoric, moral philosophy, poetry

and history. At the same time, the Iberian peninsula was gradually being reclaimed from the Moors and many ancient texts such as those of Euclid, Plato and Aristotle, long forgotten by Western civilization, came back to light.

Florence had begun a building boom during the 1300s, the like of which had not been seen since the time of the ancients. The city, which prided itself on its democracy, had a population of around 50,000, roughly the size of London's. It also had a major, intractable problem: it had on its hands the world's most impossible architectural commission.

Work on the cathedral of Santa Maria del Fiore – Saint Mary of the Flowers – had begun in 1296. In the exciting, tumultuous atmosphere of the Florentine republic there had been many bitter arguments over the design. It was intended to be the largest in Christendom: it would have a dome larger than the world's most spectacular church, Constantinople's Santa Sophia, constructed 900 years earlier. Unfortunately, things weren't going to plan. In 1347, the plague arrived in Italy with the Asian black rat, hidden in the holds of Genoese trading ships.

Four-fifths of the population of Florence died, and Tartar and Circassian slaves had to be imported to ease the labour shortage. A 280-foot campanile had been designed and built over two decades by the painter Giotto, but by 1418 there was still no workable design for the cathedral's dome.

Nothing like it had been built since antiquity: creating an eight-sided vaulted dome of this size and weight without using any exterior buttressing defied contemporary building technology. The plan was to start building the cupola at the incredible height of 170 feet – higher than the tallest Gothic vault ever constructed, the vault that had once topped the Cathedral of Sainte-Pierre in Beauvais. But Sainte-Pierre had completely collapsed, in 1284.

In the Middle Ages, it was not uncommon for a tall building to fall down. The superstitious would blame the hand of God, which was lucky for whoever had built it. Florence was not unaware of the fact that the bell towers of rival towns Bologna and Pisa had both begun to lean, because of subsidence in the inadequate foundations – although the Commune was more likely to place the blame at the feet of the architect. In short, building

# Key Dates

**1300** Florence is established as the banking centre for Europe, making its coin, the Florin, the first international currency; Paris is the largest city in Europe with a population 200–300,000 strong.

**1308–21** Dante Alighieri: *Divine Comedy*.

**1374** Death of Petrarch.

**1381** The Peasants' Revolt led by Wat Tyler.

**1406** The construction of China's Forbidden City begins.

**1400–1500** The Renaissance, also known as the Quattrocento and sometimes Early Renaissance.

**1434** Filippo Brunelleschi completes the Duomo (Santa Maria del Fiore).

**1438** Origins of the Inca Empire, Peru.

**1444–60** The Palazzo Medici is built.

**1450** Gutenberg publishes his Bible.

**1450** Leonardo da Vinci, painter, sculptor and visionary is born, Florence.

**1451** The Vatican Library is founded.

**1453** The Ottomans take Constantinople.

**1455–85** The Wars of the Roses, England.

**1471** In Pec, Kosovo, the Qarshise Mosque is built. It was to be destroyed by Serbian forces in 1999.

**1476** The first edition of *The Canterbury Tales* is printed by William Caxton in England.

**1483** Botticelli: 'The Birth of Venus'.

**1492** Christopher Columbus discovers America.

**1493** The construction of wooden buildings is banned in the old city of Moscow by Ivan III after a massive fire.

**1494** French invasion of Italy.

**1498** Leonardo Da Vinci: 'Last Supper'; toothbrushes with hog bristles are invented in China.

**1500** Antwerp Cathedral completed after 148 years of construction; the world population reaches 400 million.

**1500–25** The Italian High Renaissance, also known as the Cinquecento.

**1504** Michelangelo: 'David'.

**1506** Discovery of the ancient sculpture, 'Laocoön and His Sons'.

**1515** Thomas More: *Utopia*; Raphael succeeds Bramante as chief architect of St Peter's in Rome.

**1517** Martin Luther posts 95 Theses on Wittenberg Church; the Madonna of the Harpies altarpiece by Andrea del Sarto.

**1519** The Château of Chambord is begun in France; it will take 30 years to complete.

**1520–1600** Mannerism.

**1520** Hernándo Cortés conquers Mexico for Spain.

**1525** Michelangelo starts work on the Medici Chapel.

**1527** Sack of Rome.

**1530–90** Henry II style develops in France (under five monarchs).

**1530** Henry VIII's divorce request is denied by the Pope. Henry then declares that he, not the Pope, is the supreme head of the English Church.

**1533–1603** Elizabeth I reigns in England.

**1538** Work begins on the Piazza del Campidoglio (Capitoline Hill), designed by Michelangelo.

**1555** Nostradamus: *The Prophecies*.

**1568** Vignola: the construction of the Church of the Gesù.

**1595–96** Shakespeare: *Romeo and Juliet*.

**1618–1648** The Thirty Years' War.

this dome was going to take an act of faith. So yet another competition was held, to find an architect for the 'impossible' commission.

The man who won was 42 years old. He had only one building to his name (above). The unkempt and by now cantankerous Filippo Brunelleschi, goldsmith and clockmaker, had been one half of the pair of 'treasure hunters' mentioned earlier – the other was his friend, the sculptor Donatello. Up to that date, the only visitors to Rome were pilgrims looking for the bones of saints – the 'finger bone' of Saint Thomas, or the 'arm' of Saint Anne. Brunelleschi and the wild hell-raiser Donatello began a new kind of pilgrimage, one that delved into the minds of the ancients.

'Pippo', as Brunelleschi was known, had grown up in the shadow of the unfinished cathedral. We don't know for certain, but perhaps he had been preparing for this challenge his whole life. He had become a celebrity in Florence for a trick that at the time seemed almost magical – the rediscovery of perspective in painting.

His designs for the dome showed that it could be built using a double shell construction, an ancient Roman technique. That is, laying the brickwork in a herringbone pattern within a framework of stone ribs. The outward shell would emphasize the height: between the two, sandstone beams held together by iron clamps would act against the building's stresses. A cupola at the very top, outwardly no more than an embellishment, cleverly anchored the points of the dome together, counteracting the immense 'push' and 'pull' forces that affect all domes.

The former goldsmith then applied himself to the task of building a model, hiring Florence's two most gifted sculptors, Donatello and Nanni di Banco for the woodwork. His eventual model, requiring 5,000 bricks, was 12 feet tall. The judges could walk right inside it. There is a story, probably apocryphal, that in order to convince the judges the grouchy goldsmith demanded that it be announced that whoever could make an unsupported egg stand upright on a piece of flat marble should win the competition. When no-one else could solve the puzzle, Brunelleschi simply took the egg, cracked it to make a depression on the bottom and then stood it on end.

Whether the story is true or not, it is certain that the dome remained an object of contention. Brunelleschi's task was certainly not made easy. His fiercest rival, Lorenzo Ghiberti, was made joint *capomaestro*, presumably to keep an eye on him, and given a half share of his six florins a month. Dodging plagues, wars, and political feuds, Brunelleschi reinvented the ancient art of architecture in order to raise 70 million pounds of metal, wood, and marble hundreds of feet into the air. Along the way the architect was denounced as a madman, but after 28 years of work Florence's cathedral was a wonder of the Renaissance world.

'Pippo' had given architecture new possibility and purpose.

Writers and philosophers had discussed the glories of ancient Rome, but until Donatello and Brunelleschi's journey it seems no-one had actually studied them in any great detail. Now architects like Leon Battista Alberti, Antonio Filarete, Francesco di Giorgio and Michelangelo would follow his lead, travelling to Rome to find inspiration in the ruins.

Using this rediscovered knowledge – as well as a natural talent for geometry and mechanical engineering – Brunelleschi had pioneered a new rationalist approach to architecture. It was as systematic – and as

**ABOVE** Alberti's new façade for the existing Gothic Santa Maria Novella, Florence. Its dimensions follow the 1:2 ratio of the musical octave: the upper storey, including the pediment, is half the size of the lower. Take a ruler to it...

**RIGHT** A detail of the *volute*, a word that comes from the Latin for 'scroll'. The geometric patterns in green and white marble derive from the Tuscan Romanesque style

**ABOVE** The Cortile della Pigna, courtyard of the pine, lies within the walls of the Vatican museums. The bronze pine dates from the first century AD and stands in front of a scooped arch by Bramante

Architects through the ages have responded to that call, not least Modernist figures like Le Corbusier, six centuries later.

Brunelleschi's breakthrough was cemented by another Florentine architect, Leon Battista Alberti (1404–72). Where 'Pippo' was secretive, Alberti, an embodiment of the impossible ideal of the 'Renaissance man', wanted to publish. The illegitimate son of a Florentine family in exile, Alberti had travelled widely and then joined the papal civil service. Athlete, writer, musician, painter and mathematician, Alberti could spring over a man's head with his feet together – and was a superb horseman. His description of architectural beauty is one of the most perfect – and intriguing – in history. He called it:

'... the harmony and concord of all the parts, achieved in such a manner that nothing could be added or taken away or altered, except for the worse.'

Through his writing, and exemplars such as the beautifully-proportioned façade for the church of Santa Maria Novella, Alberti put forward a system of simple proportion that would inspire generations of architects. He rediscovered the theory of harmony developed by ancient architects and mathematicians, drawing visual lessons from the laws of music. A musical string that is depressed at its midpoint will yield a tone an octave higher than the whole string would produce. Depressing the string two-thirds or three-quarters of the way along will produce a fifth or a fourth. Extrapolating from this, Alberti deduced that rooms conforming to the same ratios would automatically be harmoniously beautiful. At Santa Maria Novella (Florence, 1470), he converted the

façade of an Italian Gothic building to an intricate, rhythmic composition with the ideal proportions of antiquity and a striking temple pediment.

Alberti's written works were immensely wide-ranging. His *Ten Books of Architecture* addressed the eternal problem of which parts of the city's fabric should be accentuated, and which parts hidden. According to Alberti:

'The beauty of the city will be greatly enhanced if various artisan workshops are built in the city districts and areas appropriate to them. There will be bankers, painters and goldsmiths around the square; near to them shops with aromatic spices and merchandise, tailor shops and those which are considered important. Ugly merchandise should be secluded in more distant places.'

Following the ideas of this sublime scholar-architect, Renaissance cities and towns rediscovered the Roman concept of town planning. Muddled medieval towns made way for planned, shaped city squares and places to meet, shop and do business. The more radical architecture took place in the service of the divine – early Renaissance papal palaces. For example, Baccio Pontelli's Belvedere of Innocent VIII (c.1485), still look medieval and military. It took Donato d'Angelo Lazzari, better known as Bramante (the word 'bramante' means 'ravenous'), to recreate the kind of bold and imaginative luxury that the Romans would have recognized. Bramante's Nymphaeum at Genazzano, modelled on the Imperial Baths, was begun in 1508 for the young Pompeo Colonna, a bishop. As in antiquity, and as specified in Alberti, it was one-storey: all that is left now is a picturesque ruin.

thrilling – as musical harmony. Buildings were to be in proportion; harmony could only be achieved by using the golden ratio, as defined by the Greek mathematician Euclid.

# The 'Gothic': the Enemy's House Style

Florence's classicist rationalism had a political, as well as an aesthetic dimension. Giangaleazzo Visconti, the Duke of the northern city of Milan, was the city's greatest enemy. The Duke had already subdued Pisa, Perugia and Siena, and now had his sights on the huge prosperity Florence had built for itself. The ginger-bearded Visconti, who espoused the Gothic style, was a real stage villain: his coat of arms boasted a viper crushing a tiny human figure to death. While

the democratic Florentines identified themselves with the Romans, and believed their city was founded by Julius Caesar, the evil Visconti was building a Gothic cathedral to rival Florence's, flying buttresses and all.

### VITRUVIUS AND THE RENAISSANCE
Leone Battista Alberti's beautifully proportioned façade for the Florentine church of Santa Maria Novella is based on

the principle of harmony. The geometric series of squares, inlaid with different marbles, cover a medieval structure and are based on classical, ancient Roman rules of proportion. The pediment and frieze are inspired by antiquity. Alberti and Brunelleschi came across radical new classical ideas when a manuscript by the 1st-century writer Vitruvius was rediscovered in a monastery. They strove to recreate a kind of architecture that represented intellectual, as well as spiritual, perfection.

# THE HIGH AND LATE RENAISSANCE

Brunelleschi and Alberti had created a bridging style between Gothic and a new, rational architecture that looked back to Italy's proud ancient heritage. Gradually, the Renaissance style was adopted outside the walls of ebullient Florence, and evolved into a confident use of classicism – what we now call the High Renaissance.

Surrounded by slender Doric columns and surmounted by a dome, Donato Bramante's sculptural Tempietto is one of the world's most perfect little structures. High on the list of the most harmonious buildings of the Renaissance, it is set within a courtyard in San Pietro in Montorio, which is said to mark the exact spot of St Peter's crucifixion.

The Tempietto – meaning simply 'little temple' – marks a high point of what is now known as the High Renaissance style. On the inside, the sanctuary is only 15 feet across. The building was not intended to be something to enter – it was more something to look at: a picture. Leonardo da Vinci had written extensively about the use of light and shade to achieve perspective. Bramante was a master of illusionistic painting, and it's as if the temple is taking a tip from Leonardo. The sharp Roman sunlight plays about its columns, the *cella* and the simple Tuscan Doric *peripteros*, making it seem ever more emphatic, ever more weighty. Pope Julius II was so pleased with it that he appointed Bramante architect of St Peter's.

The Tempietto has been endlessly copied, from the 'eyecatchers' of 18th century gardens to the enormous peripteral dome of Wren's St Paul's. Perhaps the highest accolade is Bernini's final work at St Peter's, in 1676. In the Chapel of the Sacrament he designed a miniature version of the Tempietto in gilt bronze, to hold the bread that symbolizes the body of Christ; the sacramental host.

Of the many extraordinary buildings of the Italian Renaissance, none is grander, or larger, than Pope Julius II's Basilica of Saint Peter in the Vatican. The endeavour spanned two tumultuous centuries, enraging the radical cleric Martin Luther and challenging even the

**RIGHT** The Tempietto San Pietro, Bramante's first major work, played subtly with classical forms. His circle of simple Doric columns topped by a semicircular dome was much copied

81

**LEFT** The Rocca Roveresca fort at Mondavio, Italy. Francesco Giorgio di Martini is perhaps the greatest military architect of the Renaissance

Colosseum of AD80. Difficulty and delay dogged the project, which frequently stalled for reasons of money, a change of pope or the architect's demise. The deaths of Sangallo and Giulio Romano – brought in after Raphael himself died – left the stage open for 71-year-old Michelangelo Buonarroti. The great sculptor, never one to hang back, denounced Sangallo's work as inferior, and set out to restore Bramante's spirit, and much of his original plan, to the basilica. Tired of fresco painting and sculpting, he devoted himself to architecture for the next 18 years. Begun in 1505 and not finished till 1626, Michelangelo's spectacular dome would eventually dwarf Rome's stately Pantheon, and be the measure against which all other domes were judged.

Most art historians place the short flowering of the High Renaissance to the time of the three great artists, Leonardo da Vinci, Michelangelo and Raphael. Mostly trained as painters or sculptors, the humanist scholar-architects of the Renaissance nevertheless thought like engineers, or the product designers of today. They wanted an architecture that was a celebration of all that man could achieve. Formed of geometric planes and spaces and organized according to number and proportion, it would be rational, but religious. It would celebrate man's intellect, in honour of God's creation.

greatest Renaissance minds. The huge task of managing its construction and decoration embroiled 27 popes.

By 1505 the walls of Constantine's ancient basilica inside the Vatican city were leaning six feet out of true. Pope Julius, typically, ordered the destruction of the oldest and holiest church in Christendom without a second thought. Enormous pits 25 feet deep were excavated for the new foundations. Tons of

building materials cluttered the streets and piazzas as an army of 2,000 carpenters and stonemasons prepared themselves for the largest construction project seen anywhere in Italy since the days of ancient Rome.

Ironically, in building St Peter's, one of the greatest buildings of Rome, the Popes pillaged 2,522 cartloads of stone from one of the ancient city's most astounding and most important classical buildings, the Roman

# The Rise and Rise of Rome

A series of ambitious popes ensured that Rome was a place of employment for artists and architects. By the end of the 15th century, popes were coming from the sort of wealthy, powerful families that were accustomed to underwriting public art and hiring their own private artists. Each in turn outspent the previous pope on elaborate buildings and works of art. Holy 'requests' were often delivered by armed emissaries: if a pope requested your presence, or asked

you to paint the Sistine Chapel ceiling – even when you were not a fresco painter – you did what you were told.

**MAN AS THE MEASURE OF ALL THINGS**
During the Renaissance there was a general belief that 'man was the measure of all things'. Because in Christian belief man was made in the image of God, it was thought that the proportions of the human form must therefore be an ideal reflection of the heavenly design.

Leonardo da Vinci explores this idea with his drawing of Vitruvian Man. The man's outstretched arms are as wide as his body is tall, and can be made to fit both into a circle and a square drawn around him. The fact that it is a near mirror image

is also significant: symmetry was extremely important to Renaissance thinkers like Leonardo.

This idea was not Leonardo's: he took it from Book III of the treatise *De Architectura* by the ancient Roman architect Vitruvius:

*'For if a man can be placed flat on his back, with his hands and feet extended... the fingers and toes of his two hands and feet will touch the circumference of a circle described therefrom.'*

Vitruvius believed that architecture should correspond to these heavenly proportions (see p.38). Many Renaissance figures such as Francesco di Giorgio Martini, designer of forts and palaces, and later Andrea Palladio developed and applied this theory to great effect.

# St Peter's Basilica, Rome

The man that many would describe as Christ's greatest disciple is thought to be buried under St Peter's Basilica in Rome. Successive popes had attempted to improve the condition of the medieval church already on the site and failed due to lack of money, will or both. Ironically it was human vanity, rather than the patient humility advocated by the church's namesake, that finally gave Rome the impetus and will to complete the greatest church in Christendom. As big as a football field and as high as a 13-storey building, St Peter's is the physical and spiritual centre of the Catholic faith.

St Peter was buried in a common grave, and so it remained until Constantine commissioned a basilica on the site in the 4th century. By the end of the 14th century, Constantine's structure was crumbling. Early in 1505 Pope Julius II began to plan his own tomb and ordered the reluctant sculptor Michelangelo to design it. The monument, though, would need a grand setting for this most demanding of popes.

Julius' project was monumental in scale and ambition. He might have been known as 'il papa terribile', or the 'terrifying' pope – he was prone to violent rages, in which he thrashed underlings with his stick – but his patronage would make any architect the star of Rome.

The stellar cast of the play included the 63-year-old Giuliano da Sangallo, who was so convinced he would win the commission that he moved his family from Florence to Rome. Then there was the flamboyant Donato Bramante. Sangallo had already built a splendid residence in Savona, the Palazzo della Rovere, for Julius. The whole of Rome waited with bated breath to see who would win. Entire careers – and vast amounts of money – rode on the decision. In 1506 Julius commissioned Bramante to devise a plan, much influenced by Hadrian's Pantheon, that had never been equalled in terms of scale and ambition. Nature intervened, however, and in 1514 Bramante died. It was to take many architectural talents and many popes before the project was completed in 1615, under Pope Paul V. The next act involved the artists Raphael, Michelangelo and later Bernini, with Antonio da Sangallo playing –

to some extent at any rate – the villain.

Many architects followed, with the work by Antonio da Sangallo described by the St Peter's website as 'disharmonious and complicated, still inspired by Gothic art'. Michelangelo struggled – and failed – to complete the dome before his death, but a rare drawing discovered recently proves that his is the solution that prevailed.

**ABOVE** Michelangelo's mighty dome was completed by Giacomo della Porta and Fontana after the great man's death. Pope Clement III raised a cross atop the dome – an event that took an entire day. It is said to contain relics of the True Cross

**LEFT** Carlo Maderno designed the travertine façade, with its statues of Christ, St John the Baptist and 11 apostles. It is said Maderno was forced to rush the design, which critics complain is out of proportion

# The 'Big Three'

Leonardo da Vinci, Michelangelo Buonarroti and Raphael Sanzio are always the first names that come to mind whenever the term 'Renaissance' is mentioned. Although they achieved their greatest fame through their art, each of these three towering geniuses also had an immense impact on architectural thinking. They were the intellectual stars of their time, men who were expected to turn their hand to anything.

Leonardo (1452–1519) worked for the son of Pope Alexander VI, Cesare Borgia, as a military architect and engineer, travelling throughout Italy with his patron. In Venice, he consulted on architecture for Isabella d'Este from 1495 to 1499. His drawing of Vitruvian Man, perhaps the most reprinted image in the history of the world, puts Vitruvius' theory of proportion to the test: he also seems to have invented the technique of drawing aerial architectural plans. Both he and Michelangelo were skilled designers of military fortifications.

Michelangelo's first patron was Lorenzo Medici and his many architectural works include the Laurentian Library in Florence for the Medici Pope Clement VII. Its windows lie in parallel bays. They are articulated by rippling pilasters that mirror the beams of the ceiling. The library is thought of as a prototype of the highly formal Mannerism. Always inventive, Michelangelo brought new sculptural styles to architecture, including 'giant' pilasters and pilasters that tapered. St

Peter's dome was constructed to his design. Despite creating the most influential fresco in the history of Western art, that on the Sistine Chapel ceiling, Michelangelo had a pretty low opinion of painting. He was therefore a bit of a reluctant mentor to Raphael (1483–1520).

Young Raphael idolized Leonardo and managed to get along with Michelangelo (which by all accounts was no mean feat). Like many before him, Raphael was commanded to become the official architect for St Peter's. His work there has been mainly superseded, but for a short time Raphael's reputation as a painter was

almost eclipsed by his fashionable status as an architect. Raphael was Rome's hottest property.

One of the most perfect of Raphael's creations is the Chigi Chapel in the Church of Santa Maria del Popolo, under a dome that represents the creation of the world. A rhythmic sequence of round-headed arches with canted corners lines the four walls. Only the entrance arch is open; the others are blind. A delicate emphasis is given to the classical Corinthian pilasters and entablature with subtly coloured marble; the festoon-decorated frieze is close to the Corinthian splendour of the Pantheon. Somehow, the architect managed to transform the tiniest of spaces into a monumental work of art.

However, Raphael's celebrity in Rome was mainly due to his fresh and inventive take on the revival of the Roman pleasure villa, in the shape of the Villa Madama. This lavish hillside retreat, consciously modelled on Pliny's descriptions of his own villa, was designed for Cardinal Giulio de' Medici. Its terraced garden had views of the Tiber; an open air theatre was excavated out of the hillside; and there was a hippodrome for races. The young

**ABOVE** The Chigi Chapel. Under a dome decorated with remarkable mosaic Raphael created a unified octagonal space, unique in the 16th century for its size

**RIGHT** The double helix staircase at the Château de Chambord in the Loire valley. Supported by eight square pillars, the staircase is thought to have been designed by Leonardo Da Vinci

architect followed the model of the Vitruvian house in the sequence of *vestibulum, atrium* and *peristylium.* Raphael's writings about the villa show that he paid as much attention to the setting of the villa as the building itself. Its forecourt and approach were followed by a series of oval and round terraces that heightened anticipation as you drew near. The Madama, the essence of educated

luxury, sums up the dreams and aspirations of the Renaissance. Palladio drew the villa when he came to Rome – the only modern building he drew there.

Raphael died at the age of 37, within a year of the elderly Leonardo, reportedly after 'an excess of sex' with his mistress La Fornarina. Antonio da Sangallo the Younger had to be drafted in to finish the Villa Madama, now a museum.

# LATE RENAISSANCE

**LEFT** In the hands of Sansovino, Renaissance style became more ornamental. The Libreria di San Marco

In 1527 the mercenary forces of the Holy Roman Emperor Charles V invaded Rome. They sacked churches and palaces, destroyed buildings and pillaged, raped and thieved. Clement VII was forced to escape to the ancient fortified Castel Sant'Angelo. With the power of the papacy on the wane, the focus of radical new architecture moved eastwards, out of Rome.

**BELOW** The medieval context: St Mark's Square, Venice dominated by the Basilica, the Doge's Palace and the Basilica's campanile. The other buildings are Napoleonic

Jacopo Sansovino, a Florentine who had worked on St Peter's, introduced classicism to the hitherto Gothic Venice when he was appointed chief architect and restorer of the ageing basilica of San Marco. The main square of Venice is one of the most majestic spaces in the world, and one of its best-loved buildings is Sansovino's sculptural Libreria di San Marco. He designed the Libreria (built 1537–88) to complement the Palazzo Ducale, across the Piazza. He also had a hotch-potch of nondescript buildings razed to the ground because they obscured the delicate, filigree-like medieval Palazzo. The language of classicism is traditionally associated with a rationalist severity and restraint. Unifying and rationalizing the space in the best Renaissance manner with San Marco, the Florentine still made his graceful arcaded library suit the Venetians' love of surface decoration.

Even relatively small Renaissance buildings have been influential worldwide. Modelled on the ancient temples of Vesta and Tivoli, Donato Bramante's tiny Tempietto San Petro in Rome has been endlessly copied everywhere from the Capitol, Washington DC, to Hawksmoor's Mausoleum at Castle Howard in England. The Roman spirit was abroad. And it would change the way we lived forever.

# MANNERISM

The transition between Late Renaissance architecture and the relatively short-lived stylistic adventure named Mannerism first pioneered by Michelangelo is best illustrated by a look at architects like Giacomo Barozzi da Vignola (1507–73). Vignola, who went on to work for François I at Fontainebleau, had been an assistant to Michelangelo and like him was to some extent a bridge between the Renaissance and the Baroque.

We owe some of Italy's best-loved villas and gardens to the Mannerists. The hugely influential Villa Guilia for Pope Julius III is one of the most delicate examples – Vignola collaborating with the writer and architect Vasari, and Bartolomeo Ammanati. Vignola was a master of suspense

and hidden drama. In 1556 he designed the pentagonal Castello Farnese at Caprarola for the powerful Cardinal Alessandro Farnese. You approach it via an extraordinary sequence of routes: first a road, then stepped terraces and finally symmetrical, arching oval ramps that set a precedent for the Paris Opéra centuries later. Critics argued that Mannerists worked in an affected 'manner' (*maniera*) and were more interested in intellectual conceits than in rigorous classicism for its own sake. Yet this sense of fun was liberating. The Villa Lante at Bagnaia (1566) is perhaps the most perfect 16th-century 'garden of surprises' and possibly of all Italy.

Attributed to Vignola, with the assistance of the hydraulic engineering genius Tommaso Ghinucci, the lyrical garden represents the tale of humanity's descent from the Golden Age. Based on Ovid's *Metamorphoses*, its geometry is inspired by the Belvedere at the Vatican. Ghinucci would go on to work with Pirro Ligorio at the Villa d'Este, the mannerist masterpiece that still delights visitors to Tivoli.

The highlight of Este's breathtaking series of terraces, with their sleeping nymphs, cascades and water jets, was Ghinucci's extraordinary gushing waterpipe organ that played music as guests and visitors marvelled.

**LEFT** The Villa D'Este: many of the statues and much of the marble used to build the extraordinary garden was taken from the nearby Villa Adriana, Hadrian's villa

**ABOVE** There is not one 'villa' at the Villa Lante, near Bagnaia, but two small houses built by separate owners in the Mannerist style. This is a garden of shapes (the Renaissance square and circle), story and ornament, not plants

**RIGHT** The Villa D'Este: visitors fleeing from the heat of Rome will appreciate the cooling combination of the hills, the shade of trees and lots of cold running water

# PALLADIO

From its staccato Florentine beginnings, the Renaissance spirit exploded across Europe and beyond. But it was a single figure who would have the most profound influence on world architecture. He did not come from Florence or indeed from Rome, but originally from Padua. In the panorama of 16th-century architecture Andrea Palladio is an exceptional figure, working not in central Italy, but the north – the Veneto.

The very word 'Palladio' conjures up a lyrical sense of calm, of serenity. To this day, the term Palladian symbolizes an idealised Venetian Utopia: the high culture and laid-back living we all associate with Italy. Andrea Palladio (1508–80) trained as a builder and stonemason – one of the few architects of his time to do so. He was also unusual in that he was not a painter by training like Bramante, Raphael, Peruzzi or Giulio Romano, nor a sculptor, like Sansovino or Michelangelo. The miller's son had a distinguished career, creating the Logge

**ABOVE** The Ponte degli Alpini was designed in 1567 by Andrea Palladio: it is named after Italy's elite mountain regiments who rebuilt it in 1948 after its destruction by retreating German troops

of the Basilica in Vicenza, the Palazzo Chiericati, the Teatro Olimpico, two great Venetian churches and a number of beautiful bridges. But the bulk of his commissions were for private dwellings – urban palazzos and, particularly, agricultural villas. No architect up to that time, not even the local hero Antonio da Sangallo the Younger, had such a huge number of enthusiastic clients lining up to ask for private villas and palaces.

Were it not for his patron, the writer and nobleman Giangiorgio Trissino, Palladio might simply have remained a highly capable and intelligent craftsman. Trissino, a linguist, had been a member of the inner cultural circle around the Medici Pope Leo X. He was also a talented amateur architect, and was remodelling his own suburban residence at Cricoli, just outside Vicenza, to bring it into line with the most fashionable architecture in Rome. By this time in Italy, an architect

**LEFT** The Palazzo Chiericati in Vicenza. The first-floor loggia, raised five feet (1.5 m) above the piazza, runs the entire length of the façade in 11 bays. The centre projects slightly

**ABOVE** Il Redontore, Palladio's great domed church on one of Venice's islands, was consecrated in 1592. It was built in gratitude for deliverance from the plague

**RIGHT** With a façade design for San Francesco Della Vigna, Palladio neatly encapsulated the newly fashionable religious ideas of St Thomas Aquinas

needed the 'right' cultural and intellectual credentials to get commissions. From the 1530s, Trissino took 'maestro' Andrea di Pietro, the name Palladio was born with, and transformed him by inventing the fine name of Andrea Palladio, a reference to the Greek goddess of wisdom, Pallas Athene. Trissino also gave the former mason a wide education in the classics and an introduction to the highest circles.

When Palladio visited Rome with Trissino in the 1540s, the trip opened his eyes to all that had astounded Brunelleschi 140 years before. He wrote:

'... as grandiose ruins, the ancient buildings still give a clear and fine indication of the virtue and grandeur of the Roman nation, to such an extent that the study of these qualities of virtue have repeatedly fascinated and enthused me; I directed all my thoughts to them with the greatest of expectations.'

From this point on, Palladio was to follow the principles of Vitruvius. Earlier Renaissance architects had pursued a very similar route. The great difference was in Palladio's response to this influx of ideas and learning. From the late 1540s onwards the Vicentine architect developed a coherent, unified architectural system of his own. While houses of similar status in countries like England were still being charmingly cobbled together by joiners (see p.93), Palladio's concept of systems and standardization – of room shapes, of hall dimensions, of the use of orders – was a great step forward for architecture as practised by architects. Palladio did not reinvent the wheel with each new building.

He saw the distance between columns as an integral part of each order: Ionic columns, for instance, should be separated from each other by two and a quarter times their diameters: the measure should be two for the Corinthian. Helped by his reading of Vitruvius and Alberti, Palladio applied Trissino's literary ideas on consistent grammar to architecture. Consciously or unconsciously, this intellectual leap was recognized by the humanist figures that surrounded him: people like his friend and patron Daniele Barbaro.

For Barbaro and his well-educated friends, Andrea Palladio offered something new: a truly rational architecture. In *I Quattro Libri dell'Architettura*, first published in 1570,

Palladio elaborated his ideas about architecture, and published a large number of detailed plans. Trissino had chosen his protégé's name well: Palladio's books plainly demonstrated his mastery of a codified, logical approach to Vitruvian ideals. He was the first architect to publish such plans, as well as the first to provide his readers with practical measurements, based on a strict system of proportion. As he wrote:

*'There are seven types of room that are the most beautiful and well proportioned and turn out better: they can be made circular, though these are rare; or square; or their length will equal the diagonal of the square of the breadth; or a square and a third; or a square and a half; or a square and two-thirds; or two squares.'*

His creation of a unified system of design – using 3s and 5s – and a grammar of forms and proportions was also to a large extent about common sense. Craftsmen and stone masons

had long been in the habit of ordering blocks in standard sizes from the quarries. They were also accustomed to using standard forms and sizes for doors, windows, and columns.

Palladio's villas met a need for a new type of country residence. To free Venice and the Veneto from dependence on imported grain, the nobility was improving land and establishing farm estates outside the city. Yet the educated and sophisticated Venetians, brought up on Virgil's *Eclogues* and *Georgics* and used to their sophisticated palazzos, would not settle for an ordinary farm complex. Venetian art of the time shows an increasing preoccupation with the ideal landscape – and Palladio offered his clients a Venetian Utopia. Palladio's inspiration came from ancient complexes like the temple of Hercules Victor at Tivoli. The same temple fronts that he would later use on churches like Francesco della Vigna were adapted to his villas, because he believed that to be the original style of

**ABOVE** The Villa Capra in Vicenza, often known as the Villa Rotonda, adapts the aesthetics of Rome's Pantheon. It is tightly symmetrical, built around a dramatic circular entrance hall

his ideal, the Roman house of antiquity.

These villas put man at the centre of a serene, ordered landscape. Porticos and loggias on all sides gave views of the countryside, much like the American porches of today. If the building was on a hill, as was the Villa Capra (also known as the Villa Rotonda), the views stretched in four directions, summarizing the confident spirit of the Renaissance. At the centre of it all – with a rational order superimposed upon nature – stood man. The villa was capped by a dome – a form symbolizing the divinity, which had always been reserved until then for churches and cathedrals.

Despite their open loggie, these villas were still the direct descendants of castles, and were surrounded by a walled enclosure

containing barns, bread ovens, chicken sheds, stables, dovecotes, living quarters for domestic servants and places to make cheese or press grapes. Palladio also gave the nobility of the future the luxury of options without much extra cost. An exterior could be given presence and dignity simply by the placing and orchestration of windows, pediments and loggia arcades, as Palladio did at Villa Saraceno and Villa Poiana.

Symmetry was a consistent design principle for Palladio. In many of his buildings he applied the Harmonic Mean – in which the smallest measurement (often the width) of a room was multiplied by its length to find the square root of that number. This would then determine the room's height. In *Architectural Principles in the Age of Humanism*, written in

1949, the critic Rudolf Wittkower makes a strong case for the theory that both Alberti and Palladio's rules of proportion are derived from music. 'Harmonic proportions' are beautiful to the ear: it was believed they were part of a higher universal design, and thus equally beautiful to the eye. Wittkower traces the evolution of this idea through Plato back to the Pythagoreans.

The architect's supreme common sense approach to designing the country estate is what must have appealed so strongly to the 18th-century English. Obsessed with classical learning and arcadias, the English had a 'thing' about their divided lives in town and country. They desperately needed practical farm houses from which to run their country estates, yet wanted them to have status and

**ABOVE** Following Palladio, the temple front became *de rigueur*, as with Colen Campbell's 1720 design for Stourhead, England, based on Palladio's Villa Emo

style. Palladio was the answer. The house designed by Colen Campbell at world-famous Stourhead (1720) was inspired by a combination of Palladio's Villa Emo and Inigo Jones' Queen's House in Greenwich (begun 1616), the very first English Palladian house. Other countries ran with Palladio's baton and many modern, particularly American, houses still use his designs as models today.

If Palladio was seeking immortality he succeeded better than he could have known. His body of work would not only make him famous in other countries but also inspire fervent homage in entirely different centuries.

**LEFT AND BELOW** The Villa Foscari, 'La Malcontenta', 1550-60 (front and back), sits beside a canal near the Venice lagoon; its name comes from an unhappy, abandoned woman who lived there

# Timber Framing

The warren-like homes of the gentlemen farmers of 16th-century England were a huge contrast to the Palladian ideal that was fast growing up in the Veneto.

An example is Little Moreton Hall in Cheshire, the moated manor house commissioned by the prosperous Moretons in the mid-15th century. Where Palladio had a co-ordinated plan for each building, with corridors creating vistas that helped the visitor to understand where they were going, finding your way about at Little Moreton is an act of intuition. There are no corridors and four narrow, winding staircases link the different levels. Cupboard-like oak-panelled rooms suddenly open on to large open spaces, the floors all now drunkenly lurching as the weight of the building pulls the structure out of shape. Half-timbered houses were extremely common in the wooded vales of the West Midlands and Welsh Marches and their quirky nature adds to their charm.

**ABOVE** Shakespeare's House in Stratford upon Avon is a popular tourist destination. The building is probably 16th century. In Victorian times, the timbers were exposed after the plaster which originally covered them was removed

**LEFT** The half-timbered Little Moreton Hall, in Cheshire. The weight of its third-storey Long Gallery has bowed the timbers, which would originally have been left unpainted, fading to a pretty silver-grey

# Villa Barbaro

Is the Villa Barbaro one of the most cultivated collaborations between architect and client in history? The distinguished patrons of the Villa Barbaro, the diplomat brothers Daniele and Marc'Antonio Barbaro were both architectural experts. Daniele, Patriarch-Elect of Aquileia, was the author of a translation of Vitruvius, for which Palladio provided the illustrations in 1556.

The undulating shape of the villa, also known as the Villa di Maser after its location in the Veneto, echoes the rolling hills that surround it. It might have been modelled on Roman antecedents, but this was a new concept of form – a beauty that dignified function. Although the Barbaro villa was a complex working farm, it was also a restrained pleasure palace, with a

temple front that emphasized the status and culture of Palladio's clients.

Palladio was the first architect to take the façade of a Roman temple and stitch it straight on to a domestic building, beginning a tradition within architecture that lasted until the 20th century. The arms and the identity of the owner could be displayed on the pediment. Palladio is his own best advocate:

'The floor of the upper story is at the same level as the pavement of the courtyard at the rear, where the mountain has been cut away and there is a fountain decorated with infinite amounts of stucco and paint. This spring makes a small lake that serves as a small fish pond. From there the water leaves and flows into the kitchen, and then it irrigates the gardens which are

to the right and the left of the part of the road, which, slowly climbing, leads up to the building. It [the water] then makes two fish ponds with their drinking troughs above the public road, from where it parts, and waters the garden that is very large and full of excellent fruit trees and various bushes. The Façade of the house has four columns of the Ionic order, the capitals and the corner ones face in two directions... On the one side and on the other there are loggias, whose extremities have dovecotes, and under these there are places to make wine, and the stables, and the other outbuildings for the use of the villa.'

The nymphaeum is an unusual feature, more in tune with Roman conceptions of the villa as a belvedere than most

functional Venetian estate villas. It's possible that the nymphaeum's statues were carved by Marc'Antonio Barbaro himself. The waters at Maser may have been put to practical use but, perhaps more importantly, they also give the villa a sense of quiet sanctity and repose.

As he did with many villas, Palladio disguised the mundane farm buildings, turning functional necessity into a positive aesthetic feature. For instance, the graceful arcaded lower floor is actually an adaptation of the traditional arched *barchesse,* intended to store farm implements and feed. The end pavilions might have large decorative sundials set into the pediments, but they contain a stable, a winery and, above, dovecotes for valuable winter meat.

Commissioned by the brothers, the villa's extraordinary frescos were by Paolo Veronese. They play a game with the spectator by showing not only mythological and sacred figures but real contemporary personalities. In the Hall of Olympus, Veronese painted Giustiniana, Marc'Antonio Barbaro's wife, with her youngest son and his wet nurse. The family

pets, a parrot and a spaniel also peek through the balustrades. With lifelike perspective, the villa's staff peer around *trompe-l'oeil* doors in the Crociera room. The boundaries between the antique and the contemporary, the mythological and the real are constantly blurred, in a way that perfectly complements Palladio's own mix of the modern and the ancient.

# AROUND THE WORLD

As Italy began to fall under foreign domination, the focus of new architecture gradually shifted to other parts of Europe. By the end of the 15th century Italian humanist ideals, particularly the use of classical details, had been enthusiastically picked up in other countries. Vitruvius' *Ten Books on Architecture,* only available in Latin in 1486, had appeared as an illustrated Italian edition by 1521. Alberti's *De re aedificatoria* was translated into Italian, French and Spanish in the 16th century.

Inevitably it was the stylish French who felt most at home with the adoption of classicism into their existing architectural vocabulary, written in the Middle Ages. The French monarch Francis I (1494–1547) had made many military expeditions into Italy, culminating in the sack of Rome. All this made skilled Italian painters and architects so unsettled with living in Italy that they decided to work elsewhere. Leonardo da Vinci was one of them – Francis carried him off like a prize of war. The two

reputedly became firm friends. Leonardo was present at the meeting of Francis I and Pope Leo X, which took place after Francis had captured Milan. It was for the French king that Leonardo was commissioned to make a mechanical lion which could walk towards you and then open its chest to reveal a fine cluster of lilies.

French architects began by adding classical details to their existing steep-roofed medieval forms, as at the royal château in Chambord (see p.74) of 1520–50. However, an Italian team, led by Giacomo Barozzi Vignola and Sebastiano Serlio had been brought together by Francis I to design the Palace of Fontainebleau. They would also introduce France to the Italian Mannerist style in interior decoration – and the patterned garden parterre. Born in Bologna, Serlio was another 'refugee' from Rome. It was Serlio who introduced the U-shaped townhouse plan that became standard for elite dwellings in fashionable Paris.

The building of the Louvre, which began in 1546 under the supervision of Pierre Lescot, and graceful buildings like the

Château of Anet by Philibert de l'Orme, demonstrated the maturing of Renaissance ideas in France. Then, gradually, the style morphed. Detail was pared down. Towers became flattened, as they did in England, into bays or pavilions: the difference was that roofs stayed tall. François Mansart, designer of the Château de Maisons (1642–6) designed such emphatic roof forms that they still bear his name – now spelt *mansard.* The French were developing their own classicist *argot,* a language they would make decisively their own.

In Spain, the early use of Renaissance ornamentation on buildings went hand in hand with adapting local traditions of Islamic art. The resulting mix was called the Plateresque. This Hispanic interpretation was also transplanted to the so-called 'New World' by the Spanish conquest. Examples include the Monastery of San Miguel of Huejotzingo, near Puebla, Mexico (1544–71),

**BELOW** The Louvre, used as an art depository from Francois I's reign. Here, the central Court Napoléon, faced by I.M. Pei's modern pyramid entrance of glass

which was probably designed by a priest.

However, the palace for Charles V (1527–68) built into the Moorish Alhambra at Granada is the earliest example of pure Renaissance monumental design outside Italy. Pedro Machuca, the architect, had studied in Italy and in a typically Italian gesture its plan features a circular, colonnaded courtyard, a circle set in a square. Later (1562–82) the Escorial (or San Lorenzo del Escorial) was erected 30 miles outside Madrid as the imperial palace of King Philip II. The architects Juan Bautista de Toledo and Juan de Herrera designed an enormous but terribly austere variation on the Renaissance cross-in-square plan.

Russia at around this time was still enveloped by its very own developing Byzantine-influenced tradition. The gaudy colours and onion domes of St Basil's Cathedral are architectural proof of the defiantly separate nature of the largest country in the world.

In 16th-century England, the influence of the Renaissance could be seen in grand Elizabethan houses such as Montacute in Somerset and Derbyshire's Hardwick Hall, (see p.100–1), although the end result was thoroughly and eccentrically English.

Even if English translations of Palladio weren't available until 1715, Inigo Jones did his level best to establish classicism as a court style in the 17th century.

Jones' near-contemporary in Holland, Jacob van Campen, was a gentleman-architect who had no need to work. But a visit to Italy inspired him – and he gave a gentle touch to the classical revival he had introduced into Dutch Baroque architecture. The fusion of the native, homely Dutch brick style with Vitruvian principles gave a new gentility to his buildings. Van Campen designed the Netherlands' first theatre, Amsterdam's Stadsschouwburg. Then, in about 1645, he designed the Nieuwe Kerk in Haarlem, a much-feted church that would later influence that classicist swimming against the tide, Sir Christopher Wren. Van Campen's best-known work is probably the large Town Hall of Amsterdam (begun 1648), now the Royal Palace in Dam Square.

ABOVE The aristocratic Jacob van Campen, designer of the Mauritshuis Nieuwe Kerk in Haarlem, had a typically restrained Dutch style

BELOW A case of Spanish taste transported across the Atlantic ocean to Mexico, San Miguel near Puebla was probably designed by a priest

By now a more exuberant form of design, the Baroque, was already displacing the orderly, restrained and symmetrical style of the Renaissance. Hedonism was about to hit architecture.

# Blinding the Architect

There cannot be a single foreign correspondent in Moscow who hasn't set up to film his news report in front of St Basil's Cathedral with its riotous confection of swirling colours. This striking structure is remarkable not just for itself but as a potent symbol of Russia's savage past, both real and imagined.

It was built between 1555 and 1561 for Ivan IV, whose behaviour later earned him the name 'Ivan the Terrible': he adopted a severed dog's head as his mascot and terrorized whole villages with random torture and massacre. Legend has it that when St Basil's was complete the Tsar ordered the architect Postnik Yakovlev to be blinded, to prevent him from ever creating anything to rival its beauty again.

Located on high ground overlooking the left bank of the Moscow River, the cathedral's history mirrors that of Moscow. Built on blood, it commemorates Ivan's successful 1552 military campaign against the Tartar Mongols, who were holed up in the besieged city of Kazan. Ivan's conquest of Kazan, followed by the khanate of Astakhan on the Caspian Sea, was a triumph for Russian Christian orthodoxy, at a time when the church still faced persistent opposition.

In Russia the central-domed church of the Byzantine east gradually became a sharply sloping tower or cone (the 'tent-type' or shatior church). Postnik's real aesthetic breakthrough with St Basil's was to combine this feature with Russia's traditional multiple domes. The entire design is based on deep religious symbolism: an architectural representation of the New Jerusalem. On the west side, the main axis was dedicated to the Entry of Christ into Jerusalem – at the same time usefully symbolizing Ivan's triumphal entry into Kazan. This led to an annual Easter ritual in which the Tsar, led on a horse instead of a donkey, re-enacted the Palm Sunday procession.

The nine individual chapels are each topped with a unique onion dome, among the earliest known in architecture. There are many theories concerning the origin of onion domes, the first of which appeared on the Cathedral of Sancta Sophia in

**ABOVE** Breathtaking St Basil's Cathedral, Moscow. It narrowly escaped destruction, first by Napoleon and then by the Bolsheviks

**RIGHT** The interior decoration is quite folkish. Inside is an intimate series of separate chapels, each filled with icons, on the east wall

Novgorod in the 11th century. One theory is that they came via India, another that the bulbous shape was taken from a late 15th-century reliquary that showed a medieval canopy over the Holy Sepulchre. These specific onion domes on St Basil's were replacements, after a fire in 1583. There would once have been gilded and twisted metallic strips running along the ribs of the main tall shatior with its gold-plated top, but what you see today is glazed terracotta. Even so, the scalloped drum reminds you irresistibly of the Chrysler Building. The charm of the ensemble lies in the way that each of St Basil's domes is decorated in a unique way.

In fact, a complex and symbolic numerological system is at work in the design. The group is dominated by the 'tent' of the central tower and is composed

on a series of octagons. To the east, each axis, each diagonal and each side of the Trinity chapel works on a system of threes (the Trinity). The eight onion dome-topped towers are positioned around a central, ninth spire, forming an eight-point star. The number eight carries great religious significance: it denotes the day of Christ's Resurrection (the eighth day by the ancient Jewish calendar) and the promised Heavenly Kingdom. The eight-point star itself represents the Christian Church's role as a guiding light to mankind.

The cathedral's star-like plan carries yet more meaning – the star consisting of two superimposed squares represents the stability of faith, the four corners of the earth, the Four Evangelists and the four equal-sided walls of the Heavenly City.

Surprisingly enough, the extravagant and brightly-coloured exterior masks a much more modestly decorated interior. Originally it was mainly painted brick red, with white seams representing mortar, a traditional brick-imitating technique known as 'pod kirpich'. Small dimly-lit chapels and maze-like corridors fill the interior space. Some walls covered with delicate floral designs in subdued pastels date from the 17th century. There was so little room inside the church to accommodate worshippers that on special feast days services were held outside in Red Square. St Basil's became a kind of outdoor altar.

Napoleon was so taken with the cathedral, so the story goes, that he wanted to transport the entire building back to Paris with him. When he realized that it was an impossible task he ordered it to be destroyed. As the French retreated, kegs of gunpowder were set up and their fuses were lit – but a sudden, miraculous shower of rain extinguished them.

The most extreme threat arrived with the atheist principles of the Bolsheviks. In 1918 the Communist authorities shot the senior priest, Ioann Vostorgov, confiscated the cathedral's property, melted down its bells and then closed it. During the 1930s, Lazar Kaganovich, a close colleague of Stalin and director of the Red Square reconstruction plan, even suggested that St Basil's be knocked down entirely, to create space and ease the movement of

tanks out on the square. Thankfully, Stalin rejected his proposal. The next time Kaganovich tried, however, Kolomenskoye Museum director Pyotr Baranovsky was actually ordered to prepare the cathedral for destruction. Baranovsky, an architect by training, refused point blank. He threatened to cut his own throat on the steps of the church. Stalin cancelled the decision – but Baranovsky's defiance was rewarded with five years in jail.

It was lucky Stalin didn't blind him. Baranovsky is the real hero of this story. Born a peasant in Smolensk, he became a construction engineer in 1912, working on industrial and railway projects. At great risk to himself, he was the single most important figure in documenting Moscow's historic architecture. Just as the newly-powerful Joseph Stalin purged all political opposition, the other potent force in the country – religion – was violently suppressed. Churches were closed, destroyed or converted to other uses. It was considered bourgeois and anti-Commmunist to try to preserve the architecture of the tsarist past.

As the Russian Avant-Garde reached its height, developing the radical new artistic styles of Constructivism, Futurism and Suprematism, hundreds of architectural landmarks throughout the country were being lost.

Fighting the tide, Baranovsky restored Kazan Cathedral in the 1920s and between 1927 and 1934 he either acquired or preserved many historic wooden buildings in the countryside. Structures like the house of Peter I from Arkhangelsk and the fortress tower of Sumskoy Ostrog on the White Sea were saved. Exiled to Siberia in 1934 for spreading 'anti-Soviet propaganda', he returned from the gulags to find his museum colleagues declared 'social aliens'.

Kazan Cathedral, later replaced by Communist officials with a public toilet, was reconstructed in 1993 following Baranovsky's secretly conserved plans. And St Basil's remains forever in the world's camera lenses, an exotic symbol of Russia's otherness – all thanks to an architect who threatened to cut his own throat.

**RIGHT** Kazan Cathedral, now reconstructed. First built in 1636, it and other churches were pulled down so that Stalin's tanks could have free rein in Red Square. It was rebuilt in 1993

# Elizabeth's Progress

**ABOVE** The Renaissance reaches England. The mellow tones of Montacute House, built by an accomplished master mason in a self-effacing style

A papal bull once declared the young Elizabeth I 'an incestuous bastard begotten and born in sin of an infamous courtesan'. She may have been England's most successful monarch, projecting an image of herself as the 'Virgin Queen', but from the time that her unfortunate mother Anne Boleyn was beheaded the young Elizabeth's life was balanced on a knife edge.

Perhaps it was this tang of danger that gave the Elizabethan era its heady extravagance. Henry VIII harvested wealth on a huge scale when he suppressed England's monasteries – Elizabeth and her court would reap the benefits. Her reign transformed English arts and architecture and launched a swashbuckling period of trade and conquest.

Adventuring types like Sir Francis Drake were given licence to plunder the seas. Seizing a fortune from a Spanish treasure ship, he did what a lot of the other Elizabethan *nouveaux riches* were doing. He bought an ancient religious building surrounded by generous lands: one of many that were suddenly on the market thanks to Elizabeth's father. Paying the enormous sum of £3,400 for a Gothic former abbey, at Buckland in Devon, the rogue sailor became a Lord of the Manor.

Great 'prodigy houses' were also built by Elizabeth's courtiers, in the hope of impressing her during her annual procession around the country – a tradition called 'The Progress'. Towns across the country would be shaken into action as the royal retinue trundled through the countryside with 400 or so carts of luggage. It must have been an amazing sight. Before she arrived in Stafford in 1575, the advance preparations included pointing up the houses, gravelling the streets and repairing the old town cross. Apparently, when the town presented her with a decorated silver cup worth £30, she said: 'Alas poor soul: other towns give us of their wealth, and you give us of your want'.

So imagine what it was like for those members of the nobility who were given the task of putting her up for the night. In a panic, the financier Sir Thomas Gresham built a whole new high garden wall for her when she visited Osterley (the house has since been remodelled by Robert Adam).

She was apparently unimpressed. The sheriff of Nottingham, Sir Francis Willoughby, hired the most daring of Elizabethan architects, Robert Smythson, to design him a whole new house, Wollaton Hall, in anticipation.

Unlike medieval homes, which turned inwards into an internal courtyard, Elizabethan houses looked boldly outwards, often with a great display of glittering glass. The Renaissance influence is there, but with an idiosyncratic edge. Among the houses that Elizabeth may have actually visited on her Progress is Montacute in Somerset, home to Sir Edward Phelips, Speaker of the House of Commons and Master of the Rolls.

In the right light, Montacute oozes colour, its creamy honey-brown Ham Hill stone gently mottled with lichens. Sir Edward's builder, a local man named William Arnold, was a master mason. His mastery shows. The original entrance front, with its rigid geometry, seems quite flat

from a distance. Three tiers of enormous mullioned windows reach across the façade: nearly 200 feet long, it is topped with graceful Flemish-style gables.

The grassed forecourt is closed on three sides by a balustrade. At each end are identical domed pavilions, each topped with a stone astrolabe. These architectural doll's houses – an Elizabethan reliqua of the defence towers that would once have flanked a medieval forecourt – are amazingly delicate and graceful. At roof level is another Renaissance-style balustrade, echoing that in the garden.

As you get nearer to the house, with its projecting porch and wings, you see a frontage rippling with detail and variety. Crossing the forecourt, you realize that the façade has an immense amount of subtle detail: windows have curved cornices, walls have scalloped niches. High on the third floor, below the balustrade, the niches are set with statues dressed as Roman soldiers. In fact, they represent the 'Nine Worthies', all parables of chivalry within their own religious tradition – Joshua, David, Judas Maccabeus, Hector, Alexander, Julius Caesar, Arthur, Charlemagne and Godfrey of Bouillon.

At the top of the house is a magnificent Long Gallery, another Elizabethan innovation. Now an art gallery, it would have been a party room, but it was also useful as a place to walk and play games during the frequently wet English weather.

Another beautiful example of a Long Gallery can be found at Hardwick Hall, the greatest prodigy house of all, which stands, imperiously windswept, on the flanks of a great hill in Derbyshire. Bess of Hardwick was born a squire's daughter, but through a dexterous series of four marriages she elevated herself to the status of Countess of Shrewsbury. The ambitious Bess built Hardwick with the express purpose of getting Elizabeth to honour her with a visit. Also designed by Robert Smythson, Hardwick's six towers thrust into the sky, their windows growing larger as they get higher. Especially at night, this makes the house look like a shimmering lantern. Bess's initials stand proud on the openwork balustrade of the roof, for all to see.

The High Great Chamber which leads on to the Long Gallery has been described as 'the most beautiful room not in England alone, but in the whole of Europe'.

Opinions may differ, but there is a huge poignancy about this faded, light-patterned space, which opens out into a vast mullioned bay. Bess must have devoted so much loving care to it. Above the Brussels tapestries that frame the walls is a faded plaster frieze of 1559, which pays homage to Elizabeth as Diana the virgin huntress. Her exotic court includes deer, monkeys and elephants; the deer guarding 'Diana' are meant to symbolize Bess's family, the Cavendishes. The effect is elaborate but delicate. The records show that although 375 workmen's names were recorded at the house, not one is foreign. This is a strong feature of Hardwick. Although much of its design is classically influenced, the results are idiosyncratically English.

When Mary Queen of Scots, Elizabeth's 'loving sister and cousin', returned home from France, the rival queens competed for power. Ironically for Bess, Mary was the only queen ever to see Hardwick. Elizabeth had her 'loving sister' imprisoned there.

# Inigo Jones (1573–1652)

It would take a real showman to become the first professional architect in England. In Italy, great artists like Michelangelo were feted for their work, but in stolid, pragmatic England architectural impresarios hardly existed. Even talents like Robert Smythson, who built Hardwick Hall, Wollaton Hall and Burghley House, were usually described as 'master masons' or 'surveyors'.

Yet Elizabeth's Stuart successors began a serious flirtation with an architectural style that would eventually turn into a love affair: classicism. The man who started it all was a flamboyant, arrogant Welshman who diverted English architecture from its essentially medieval riverbed into the European mainstream. Many of his architectural projects were vast in scale. But Inigo Jones lived in turbulent times. Only seven of his buildings are left, and they are all much altered.

How Jones hauled himself out of the working class – he was the son of a cloth worker – and began moving in the highest circles in the land is a total mystery. The information we have is scanty. He first crops up in history as the designer of remarkably elaborate theatrical feasts, called *masques,* which he staged for the court with the playwright Ben Jonson. We also know that Jones had travelled in Italy, probably in the company of aristocratic patrons, and that there he bought many of Palladio's drawings.

Jones fell out with Jonson in spectacular fashion, yet remained in favour with the royal court: his 'pictures with light and sound' had done so much to cement the authority of the new monarchy. In 1615 James I appointed him Surveyor of the King's Works, effectively making him the chief architect to the Crown. He held the position until 1642, when civil war broke out under Charles I. We know the pay of this important new post: 8s. a day for his entertainment, 2s. 8d. a day for riding and travelling expenses and £80 a year for what was described as his 'recompense of avails', or salary. This regular income amounted to an enviable £275 a year.

His duties were much more general than just those of an architect. London's

water supply and sanitation, public nuisances of all kinds, overcrowding and repairing the many royal palaces scattered up and down the country also became his responsibility, as did preparing for the royal progresses.

The earliest of Jones' surviving buildings is the Queen's House at

**ABOVE** The Banqueting House in Whitehall. Inspired by Palladio's ideas, Jones brought Italianate sophistication and, above all, restrained simplicity to London. Its like had never been seen before

Greenwich, a project he undertook for Anne of Denmark in 1616. It was completed in 1635. However, the severe building we see today, a simple rectangle, is not the one Jones created – except perhaps in its grace, symmetry and restrained classical detail. Built on an H-plan, like many Elizabethan houses, originally it actually straddled the main Dover Road. A bridge between the two sides of the 'H' allowed the court ladies to visit the park without having to cross the noisy, muddy and busy thoroughfare, or rub shoulders with the drovers and hawkers on the London road.

To Londoners who had never travelled

**ABOVE** The Banqueting House. A great performance space used for balls and masques, often designed by Jones himself. Charles I had an underground drinking den here

**RIGHT** The famous 'Tulip' staircase of Jones' Queen's House in Greenwich, London, the first geometric self-supporting staircase in Britain. The ironwork is original

**RIGHT** St. Paul's church, Covent Garden, which has two cats, Inigo and Jones. This is the rear façade: at the front Jones designed a grandiloquent Tuscan portico, with alternating square and round columns

abroad, the Queen's House must have seemed revolutionary. But perhaps Jones's most famous building is the Banqueting House at Whitehall (1619–22). Intended for state functions, it is a sophisticated manipulation of Italian classical elements that owes much to Palladio. In Stuart England, this blocky, palazzo-like stone building was almost shocking. London was

largely timber built. Even the grandest people lived in quite modest, medieval-style houses. The monarchy's London palaces were not much better, being low, unassuming buildings built in red brick rather than stone.

The Banqueting House's Palladian influence lies in its double-cube proportions and the way the main facade

of seven bays and two storeys is gracefully unified in an elegant, rational pattern of classical columns and pilasters. In Roman fashion, the capitals are linked by carved stone garlands. The interior is a single room. Its ceiling is especially simplified in comparison with the usual contemporary fashion of an interlocked Jacobean grid of lozenges, squares and stars. Taking advantage of this simplicity, paintings by Peter Paul Rubens, in which the King points to 'Peace' and 'Plenty' embracing under his rule, were installed in 1635. Little did Rubens know.

Jones' great building would be the scene of his patron's undoing and the end of his own career. The bitter period that followed saw the elegant monarch lose two civil wars and face trial for high treason. On January 30 1649, Charles I was taken from St James's Palace to the Banqueting House. He stepped out of a window – we don't know which one – to his scaffold. Jones's world, a world of the divine right of kings, of banqueting and lavish ceremony, of an architecture of luxury, disappeared with him.

Jones' influence, however, lived on. Buildings like the Banqueting House and his imposing classical design for St Paul's in Covent Garden (still there, but much altered), the first classically styled English church, would inspire a new generation of Palladians in England.

**LEFT** The Queen's House, Greenwich, spare and restrained. This was the first of Jones' innovative double-cube buildings. A loggia overlooks the park. Palladio himself would have approved

# BAROQUE AND BEYOND

Think of Handel, Bach, Scarlatti or Vivaldi and detailed, beautifully intricate sequences of music come to mind – highly ornamented, complex patterns, infused with a sense of fun. Baroque composers took great pleasure in display, in the formality of counterpoint and elaborate harmony. In Baroque architecture, harmony and counterpoint are just as crucial. The Baroque is a study of contrasts and opposites: between small and large forms, close and distant, light and dark. Movement, energy and tension are the watchwords. Spectacular and ornate, it is sometimes a bit perplexing to the modern mind, used to modern architecture with its emphasis on simplicity. Perhaps the word to unlock and understand the Baroque is 'joy'. Pure, religious joy.

The Catholic Church encouraged the Baroque and Rococo, believing that they embellished daily life: this is the library of a Cistercian monastery in Waldsassen, Bavaria, dating from 1725

# ECSTASY

The visual intensity of the art and architecture of the period mirrors the religious changes sweeping through Europe. Martin Luther had already nailed his Protestant colours to the church door in Wittenberg in 1517, leaving the Catholic faithful determined to prove their strength and legitimacy. This came at a time when a new spirit of scientific rationalism was also threatening the power base of the Church.

The artists and architects of the Renaissance had worked at a time when the Church was strong enough to tolerate secular and intellectual impulses. But following Copernicus' heretical revelation that the earth revolved around the sun and René Descartes' contention that reason alone determined knowledge, the Church felt increasingly under threat.

Particularly in its first stages, the Baroque was directly linked to the Counter-Reformation. Baroque artists and architects took the humanist visual vocabulary of the Renaissance and developed it. The architectural 'language' is intense and intricate; it expresses the power of an absolutist Church, and following that, the State. Important commissions came from new religious orders like the Jesuits, who were to spread the new, flamboyant style through much of the world, especially Latin America. Soon, Spain, Hungary, Austria and those regions of Germany that were still strongly Catholic had all developed their own variations on the new style. But there were important exceptions. A permanent religious rift between Catholic Italy and the Protestant nations – Holland, England and much of Germany – meant that the Protestants would not accept this new style unadulterated. In Protestant hands, Baroque would take some very different directions.

As with the Renaissance, architects were often sculptors and painters. Both Michelangelo and Bernini had combined theatricality in architecture with a sensual, not to say sensational, use of painting and sculpture. Michelangelo, always a law unto himself, had prefigured the Baroque with his almost heroic handling of massive volumes, especially with his work for the Vatican. Gian Lorenzo Bernini's love of curves and dramatic lighting, along with his incredible sense of

**ABOVE** Bernini produced the overall design for St Peter's Square, including the colonnades which symbolize the 'enfolding arms of the church'. This huge task took him from 1656 to 1667

**RIGHT** St Peter's baldachin by Bernini, once claimed to be the largest piece of bronze in the world, has four spiral columns about 98 feet high (30m), each one supporting an angel

theatre, were to make him the early crown prince of this regal style. If Bernini can lay claim to some of the most moving religious sculpture in the world, the same could be said of his architecture. St Peter's baldachin (1624–33), the sublime bronze canopy in St Peter's Basilica in Rome, was his first work for Pope Urban VIII, but he was soon in charge of all the works in the basilica. The grand sweeping Papal piazza and colonnades, where the thousands of faithful gather to see the Pope to this day, are Bernini's creation.

The next step came about almost by accident. It was by an act of fate that Michelangelo's style would gain a new importance well after his death. His pupil, Giacomo della Porta, was asked to redesign a façade for a church in Rome: the church of Il Gesù, the mother church of the Jesuits. The order that commissioned him was to have an immense impact on history.

It is a remarkable structure. Della Porta was asked to add a pedimented façade to what was already a radical plan by Giacomo Barozzi da Vignola. The façade is that first link between the Renaissance and the Baroque. It unites the building's two storeys with volutes, scrolled sections that make you think immediately of Alberti's S. Maria Novella. But where Alberti's façade was flat, Della Porta's was sculptural, anticipating what would become a Baroque norm. The Church of the Gesù was a model, inspiring buildings throughout Europe, from the Church of St Michael in Munich (1583–97) to the Corpus Christi Church in Niasvi, Belarus (1587–93). Eventually, through missionary zeal, its influence would spread to much of the world.

Francesco Borromini, a major rival to Bernini, was one of the greatest figures of the Italian Baroque. The corner is the enemy of all good architecture, according to him: he worked in unconventional ways with spheres and ellipses and his façades seem to ripple

# Key Dates

**1600** Advocate of Copernican theory Giordano Bruno is burnt at the stake by the Vatican.

**1603** Carlo Maderno completes the façade of the church of Santa Susanna, Rome.

**1604** Shakespeare's *Othello* premieres at Whitehall Palace, London.

**1605** The Gunpowder Plot is uncovered in London; Guy Fawkes is arrested.

**1620** The Pilgrims sail from Plymouth, England for America.

**1637** René Descartes publishes *Discourse on Method*.

**1640–50** Borromini works on the idiosyncratic Sant'Ivo alla Sapienza, Rome.

**1642** The Château de Maisons near Paris by François Mansart.

**1645–52** Bernini's Ecstasy of St Teresa and the Cornaro Chapel.

**1656–67** St Peter's Square is redesigned by Gian Lorenzo Bernini.

**1658–78** The Church of Sant'Andrea al Quirinale, designed by Gian Lorenzo Bernini.

**1661** Louis XIV, along with the architect Louis Le Vau, begins their plans to renovate and enlarge the Palace of Versailles.

**1666** Moliere's *Le Misanthrope*.

**1670** Louis XIV orders a hospital and retirement home for war veterans, Les Invalides, Paris. The Église de Dome, inspired by St Peter's Basilica and designed by Jules Hardouin-Mansart and Libéral Bruant, is a 'triumph of French Baroque'.

**1675** Charles II lays the foundation stone of the Royal Greenwich Observatory.

**1685–88** James I rules Stuart England.

**1687** Clocks are made with two hands for the first time.

**1693** The city of Noto, Sicily is destroyed by an earthquake and rebuilt in Baroque style.

**1719** University of Valladolid in Spain: Diego Tome.

**1703–11** The so-called 'radical Baroque' of the Church of St Nicholas in Prague.

**1705** The first Capitol Building in Williamsburg, Virginia. It burnt down in 1747 and had to be rebuilt.

**1708** St Paul's Cathedral opens on architect Christopher Wren's 76th birthday.

**1726** Nicholas Hawksmoor's Christchurch is completed in London's Spitalfields.

**1741** Handel composes his *Messiah*.

**1743** The Frauenkirche in Dresden is completed.

**1754–62** The rococo Winter Palace of the Russian tsars by Bartolomeo Rastrelli.

**1764** Construction begins on the Madeleine, Paris.

**1776** The Declaration of Independence in America.

**1778–88** The Neo-classicist Étienne Louis Boullée teaches at the École Nationale des Ponts et Chaussées. His 'speaking architecture' is hugely influential on the later Beaux Arts movement.

**1793** Old East, the oldest public university building in the USA in North Carolina.

**1796** The Neoclassicist Somerset House opens in London, designed by William Chambers. It replaces a Renaissance building.

**1797** The Mission Church of San Xavier del Bac in Arizona.

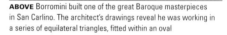
**ABOVE** Borromini built one of the great Baroque masterpieces in San Carlino. The architect's drawings reveal he was working in a series of equilateral triangles, fitted within an oval

with energy. He and Bernini worked together at the Palazzo Barberini, a much-loved building that is now home to one of the best art collections in the world. For popularity at least, Borromini's famous elicoidal staircase would probably win any battle between the palace's architectural features.

Son of a stonemason, his first break as an architect was at St Peter's, where he began working for his uncle, Carlo Maderno. The sinuous outline of San Carlo alle Quattro Fontane (1638–41) makes it seem almost alive: the wall plane is twisted, an intricate play between convex and concave surfaces. Borromini had to work his church, often called San Carlino by the Italians because it is so small, into a tiny space. Each storey has three bays, divided by Ionic columns with

capitals adorned with shells and festoons. Smaller columns punctuate the semicircular niches on either side and the columns support an unusual, undulating entablature, setting up a rhythm of opposites.

In Italy, the 17th century was the era of grand public spectacle, of vast state funerals and flamboyant public festivals. The invention of opera was a catalyst. Teatro San Cassiano in

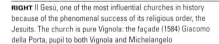

**LEFT** Now an art gallery, the Palazzo Barberini was owned by Maffeo Barberini when he was Pope Urban VII. Its grandiose, two-storey central hall has been copied worldwide

**RIGHT** Il Gesù, one of the most influential churches in history because of the phenomenal success of its religious order, the Jesuits. The church is pure Vignola: the façade (1584) Giacomo della Porta, pupil to both Vignola and Michelangelo

Venice was the first public opera house, opening in 1637. By the end of the century, there were 11 opera houses in Venice alone. The theatres became bigger and the staging more elaborate. The astonishing lavishness of Baroque had its zenith in Rome, the eternal city, with extraordinary public events. Whole city squares were turned into theatrical sets, in the spirit of the Colosseum.

The Piazza Navona, once the stadium of Emperor Domitian, was spruced up with Sant'Agnese – another church by Borromini – and three new fountains, including Bernini's Fountain of the Four Rivers. Papal power is symbolized by the dove atop the ancient column at the centre of the flowing feast of

carved travertine marble. On feast days the Piazza would be flooded, sometimes to emulate famous sea battles, but more often to symbolize Noah's flood. On hot August Sundays, the aristocrat's favourite new status symbol, the coach, would be driven round the Piazza in two to three feet of water, to the sound of music.

The Baroque also took hold beyond Italy, often outside the rarefied world of the church. It was mainly expressed in the form of grand palaces – first in France, as in the Château de Maisons (1642) near Paris, designed by François Mansart, and then throughout Europe. Sometimes its influence travelled even further, arguably as far as the Taj Mahal.

# Il Gesù

In previous churches, the faithful would enter the main body of the church via a narthex, a kind of holding space. Rome's Il Gesù has no narthex and no aisles: the congregation is plunged directly into the nave. Its frescoed ceiling was completed later by a 22-year-old, Giovanni Battista Gaulli, with the guidance of Bernini. The *Adoration of the Name of Jesus*, a whirlwind of religious devotion, was a triumph of illusionistic painting. Gaulli's figures spill out of their frames, creating a vertiginous world of heavenly ecstasy. It inspired the fashion for the *quadratura* (*trompe-l'oeil*), architectural illusionism that opened up 17th- and 18th-century ceilings to astonishing feats of perspective.

# A Tear on the Cheek of Time

The poet and philosopher Rabindranath Tagore once described the Taj Mahal as 'a solitary tear, suspended on the cheek of time'. One of the most ethereal and almost 'feminine' structures in the world, it sits in the city of Agra, on the great northern plains of India. You approach the mausoleum over a long road on the banks of the River Yamuna, through great mounds left by ancient ruins. Then gradually you see it, rising like a mirage out of a host of mirrored reflections. It seems so delicate, so other-worldly, that at any moment you expect it to vanish into thin air.

The monument was built for Mumtaz Mahal, the favourite wife of Mughal emperor Shah Jahan, who died in 1631 giving birth to their 14th child, a daughter. It is said that the building of her tomb kept 20,000 men employed for 22 years.

Construction of the tomb began in

**LEFT** The Taj Mahal was built as a symbol of eternal love and it is intended to evoke serenity and awe. It changes colour according to the time of day and season, sparkling like gold in the moonlight

**BELOW** A ceiling at the Taj Mahal. Like much Islamic art, it plays with mathematics and geometry, and features interlocking stars

**ABOVE** A *jaali*, an extraordinary trelliswork marble screen, surrounds the cenotaph. Above the tombs is a Cairene lamp, the flame of which is supposed to never burn out

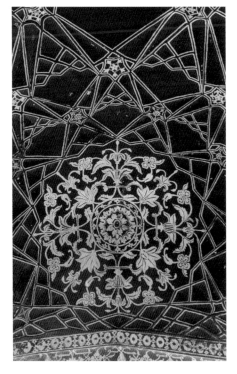

1632. Ustad Ahmad Lahauri, a mathematician and astronomer of high repute, is the most likely candidate as architect. He had already designed the nearby Red Fort. However, court histories emphasize Shah Jahan's personal involvement. His reign represented the golden age of Mughal architecture and he was passionate about the subject, holding daily meetings with his architects and supervisors.

The graceful tomb sits on a raised platform, surrounded by four minarets, the culmination of a harmonious game of perspective confused by the shimmering image seen in the intersecting canals. Rising to 35 metres above the mausoleum, the marble dome is equal in height to the base of the building. The very top of the dome is decorated with a lotus, accentuating its height. Tall decorative spires named *guldastas* extend from the the base walls, for visual emphasis.

The careful balance of the image is enhanced by the way the marble surfaces change as the sun gradually crosses the sky. The four canals are symbolic of the four rivers of Paradise mentioned in the Qur'an, which were seen by the Prophet Muhammed during his ascent to Paradise. Many scholars think of the tomb as an architectural allegory, depicting the Throne of Allah floating above the Garden of Paradise on the Day of Judgment.

Calligraphy adorns the exterior, the geometric friezes on the white marble inlaid with jasper inscriptions in script created by the Persian calligrapher Amanat Khan. Twenty-two different Qur'anic verses are inscribed with heraldic precision. Inside, the marble walls are adorned with intricate patterns of delicate inlaid precious stones. A riot of stone flower motifs with a surprising stamp of freshness and realism cover the imperial cenotaphs. These floral motifs are sculpted in simple uncoloured or 'sober' relief (*munabbat kari)* or inlaid with semi-precious stones like jasper and jade (*parchin kari*). They are designed to reflect the light, in much the same way as the waters outside reflected the roses and jasmine of the gardens. The technique is not unlike that of *pietra dura*, in which thin shards of precious or semi-precious stones are cut with extreme care and then shaped into tendrils and floral arabesques.

Sadly, though, this crown jewel of Mughal architecture has been pillaged over the years. The entrance was originally guarded by silver doors studded with 1,100 silver nails, each with a head made of a Sonnat rupee. In the 18th century the Mughals' former enemy, the Jats, melted down the silver gates and removed many of the jewels in the tombs.

But worse was to come. The final phase of Mughal rule in Delhi ended with the British sack and siege in 1857. According to a French visitor in 1863:

*'It would be difficult today to find a single flower, a single ornament intact. Many of the delicate flowers, with their Cornelian or amber petals are mutilated, chiselled out with the tips of soldiers' daggers or bayonets...'*

Lahauri may have built the embodiment of order and harmony, beauty and perfection, but life rarely follows the same pattern.

When Shah Jahan fell ill his four sons competed for his throne. Unfortunately for him his favourite, Dara Shukoh, failed to win the bitter struggle and the victor, Aurangzeb, imprisoned his sick father in the Agra fort. Legend has it that on his deathbed Shah Jahan kept his eyes fixed on the Taj Mahal, which was clearly visible from his cell. After his death, the emperor was buried beside his beloved queen.

# THE SPIRIT OF ENTERPRISE

In the time of Galileo and Newton, Descartes and Liebniz, it is not surprising to find a fascination with opposites. In faith, Europe was split into two parts: Protestants in the north and Catholics in the south. So too was architecture divided. In Holland, just like today, efficiency and comfort took precedence over any kind of grandeur. Instead of boulevards, practical Holland had canals. Here, the way in which space was used was dominated by water. In Amsterdam, which occupies the two banks of the Amstel, a dyke was built to block the water; soon afterwards a master plan was approved to dig three canals concentric with the 16th century walls. The charming individuality of the houses seems to suit that Dutch spirit of enterprise.

In southern Germany, Austria and Bohemia, which were suffering the disruption of the Thirty Years War along with Ottoman pressure from the East, there was little building until the early 18th century. At this point, an extraordinary, almost licentious mood took over church architecture in particular. The Asam and Zimmerman brothers, Balthasar Neumann and others decorated everything, from windows to doors, to altars and pulpits, in a riotous fugue of spatial point and counterpoint.

In Spain, the three brothers of the Churriguera family were recognized as the leading architects of their time, so much so that the term Churrigueresque is often used to define the Spanish Baroque. Their highly

**ABOVE** The Brouwersgracht canal, built largely during the Dutch Golden Age, the 17th century. The tall, narrow canal houses and gently arching bridges are typical of Amsterdam's picturesque beauty

sculptural architectural ornament was fashionable up to about 1750. The main altar in the church of St Stephen in Salamanca is a good example of the highly intricate style of the most famous of the brothers, José Benito de Churriguera.

Churriguera frequently used an unusual form of column (see far right), which is such a strong feature of Spanish architecture at this time, you might think of it as specifically an Iberian development. But the highly-decorated, so-called 'Solomonic' column has an astonishing pedigree. Constantine the

**LEFT** The Asam Brothers' Asamkirche in Munich, which they built for themselves as a private church, is worlds away from the calm, contemplative design style of much of Europe

Great rescued some of the original columns from Jerusalem's Temple of Solomon, destroyed by the Babylonians in 586BC. Twelve were brought to the original St Peter's Basilica. Only eight of those original twelve still remain, the others being somehow lost to history. Two of them, covered with spiralling twist-fluting and relief carvings of leaves, can be seen high on a pier right behind Bernini's famous baldachin. Bernini directly imitates their curving, sinuous form.

The Churrigueresque was far from being the only Spanish style during this period: the Moorish influence and the Plateresque had never quite gone away. Seville's Hospital de Los Venerables Sacerdotes (1687–97) by Leonardo de Figueroa is formal Moorish revisited by the Renaissance. Its arched galleries, with restrained used of colour, are delicate and elegant: an inspired synthesis of Italian and Mudéjar elements. The sunken fountain that is the focal point of the central courtyard is made from concentric brick and tile steps. Alonso Cano's facade for Granada Cathedral (designed 1667), meanwhile, is classical in structure but points the way to the Rococo.

But it was in Spanish-influenced Mexico that the Baroque would reach the dizzying heights of transcendent religious ecstasy. Perhaps the most visually intoxicating form developed in Mexico City, where the Spanish-born Lorenzo Rodriguez built a masterpiece, the Sagrario Metropolitano (1749–69). His façade takes the typical Baroque shape of the volute to castellated extremes, but somehow the Sagrario still ends up as a building with great dignity.

**LEFT** The Hospital de Los Sacerdotes in Seville is typically Andalusian in its Islamic influence. Seville is rich in Gothic, Mudéjar and Plateresque as well as Baroque masterpieces

Through the missionary activity of the Jesuits, the Spanish Baroque attained its own independent life in the Americas, spreading right up into vernacular architecture in the southern United States. The Mission Church of San Xavier del Bac in Arizona was probably built in 1797 by the native Tohono O'odham tribe, well past the point where the established Baroque had gone out of fashion. Made of kiln-baked burnt bricks similar to adobe, packed with volcanic rubble then covered with white lime plaster, it outlasted many of its adobe fellows. It is also one of the most famous examples of 'Frontier Baroque', a symbol of beauty and survival in a harsh desert climate. The design fuses Spanish Islamic with Mexican influences. After the usual struggle to find money, it received a $1.5 million

**ABOVE** Frontier Baroque: the Mission Church of San Xavier del Bac, Arizona, a prime example of Spanish colonial architecture

restoration in the 1990s. Inside, charming Native American motifs mix with the silvery extravagance that is Mexican baroque, all within a dazzling array of wall paintings and gilt, where countless sculptures of friendly angels dance among the arches.

# Flights of Fancy

**A**lberti recommended that the smaller the stairs were in a building, the better. After all, staircases are purely functional items, aren't they? They take up a lot of room, space that you don't actually use that much. Yet architecture is as much about space and illusion as it is about practicality. Later designers – just think of the set designers on *The Battleship Potemkin* by Eisenstein or *Rebecca,* by Hitchcock – were to see far more potential in a humble set of stairs. For a start, they could be used to emphasize hierarchy, and heighten that delicious sense of suspense.

Baroque architects were not the first, but they were certainly amongst the most inventive designers of this powerful emotional device. They delighted in creating vast entrance halls specifically for that dramatic entrance: the ladder to the stars. These expansive, space-eating creations showed exactly how wealthy and

important the client was. The Prince-Bishop's Palace, created by two different architects before Balthasar Neumann got his hands on it, was a truly spectacular example of self-importance. The wide centre pavilion had three vast doors, so that on dark rainy nights the prince-bishop could drive right inside the building in his coach and alight at the foot of the stairs, without getting a drop of rain on his magnificent clothes. The staircase itself is built to what is called an 'Imperial Plan': the initial, central flight ends in a landing, and then the flight splits into two, doubling back and taking you up to a higher level. This is all designed to slow progress, so you can savour the moment.

The Venetian painter Tiepolo painted wonderful frescoes for the ceiling vault. Imagine the powerful image of the Prince-Bishop of Speyer dressed in ceremonial robes at the top of Neumann's stairs, his

guests all watching rapt as he descends.

Bernini had begun this trend for the grand with his extraordinary Scala Regia in the Vatican Palace, which symbolically leads you towards the Pope, the earthly embodiment of God. It was the main entrance to the Vatican, as well as the principal connection between the palace and St Peter's basilica. The monumental staircase combines art and architecture, sculpture and decoration in a riot of stop-dead spectacle. The barrel-vaulted colonnade becomes narrower towards the end, emphasizing distance through perspective.

A major preoccupation of architects at this time was playing with space: setting up and then distorting illusions. So a favourite Baroque trick at the end of a stair is moulding sequential spaces, making them alternately light and dark. Another is playing with a sense of opposites: cramped rooms that then open up into grandeur.

**BELOW** The grand stair by Balthasar Neumann at the Würzburg Residenz, named the 'nicest parsonage in Europe' by Napoleon. Neumann initiated a unique Austro-German style of Baroque

**RIGHT** The Vatican's Scala Regia is one of the most humbling staircases in Europe. It is unrivalled in scale

# THE MIGHT OF FRANCE

If Rome was still the capital of Catholic Christianity, then Paris was the political fulcrum of Europe. With a population of 20 million, France was the largest European nation. Yet the place appears to have run like clockwork. Architecture was seen as a state business and it was ruled by civil servants. Louis XIV's minister Jean-Baptiste Colbert founded an Academy of Architecture in 1666, and as the architectural focus shifted from Italy to France, style would become a matter for control. Trades were set up in craft workshops and regulated by the state, including tapestries, furniture and glass.

**G**ian Lorenzo Bernini, sublime master of the dramatic gesture, is our initial connection to France – although he did not last long. After an annoying and tense courtship period, Louis XIV finally managed to hire Bernini as an architect, with the Pope's permission. The artist arrived in 1655, but had barely hit his stride before he lost favour, tactlessly declaring that one painting by Guido Reni was worth more than all of Paris.

You could never accuse Louis XIV of not knowing his own mind. Bernini's ideas for the Louvre would have called for the destruction of much of the existing structure, replacing it with an Italian summer villa which might have looked awkward in the centre of Paris. In his place, Louis chose Claude Perrault, brother of the famous writer who revived the fairy tale Cinderella. Perrault's work couldn't be less fanciful: severe is the term. The Perrault Wing is crowned by a distinctly non-French classical roof, and cut through the centre is a pedimented triumphal arch entrance. And so the Baroque was ousted for good, in favour of the disciplined, ordered classicism that came to define the architecture of 17th century France.

So although there was a brief 'Baroque' period in France, the French ability to formalize logic into discipline meant the arts, literature, painting and architecture were all given a coherent body of rules by the new Academies. This was a golden age for France, a time of increasing political power and the rise of illustrious names such as Molière, Colbert and Racine. To that list add the names of the great architectural classicists, like Jules Hardoin-Mansart and Jacques Lemercier. In architecture, as in art, the Academies valued clarity, beauty and dignity above all. French classicism became cool, intellectual and controlled.

The French Royal Court, the sublime centre of nationalist power, had to be of 'unique and perfect beauty'. It was the 'Sun King' Louis XIV who initially moved the French court to Versailles, in 1682, to give himself absolute control over the government, while keeping well away from Paris. By contrast, St James's, the official residence of the monarchs of England, was far from grand. In 1725, Daniel Defoe described it as 'low and mean'.

The Château de Vaux-le-Vicomte, a sublime château at Maincy just south of Paris, was Louis' model. It marked the beginning of a new order. Gardens, buildings and interiors would all be designed in concert, like a piece of music, and all would work in total harmony. The team at Vaux-le-Vicomte, which was built for the King's powerful finance minister Nicolas Fouquet, was the top talent in France: painter and decorator Charles Le Brun, garden designer André Le Nôtre and architect Louis Le Vau.

With the proud Vaux-le-Vicomte, set like a prince's castle in a rectangular moat, Fouquet had made the mistake of his life: Louis XIV was, of course, not to be outdone. The lavish Vaux-le-Vicomte became a centre for fine concerts and elaborate parties, the talk of society. The King had Fouquet arrested shortly after a famous celebration on 17 August, 1661, at which Molière's play *Les Fâcheux* was performed. The King seized 120 tapestries, the statues and all the orange trees. He then got hold of the team of artists (Le Vau, Le Nôtre and Le Brun) – and sent them to Versailles.

After Fouquet's famous fête, Voltaire wrote: 'On 17 August, at six in the evening Fouquet was the King of France: at two in the morning he was nobody.'

The château of Versailles was in effect a

royal town, built in total obeisance to the crown. Most of it was taken up by the royal palace and its gardens. It was begun in 1669, when the architect Louis Le Vau, along with landscape architect André Le Nôtre, began a renovation of the old château built by Louis XIII in 1624. Now a tourist honeypot and the set for innumerable period dramas, the walls of the sumptuous palace still hang heavy with the weight of the stories they have witnessed.

Versailles is mainly the work of three men: de Brosse, Le Vau and Jules Hardouin Mansart. Some visitors may find its horizontal lines disappointing; Mansart was unhappy with Louis XIV's insistence that he extend Le Vau's original palace. Visit on a cool day, head first for the garden fountains and then the sublime interiors.

Versailles has seen the best of times, and the worst. Halcyon days of excess and grandeur under the 'Sun King' are etched into these stones, along with the tragi-heroic years of the French Revolution. Only a century later a throng from Paris invaded the chilly halls here and Louis' hapless successor and his queen were driven back to the city. The invasion of this hallowed ground heralded the bloody destruction of the French monarchy.

The philosophy behind Versailles is straightforward. It's about power, pure and simple. Louis XIV commissioned countless pictures of himself in which he was portrayed in robes much like those of a Roman emperor.

**ABOVE** The French court was established at Versailles in 1682. The palace was purpose-built as a seat of power, dazzling in its wealth and suffocating in its rituals, designed to enforce obedience

But the most visible expression of his prestige, at least to the French people, was Versailles. And as the planets revolve around the sun, so should the court and the nobility revolve around 'Le Roi Soleil'.

You wonder if Le Vau, who abandoned the normal steep French roof style at Versailles for an Italianate flat balustraded roof, was trying to evoke the powers of the Roman Caesars. If so, the symbolism didn't stop there. Inside the château a grand procession of rooms with allegorical paintings

# Neoclassicism marches on

**LEFT** Vaux-le-Vicomte in Maincy, south of Paris. It set a standard for classical French architecture, but its ambition landed its owner in a whole world of trouble

In France, Claude Nicholas Ledoux designed a pavilion in 1771 for the Comtesse du Barry at Louveciennes and a series of city gates (1785–9) for Paris. Both exemplify the early phase of French Neoclassical architecture; his later works, however, consisted of projects (never executed) for an ideal city. When Napoleon became emperor in 1804, his official architects Charles Percier and Pierre François Fontaine were given far more rein, and worked to realize his wish to transform Paris into the foremost capital of Europe by adopting the intimidating opulence of Roman imperial architecture.

The 'Empire' style in architecture is epitomized by such imposing public works as the triumphal arches at the Carrousel du Louvre, designed by Percier and Fontaine and the Champs-Élysées, designed by Fontaine and started the same year. These grandiose *projets*, begun in 1806, were far different in spirit from the visionary work of Ledoux.

Greek-inspired architecture in England was exemplified by the Bank of England rotunda in London (1796) by Sir John Soane and the British Museum portico (1823–47) by Sir Robert Smirke. The Greek Revival was often softened and modified in Georgian England by the existence of the light-hearted Regency style, notable architectural examples of which are the façades for Regent Street in London designed by John Nash and begun in 1812 and his Royal Pavilion in Brighton (1815–23).

The Neoclassical architecture of Edinburgh, Scotland, was a highly individualistic interpretation and earned that city the name of the Athens of the North. Elsewhere, the Neoclassical impulse would be taken up wholeheartedly by the German Karl Friedrich Schinkel.

depicting royal victories ended in an ecstasy of art in the 'Room of Apollo'. La Chambre du Roi, the central room of the long extensive symmetrical range of buildings, was the axis of the entire design. At the very centre of the Versailles universe was the state bed, the very fulcrum of the power system of France. No wonder Louis XVI found it difficult to consummate his marriage to Marie Antoinette. The nobility referred to the Palace complex as *'ce pays ici'*: Versailles was a country in itself.

The château itself is an authoritarian, unforgiving-looking building. It's not blocky, like a prison. On the contrary, it's delicate – except for its size. But it's also somehow emotionless. As a symbol of the absolute power of the *ancien régime* – and of what the French felt they needed to overthrow – it could hardly be bettered. Perhaps for that very reason, Versailles had a lot of influence. It inspired a rash of palace building throughout Europe. Le Nôtre's plan, with its intersecting diagonals and radii, would be imitated in gardens from Austria to St Petersburg. The influence of Versailles can also be seen in many other places, from the grandeur of Washington's public buildings to John Nash's sweep of terraces around Regent's Park in London.

The interior of the château is justly famous: particularly the Hall of Mirrors (the Galerie des Glaces), the largest room in the entire palace. The Galerie is humbling, literally so. It makes you want to tiptoe invisibly down its entire length, as if you never truly existed. For beauty-lovers and antiquarians, the glass in those low-slung chandeliers, which refracted the Sun King's light in a delicate dance as he moved, is exquisite. Each of the 17 arcaded windows overlooking the gardens contains 21 mirrors.

Many a copy of Versailles exists, like Luigi Vanvitelli's Palace of Caserta for the Bourbon kings of Naples, (1752–80), the largest palace erected in 18th-century Europe. It is described

now by UNESCO as 'the swan song of the spectacular art of the Baroque'.

The Baroque, though, had had its day once a development called Rococo took hold. Sweeping away colossal pilasters and Corinthian capitals in a light 18th-century breeze, Rococo became dominant in France, southern Germany, northern Italy and central Europe during the first half of the 18th century. It's a playful, sometimes excessive interlude between the dramatic fugue that was Baroque and the symphony-like severity of Neoclassicism that was soon to come. The word Rococo itself comes from the French *rocaille* – which refers to the shells and water-

worn rocks that were a favourite inside the garden grottoes of the rich.

The most important of all Louis XV's mistresses, Madame de Pompadour, is often credited with being the movement's prime patron. However, in reality, although she did have access to the King's purse, the style was in full swing well before she caught the king's eye. The style began as the heavy scrolls of Louis XIV's interiors suddenly became snaky S-curves. The Baroque had gradually transformed from being an intense art of excessive religiosity to one simply of excess. Rococo is all about the pleasure principle, and in many ways it is calmer, more rational than

# Hierarchy of Ornament

Hierarchy was the name of the game in 18th century Europe. Jacques-François Blondel, who ran architecture courses at the Ecole des Arts and was appointed architect to Louis XV in 1755, argued that the client's rank should be 'the source from which the Architect determines the genre of his decoration'. The Ionic order, he proposed, would be appropriate for clergymen, because it suggested temperance. The Composite mixed delicacy with moderation, so it was perfect for judges. The Tuscan order, which had been carefully described by Palladio, didn't meet with his favour. In fact he complained that the Tuscan was too rustic to be used for the town house of a nobleman.

RIGHT The intricate splendour of Rococo: here at the Amalienburg hunting pavilion in Munich

LEFT The Amalienburg Hall of Mirrors, inspired of course by the grandeur of Versailles. François de Cuvilliés had studied in France

BELOW Claydon House in Buckinghamshire, the home of Sir Harry Verney and Florence Nightingale's sister, Parthenope, is also home to extraordinary Rococo, Gothick and Chinoiserie decoration. Here, a Chinaman entertains a guest to tea

the Baroque. Many of the motifs are exactly the same, but the obvious differences in the interior were the frequent use of a white and gold colour scheme and painted panels over doorways. Motifs from the natural world, like plants, shells and vines were combined with the 'grotesques' – called that because they were often found in grottoes – of Roman ornament. Walls, window recesses and cornices would be emphasized with gilded mouldings.

One of the most appealing examples is Amalienburg, a tiny hunting pavilion built for Charles VII and his wife the Electress Maria Amalia, in the park of the Nymphenburg Palace in Munich. The skills of the court dwarf, François de Cuvilliés, helped make the Rococo the style of the moment. Working with the talented brothers Zimmermann, he built and designed Amalienburg between 1734 and 1739. It is quite restrained and formal on the outside. Inside, the pavilion is dominated by an ethereal, circular Hall of Mirrors in the Bavarian national colours of silver and blue. Its walls are pierced with large windows and doors, and the flood of light is magnified, as at Versailles, with mirrors. Frostings of delicate silver stucco relief flutter around a dancing cornice that is (almost) alive with gilded birds reaching up to the sky-like, domed ceiling. The tiny lodge is possibly the grandest kennel for hunting dogs ever known.

A fashion for entire interiors reached its height at the same time as Rococo. 'Chinoiserie' would often be used as an exotic

variation in the interior design of a house. Asymmetrical, and also pretty riotous, Chinoiserie often cropped up in glamorous bedrooms, featuring birds with gorgeous plumage, or fanciful 'islands in the sky'. The arch priest was Jean Pilement, who somehow managed to publish his fanciful engravings of Chinese huts or ladies on swings 'in the Chinese manner' in both London and Paris in the middle of the Seven Years War.

At Claydon in Buckinghamshire a mysterious designer called Luke Lightfoot created probably the world's most spectacular and idiosyncratic Chinoiserie room. The Chinese tea ceremony is played out in plaster with real bells, and alarmingly large, mustachioed Chinamen support pagoda-like doorcases. We know virtually nothing about poor Lightfoot, except that he got fired. The style fell from favour in the late 18th century, but the odd serious outbreak did recur. The Brighton Pavilion, where the Prince Regent would woo his Mrs Fitzherbert, far from the prying eyes of London, was a particularly serious attack, completed by Nash in 1822.

The Rococo lent itself to sybaritic pursuits. In Britain, the style was thought too flighty to be used outside, but worked for ceilings or anything frivolous. The Music Room in Norfolk House was designed by Giovanni Battista Borra as a hub of cultured society, in the middle of St James', central London. The house is no more: but after decades in storage you can see the room today, perfectly preserved and redecorated to its original scheme of pure white paint with gilt, carved woodwork; it was moved lock, stock and barrel to London's Victoria and Albert Museum.

# The Man Who Never Was

The scene: the landlocked state of Minas Gerais, in Brazil, a gold-rich mountainous region east of Rio, on the cusp of the 18th and 19th centuries. Was this the backdrop for the emergence of a true 'Brazilian' school of architecture? Was there in fact a black artist/architect, born of a slave mother and a Portuguese father, who created unique Baroque masterpieces worthy of the *ouro preto* (black gold) of his home country?

Ouro Preto is said to have been founded in 1698, on the very day that pioneering explorers from São Paulo first discovered that the fabled black gold, covered with a layer of iron oxide, did in fact exist. There was a sudden, massive gold rush. Entire villages from northern Portugal crossed the Atlantic to mine the newly discovered Eldorado. The town they built, Ouro Preto, was built from scratch in a single style: Baroque. As a result, it is one of the world's most architecturally coherent places. And with gold almost pouring out of the ground, no expense was spared when it came to gilding the extravagantly carved Baroque interiors. Local soapstone became a substitute for European marble and behind the relatively simple façades are elaborate, effusive interiors teeming with sculptures of angels, mythological beings, saints and biblical scenes.

The town is worth visiting for its wealth of Baroque architecture, as well as for the cobblestone streets and steep hillsides. Yet it is also the scene of an intriguing architectural mystery. Ouro Preto's architectural uniformity can be attributed largely to the fact that so many of its buildings are the work of a single architect: but if so, who was it? The San Francis of Assisi Church; the Church of Our Lady of Carmo; Saint Joseph's Church; the Cathedral of Our Lady of Pilar; the Public Fountain of Pissarrao; the Governor's Palace – all are gems of South American Baroque.

With some oddly military features, the Church of St Francis of Assisi (Igreja de São Francisco de Assis), first begun in 1776, is particularly original. Its tall cylindrical towers look like watchtowers, its roofs resemble helmets and are adorned with spears. It is seen as a masterpiece. But

here the plot thickens. Local lore has it that the church's architect was the mysterious Antônio Francisco Lisboa, nicknamed Aleijadinho. The nickname means 'little cripple', and Aleijadinho's story is one which combines the greatest physical suffering with the highest expression of the Brazilian Baroque.

Antônio Lisboa was the son of a white architect Manoel Francisco de Costa Lisboa and a black mother, his father's slave Isabel. Brought up with his half-siblings, the young boy learned the fundamentals of sculpture and architecture from his father – and soon outstripped him in ability. His first commission was the Chapel of the Third Order of St Francis of Assisi, where his carvings include a skilled bas-relief, depicting St Francis receiving the stigmata. Tragically, if we are to believe the official

RIGHT Aleijadinho, or 'the little cripple' first appears in the official records as a labourer at the Church of Our Lady of Carmel in Ouro Preto, designed by his father

LEFT Church of the Third Order of St Francis, which sits atop a hill in Ouro Preto. The circular bell towers were an innovation in the Brazilian town

BELOW The Sanctuary of Bom Jesus of Matosinhos at Congonhas, where Aleijadinho's masterly twelve prophets were sculpted by having his assistants strap hammer and chisels to what remained of his hands

The big question is, did this larger-than-life figure, who suffered terrible tortures for his art, ever actually exist? The issue of whether Aleijadinho is simply a myth was first raised in the 1960s by the Brazilian art historian Augusto de Lima Junior. After years of research, Lima Junior was unable to find any evidence that Aleijadinho had ever been born. His birth and death certificates are reported in only one book, written by a government official long after the architect's death. The birth date of August 29, 1730 does not match the one reported to be on his death certificate. As for church records, there do appear to be receipts for the expenses of someone named Aleijadinho: occasionally, the records state his involvement in one or another building. Frustratingly, none of these name Aleijadinho himself as either sculptor or architect.

Could there be another truth that lies behind the large body of work attributed to this legendary figure? Are Aleijadinho's many buildings in reality the creation of many others, who were working at the same time? Some scholars argue that Aleijadinho, the mixed race child of a slave, is no more than a useful folk myth, a 'national narrative' created by a new republic striving to forge a cohesive national identity.

The argument centres on the publication of the only significant near-contemporary account of the architect: *Traços Biográficos de Antônio Francisco Lisboa*. The original text was republished as *O Aleijadinho* by the Ministry of Education in 1949, with an introduction by Lúcio Costa (1902–98) praising the work of Brazil's great architect.

The poet Mario de Andrade wrote:

*'Brazil had in Aleijadinho its greatest artistic genius, a grand human manifestation. Of anyone from the colonial period, only he could be called national, because of the originality of his solutions. He was already a product of this land, of his suffering, and a psychological extension of his time.'*

Allegory, or architect? The jury is still out. Perhaps we shall never know.

account, Antônio was soon to deal with stigmata of his own – a dreadful degenerative disease.

Slowly, disease deformed and atrophied his whole body, until he became not Antônio but Aleijadinho. The pain in his hands became so great that he cut off some of his own fingers. It seems to have been a form of syphilis – or perhaps even leprosy. Gradually, as his body became progressively more deformed, the architect lost all his fingers, his toes and eventually even his lower legs. Undeterred, and determined to carry out his architectural vision as far as he could, the story tells us that he made his assistants strap instruments to his hands. He worked only at night, under a canopy, as the heat of the day made his suffering worse. His real name forgotten, the little cripple would be carried through the streets by his slave assistants in a covered palanquin. His artistic martyrdom was biblical in proportion; it must have appealed to a Catholic sensibility.

Aleijadinho's most famous work is a series of majestic soapstone statues of the Twelve Prophets at the Sanctuary of Bom Jesus do Matozinho in the neighbouring town of Congonhas. The statues are a mournful, evocative expression of a haunted man who found solace from his terrible pain in his deep Catholicism. The Sanctuary was declared a UNESCO World Heritage Site in 1985. The statues are symmetrically arranged on the steps and terraces, among pavilions that symbolize the 12 stages of the Cross. The Sanctuary seems to symbolize the slow agony of its creator, and the Christ-like way he pushed himself beyond endurance.

# THE AMATEUR ARCHITECT

The direct British answer to Versailles was Blenheim Palace, built as a national monument for Louis XIV's powerful nemesis, the Duke of Marlborough. 'What a great heap of stone,' exclaimed the French satirist and playwright Voltaire when he first saw it. A great heap indeed.

The Duchess, it is said, wanted Wren. The Duke, however, wanted someone of a different cast – a man of action. The charming, witty John Vanbrugh was just such a man. More than just a playwright, his journey through 17th- and 18th-century society had been an astoundingly picaresque affair, worthy of a soap opera.

Vanbrugh had many a provocative tale to tell. He'd worked for the East India Company, in Gujarat. An undercover political activist, he'd been imprisoned in France for four and a half years, some of that in the infamous Bastille, for spying. He'd spent some time in the army, seen battle and then inexplicably turned up again in London as a playwright and theatre manager. Founder of the Haymarket Theatre, and a popular member of the famous Kit-Cat Club, his plays *The Relapse* and *The Provok'd Wife* were satisfyingly scandalous.

The Duke met the former spy at a playhouse – and commissioned him on the spot. Still only 43, Vanbrugh had already completed parts of Castle Howard, near York, with his friend and collaborator Nicholas Hawksmoor. In Italy, the Baroque had been used for personal residences like Guarino Guarini's Palazzo Carignano in Turin for some 60 years. In Protestant Britain, though, this raunchy stylistic venture was new and very daring. Everyone was talking about the flamboyant Castle Howard and this new European style. With its coronets, cherubs and urns, together with Doric pilasters on the

north front and Corinthian on the south, Castle Howard brought a breath of sophisticated Europe to the north of England. Its interiors were heart-stopping and operatic, particularly the Great Hall, which soars into a central cupola.

By contrast Blenheim, with its towering stone belvederes, became more of a castle than a gracious home. The process of building it, with Sarah Churchill interfering almost every step of the way, was an unhappy one. The amateur architect was turned out on his ear before the monumental work was completed: to monitor progress, he had to sneak back in secret when the Duchess was absent. A few years later, Vanbrugh was even refused admission when he, his wife and the Earl of Carlisle – owner of Castle Howard – turned up as paying visitors in 1725. Embarrassing? It must have been searing.

## The Rise and Fall of a Reputation, Sir

Blenheim Palace is yet another instance of a house that ruined reputations – in this case, three of them. The land, near Oxford, was a gift from a grateful nation to the 1st Duke of Marlborough after the defeat of the French at the Battle of Blenheim in the War of the Spanish Succession. Sarah Churchill, the Duchess, was a close childhood friend of Princess Anne. The Duchess became the Queen's Mistress of the Robe – and seems to have been a very domineering, bullying one. She also spent a lot of time and effort scheming to get the money needed to build the house.

The Duchess wanted Christopher Wren to be her architect. The Duke, meanwhile, met Vanbrugh at a play – and without asking the missus, commissioned him instead. The forceful Duchess was furious, and decided to dislike the perfectly innocent Vanbrugh. But there were more problems ahead. The Churchills had assumed that the building would be paid for by the Crown. The precise agreement is unresolved to this day. A warrant appointing Vanbrugh as architect, dated 1705, was signed by the Parliamentary treasurer. Unfortunately, it outlined his remit but did not mention either the Queen, or the Crown as paymasters. The scene was set: meltdown.

The playwright was being asked to create a family home, a mausoleum and a national monument in one. It proved an impossible commission, particularly as the project kept running out of money. Sarah eventually threw him out and banned Vanbrugh from the site. She and the Duke, meanwhile, were forced into exile abroad after the Duke was accused of embezzlement and Sarah had a bitter quarrel with the Queen.

The whole episode did terrible things to Vanbrugh's reputation, and contributed to the short-lived nature of English Baroque. The nation quietly breathed a sigh of relief and returned to a more comfortable version of the Palladian.

# The Trials of Greatness

When he first saw Wren's majestic design for The Royal Hospital Chelsea, a home for military pensioners, the Victorian thinker Thomas Carlyle declared: 'This must have been designed by a gentleman.'

Christopher Wren is the epitome of that 17th century phenomenon, the gentleman architect. Architecture was not seen as a profession: it was the province of talented amateurs. Yet what a talent – Wren's rise to fame was meteoric. His natural abilities were those of a Renaissance man: he may have only been five feet tall, but as intellects go, he was a giant. As a young man he made models that mapped the moon and the solar system. He also invented a device for writing in the dark. Described by Isaac Newton as one of 'the greatest Geometers of our times', by the age of 25 he was a professor of Astronomy at Oxford.

By the time he began to dabble in architecture, Wren was already famous throughout Europe as a mathematician, an astronomer and an experimental scientist. He'd even performed the world's first-ever injection – into the bloodstream of a dog. Architecture was then widely accepted as a practical application of mathematics. Although we don't know how close the connection was between Wren and the future Charles II, his father was the Dean of Windsor and the two were brought up in the royal town at the same time. When the monarchy was restored, Charles II insisted on Wren as Surveyor-General.

In the spring of 1666, Wren made his first design for St Paul's, building on Inigo Jones' work. Accepted in principle on August 27, 1666, it was a weak design, a compromise. Fate stepped in. Shortly after midnight on Sunday, 2 September a fire started at the bakery of Thomas Farriner (or Farynor) in Pudding Lane. The Great Fire of London reduced two-thirds of the City to a a dense mass of charcoal and old St Paul's to a ruin. Together with his close friends the architect Robert Hooke and the diarist John Evelyn, Wren took on the task of surveying the extent of the damage. He produced a plan for the city which would create new open spaces along the main thoroughfares. Although this plan could not be carried out completely, Charles II admired the design.

The king decided that all the churches that had been destroyed in the fire must be rebuilt – and that Wren was just the man for the job. It was not just the opportunity of Wren's lifetime, but perhaps one of the greatest opportunities any architect has ever had. He set about the task with gusto.

Out of 86 churches that had been

**BELOW** During the Blitz, St Paul's came to symbolize the unbeaten spirit of the Brits against the odds in World War II. This image was taken by *Daily Mail* photographer Herbert Mason

**ABOVE** The Royal Hospital, Chelsea, founded by Charles II to take care of sick or injured soldiers, the 'Men in Scarlet'

**ABOVE** The dignified oak-panelled dining hall of the Chelsea Hospital, a reminder of the medieval manor hall

destroyed by the Fire, 51 were rebuilt by Wren and a talented cadre of friends and disciples that included Nicholas Hawskmooor and Robert Hooke. The rebuilt churches ranged from St Bride Fleet Street and St Mary-le-Bow to St Stephen Walbrook and St Magnus Martyr.

They were built in a style that has come to be known as distinctively English Baroque – pragmatic and somehow sparer than its continental forbears. However, Wren never thought of himself as a 'Baroque' architect: instead he saw himself as a classicist.

But while the city-wide church building programme was a huge success, the rebuilding of St Paul's became a near-impossible task, due to all the usual problems – political infighting and bureaucracy. The clergy condemned Wren's first plan for the cathedral outright. It was 'too modern' and too modest. Undeterred, Wren came up with a second design in 1675, this time in the shape of a Greek cross, with a dramatic, soaring dome. This, his 'Great Model' was an inspired design, yet the Church fathers still rejected it. This time it was too modern *and* too 'Italian' – by which they meant, 'too Catholic'. Wren was

ordered to prepare something different.

In desperation, Wren sought an audience with the king, taking with him the 20-foot-long (6 metres) Great Model he had painstakingly built to illustrate the design. The bond between Wren and the king was to last throughout their lives, but it would still not make Charles defy the Church commissioners. Shaken by the ability of the clergy to block a plan favoured by the king, Wren vowed, in the words of a memoir written by his son, to 'make no more models'. He is said to have knelt down and wept.

The third time around Wren gave the clergy what they wanted: a nice, old-fashioned Gothic cathedral with a long nave and a tall spire. To this uninspired design – known as the 'Warrant' design – the king gave his approval. Work started. But the king had told Wren that he was free to make 'variations, rather ornamental than essential' to the approved design. A nod's as good as a wink, and Wren did what many

architects have done when faced with a poor, compromised design: resorted to subterfuge. Shrouding the construction in scaffolding, he began to build a cathedral uncannily like the one that had been rejected, quietly removing three bays, raising the height of the walls, dropping the spire and building a striking, wide dome, the first of its kind in England. When the clergy found out what he was up to, they were predictably furious. Funds dried up – along with Wren's salary. Work stopped, and then started again, continuing in this staccato fashion for the next 33 years.

The cathedral unveiled in 1711 is a triumph in Portland stone – and the only one of Europe's major cathedrals that had been designed by a single architect and built within his lifetime. It is the building of a mathematician, and it shows. Within a rectangular outline nests a square, divided by two tiers of paired Corinthian columns, 12 columns below and 8 above. The elegant dome is peripteral – surrounded with a ring of columns. Together with the two rippling towers that frame the ensemble – rather like Borromini's church of S. Agnese in Rome – the dome sets up a swirling dynamic to the façade. The interior, an

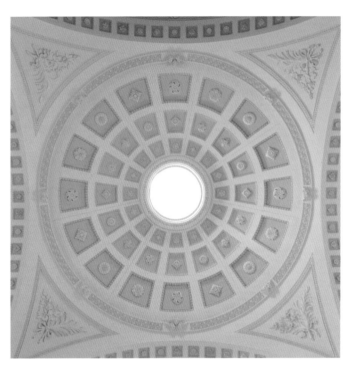

ABOVE The ceiling of St Mary-at-Hill, one of a satisfying ring of contemporary churches in the City of London. Unfortunately, some were bombed in the war

LEFT The quiet calm of St Stephen Walbrook, one of Wren's finest interiors, where he used the device of the Byzantine squinch – corbelling at the corners – for the dome

expressive flow of light and space, uses colour and ornament in a decidedly un-English way, with the best craftsmen of the age drafted in to help. Jean Tijou designed the magnificent wrought-iron gates, Grinling Gibbons carved the choir stalls.

Yet for Wren, St Paul's had become a cross to bear, one that had dominated an otherwise stellar career. He had introduced new architectural forms to England and he was the author of many remarkable buildings – the Monument commemorating the Great Fire, the Royal Observatory, and

the library at Trinity College, Cambridge among them. Yet it is hard to imagine how he must have felt about his career with St Paul's the touchstone of his reputation. Humiliation piled upon humiliation. Parliament had withheld his salary for 14 years since 1697, apparently attempting to speed up the cathedral building programme. Worse, his cathedral was now the object of scorn.

By the time the scaffolding came down, fashions had passed on. Palladianism was now all the rage. Critics

complained that his great cathedral was a 'Catholic' intrusion into Protestant England, a Gothic building in classical clothes. Wren himself might have been unhappy with the design he had been building for 35 years. The dome is ingenious – a hemispherical vault is surmounted by a brick cone upon which the outer light shell, made of lead-sheathed timber, rests. But he knew that he'd got his calculations wrong. He famously commissioned a vast chain to hold the whole thing together.

Just a year after the unveiling, in 1712, the third Earl of Shaftesbury dealt Wren a body blow – he challenged Wren's level of influence on London, and proposed a new British style of architecture. In the *Letter Concerning Design* Shaftesbury questioned Wren's cathedral, his taste and his long-standing control of royal works. Then, the bitterest blow of all came – the great man was dismissed. The great architect was seen weeping inside his cathedral, a broken man.

There is a coda, however, to this story. Gradually, myths built up around Wren's heroic story of dedication. The favourite Victorian tale was that the chain on the

drum around the dome was insisted on by the Dean and Chapter – and that Wren, knowing his dome wouldn't fall down, crept up there in the dead of night and snicked open one of the links. It's not true – Wren commissioned the chain. But the stories showed how Londoners, at least, held Wren's reputation up high. And he did have an architectural legacy.

The great Sir Edwin Lutyens, the man who led the alternative wave to the Modernists in the 20th century, referred to his own architecture as 'Wrennaissance Style'. Although badly damaged after German bombing raids in the Second World War, St Paul's survived. The famous photograph of the dome rising above the burning city in 1940 shows just how important Wren's building is to the spirit of London. Christopher Wren is buried in the crypt of St Paul's, along with the Great Model. His son Christopher wrote his epitaph: 'Reader, if you seek his monument, look around you.'

## The Chequered History of St Paul's

Given the history of its predecessors, it's a bit of a miracle that Wren's design for St Paul's Cathedral ever got built. Or that it has remained in one piece.

There have been five cathedrals at a rough count. Fire destroyed the first church, built by King Ethelbert of Kent in AD604. In 962, a Viking raid put paid to its successor. Following a second fire in 1087, the Normans set to work on a new, stone replacement which became known as 'Old St Paul's'. It took the best part of 200 years to build, but at 489 feet it did have the tallest spire in Europe for its day. Sadly, this meant that it attracted lightning.

Things got even worse during the Reformation, when Protestant mobs smashed the high altar, ransacked the interior of the Catholic Old St Paul's, and destroyed many of the ancient tombs.

As a final insult to the old faith, market traders were allowed to set up stalls in the nave. In the 1630s, Charles I commissioned Inigo Jones, his Surveyor of Works, to set the old cathedral back to rights. Jones remodelled the north and south walls of the nave and transepts, built a striking new West Front in a classical style and refaced much of the building in Portland stone.

While his work was greatly admired at the time, admiration counted for little during the English Civil War. Roundhead troops used the cathedral as a cavalry barracks. They also broke up what they could of the structure and sold it on as building materials.

Come the Restoration, things looked as if they might take a turn for the better. Charles II appointed a promising young architect named Christopher Wren to restore the structure to its former glory. Wren had only just got started when the Great Fire of London broke out, on 4 September 1666. Four days later, Old St Paul's was a heap of smoking rubble and Wren had his great opportunity.

# THE NEW CLASSICS

Richard Boyle, 3rd Earl of Burlington, first got involved with architecture when he commissioned James Gibbs to do a small amount of renovation work. Gibbs probably didn't realize that here was the individual who would become the principal patron of architecture in England. But then, Burlington was the grand old age of ten.

**ABOVE** The Royal Naval College in Greenwich, designed by Wren and built 1696–1712 is in truth very handsome. Jones' Queen's House can be seen in the gap

**RIGHT** Burlington's 1726 design for his own home, Chiswick House on the outskirts of London, was directly inspired by Palladio's Villa Rotonda

It was Inigo Jones who had first introduced a formal, integrated notion of classicism to Britain – then exclusively a sophisticated, court taste. The Queen's House at Greenwich (1616–35), all white minimalism, underlines the huge difference between the phlegmatic spareness of English building and Italian architecture of the time, like Borromini's S. Carlo. Yet at this stage in British architecture this was a pretty refined taste: classically-inspired architecture would take a long time to break through the hard, isolationist shell of British taste.

A quarter of a century later, with Christopher Wren, the classical language hit the big time. Wren was in many ways Britain's latter-day Renaissance man, and through his many churches and influential buildings like Hampton Court he brought a peculiarly English, rational quality to Baroque.

But where Italy was all light and air, British architecture – Wren and Nicholas Hawksmoor aside – was pretty big-boned and raw; even ugly, as at Blenheim. At its best, though, as at Castle Howard, the English baroque spirit was brooding, heroic. It was almost romantic. This spirit would be picked up in France towards the

end of the century by architects like Ledoux, and at home by the new Gothicists.

But in the meantime, the Baroque was beginning to look 'decadent': buildings by Vanbrugh and Hawksmoor became identified with royalist or Tory causes. A new definition of classicism was abroad. Literally – in the form of 'the architect Earl'. Like all young men of money, Richard Boyle, Lord Burlington, did the Grand Tour – more than once, in fact. His first trip was made at the age of 20 and then he took three further trips, with a fourth to France. Burlington was the sort of man who stood out, a man of determination as well as intellect. Georg Friedrich Händel dedicated three operas to

him, while staying at Burlington House: *Il Pastor Fido*, *Teseo* and *Amadigi di Gaula*.

In contrast to France, where architecture was the province of the professional, in England architecture was a cultured man's plaything. Yet Lord Burlington was serious. Deciding to follow only the work of Vitruvius, as interpreted by Andrea Palladio in his *I Quattro Libri dell'Architettura*, he was instrumental in the revival of Palladian architecture.

William Kent set to work to transform British architecture into a model of restraint and decorum. Kent's interior for the entrance hall at Holkham Hall, the immense country house of the Earl of Leicester, is a masterstroke. It takes a Palladian basilica, with its apse and stairs

leading into it, and adapts it into a grand entry with a raised interior colonnade. Kent turns copy-catting into something new and original. In gardens, where Kent had huge influence, there was a parallel reaction to the formalism of Le Nôtre's Versailles. Englishmen were free; England was a democracy. By extension, an Englishman let nature itself run wild. As interest in history and ruins grew, so did garden buildings. They often took the form of ruins or mock-ruins, temples and grottoes, 'rustic' retreats and even hermitages, sometimes complete with a fully paid-up resident hermit.

In 1721 J.B. Fischer von Erlach published a book which not only contained the seven wonders of antiquity, but images of the Parthenon and Arab and Turkish buildings. His would not be the last study: James 'Athenian' Stuart travelled on foot to Italy, paying his way as a *cicerone* (guide). With the nobleman Nicholas Revett, he published *The Antiquities of Athens and Other Monuments of Greece*, in 1762. There were more than 500 subscribers to its first volume. Piranesi's exquisite engravings of the buildings of Rome were published the same year as *Vedute* (Views). The new archaeological finds of Herculaneum, Pompeii, and Athens were followed with bated breath by an entranced Europe. Architects believed that in uncovering the old, they were rediscovering the elemental first principles of building. They were also extending classical architecture's formal vocabulary. That vocabulary was adopted with a new eye by the Scot, Robert Adam.

**ABOVE RIGHT** Holkham Hall breaks the mould. The Marble Hall is modelled on the idea of a Roman basilica. Kent's rich interior contrasts with a severe Palladian exterior

# Elaborations on a theme

### MEANWHILE, IN FRANCE...
The first prominent proponent of Neoclassicism in France was Claude-Nicholas Ledoux. He is a cult figure for architects, his work taking abstraction so far that it often feels like an exercise in pure geometry. In the years just before the French Revolution, France produced some of the most fascinating examples of Neoclassicism. As far as Ledoux is concerned, architecture was also about town planning, just as the Romans had done. He is perhaps best known for the highly original ideal working city for the Royal Saltworks at Chaux and the Palace of Justice, Aix-en-Provence.

### OUSTING THE BEASTLY BAROQUE:
The Baroque style never really seemed to suit the English, even that of the best, highly individual British practitioners like Nicholas Hawksmoor and Wren. So when a series of books was first published opening the door once more to classical knowledge, the British sat up and took notice. Suddenly, architects and dabblers alike could get their hands on detailed classical drawings:

*De Re Aedificatoria,* Leone Battista Alberti, re-published in 1726
*I Quattro Libri dell'Architettura,* Andrea Palladio English translation 1715
*The Designs of Inigo Jones... with Some Additional Designs,* published by William Kent, 1727
*Vitruvius Britannicus,* Colen Campbell on the great Roman engineer, 1715

### PALLADIAN BRIDGES
Bridges such as those at Stowe Landscape Garden (see p.134) and that at Prior Park near Bristol have always been called 'Palladian', but this is a misnomer. At least, they are not based on any known design by Andrea Palladio. The first seems to have been one put up at Wilton House near Salisbury by the architect Roger Morris, in collaboration with his patron the 9th Earl of Pembroke. There, parts of the house were rebuilt in the English Palladian style: perhaps the bridge was assumed to belong to the same school of thought.

# TOWER OF THE WINDS

This white marble octagonal tower, built in the first half of the 1st century BC by an astronomer, has had a huge effect on the architectural imagination. It has inspired tombs, garden buildings and gentlemen's gambling dens from Ireland to Sevastopol.

Its designer, Andronikos of Kyrrhos (or Cyrrhestes) was a Macedonian. According to Vitruvius he constructed the 'Horologian' – an early form of clock – for the marketplace in Athens. It showed shoppers the time by means of sundials or mechanical hour indicators. There was also a weather vane to indicate which of the eight winds sculpted in deep reliefs on its sides was prevailing (thus the tower's name). A clepsydra inside – a device that measured time by marking the regulated flow of water through an opening – was driven by water from the Acropolis. The roof was originally topped with a bronze statue of Triton and the building itself was made of durable Pentellic marble, also used for the Elgin Marbles.

With an internal measurement of just over 22 feet, the building was an ideal model for the English garden buildings that served as genteel distractions for the rich. One of the most famous copies, a folly of about 1765 in the grounds of Shugborough Hall in Staffordshire, was designed by James 'Athenian' Stuart. It was used as a banqueting house – although the lower two storeys were converted into a dairy in 1805. The building made free with the original design – for instance, it now had windows. Complained Joseph Banks, a future President of the Royal Society:

*'He has left the ancient design, making two Porch entreys instead of one, and leaving out that most elegant freeze said to be the work of Phideas, to which the Building certainly owes the most of its beauty in the original… as this plainly shews. For want of it appears scarce more Beautiful than a common Octagon Pidgeon house.'*

The interiors were in fact much more grand: for instance, the ceiling in the first floor 'banqueting room' is based on one from Nero's Golden House in Rome.

ABOVE The Temple of the Winds at Dashwood House, 1759, is one of the earliest English attempts to recreate a monument of Greek antiquity

BELOW The mania spread far and wide: built in 1849 at Sevastapol by the Black Sea, this Tower of the Winds is now a tourist attraction

LEFT The Tower of the Winds below the Acropolis is supposed to have been built by Andronikos of Kyrrhos around 50BC; in its heyday it was topped by a weathervane. The frieze depicts the wind deities

BELOW 'Scarce more Beautiful than a common Octagon Pidgeon house', James Stuart's Shugborough Hall folly

# THE ADAM STYLE

Born in 1728, Robert Adam was the son of a noted Palladian architect. He grew up, as did his fellow architect brothers, with the principles of his father William and the Palladian school. From 1754 to 1757 Adam embarked on the Grand Tour, later joined by his brother James. He was taught by Piranesi and he befriended Clérisseau. When he returned to England, he set up his own practice with his brother James. In 1764 he published his own studies of the Roman ruins at what is now the city of Split – the *Ruins of the Palace of the Emperor Diocletian*. He was issuing a manifesto: the Palladians would not have the last word.

However, Palladian design was popular, and Robert designed a number of country houses in this style. But Adam's brilliance was such that his name applies to an individual style – a rare achievement. The Adam style was innovative when it came to ornamentation, lighter and more ingenious than many contemporaries. He was inspired by the same classical Roman designs as Michelangelo had been, as well as influences from Greek, Byzantine and Baroque sources.

One of his trusted collaborators was Thomas Chippendale, and the partnership brought together many a beautifully unified interior. Adam's wall panels with 'grotesque' ornament were particularly fashionable, although he did find it difficult to get English workmen to give up 'their angly Stiff Sharp Manner'. In France, meanwhile, his friend Clérisseau was busy with the salon of the Hôtel Grimod de La Reynière, Paris, the earliest revival of the grotesque in France.

Adam gave a light touch to a style that in other hands loomed dour and heavy in the

**ABOVE** Osterley Park, an individualist's approach to the Palladian portico. Adam spent 20 years working on this house and its interiors. The red brick echoes the original Tudor stableblock

**LEFT** Like Wedgwood, Adam was interested in antique decorative styles. The Etruscan Dressing Room at Osterley shows the inspiration of Adam's friend Piranesi

131

**LEFT** Robert Adam had just been travelling in Rome when he designed Kedleston Hall in 1760. This is the view into the Saloon, inspired by the Pantheon with its sky-lit, coffered dome

**ABOVE** The massive south front at Kedleston Hall, Derbyshire, with a Baroque-style grand entrance stair. The young Adam arranged it so that guests' first sight inside was an astounding, monumental marble hall

English landscape. He was also adaptable – he combined the Grecian Ionic order when working for the banker Robert Childe at Osterley Park, outside London. Horace Walpole described the drawing room at Osterley as 'worthy of Eve before the fall'.

Adam called the heavier style of early classicists like Burlington and Kent 'ponderous', and felt that the Palladian style depended too much on Inigo Jones' precedents: it was nothing but 'bastard Renaissance'. 'Movement' relied on dramatic contrasts and diversity of form, and drew on the picturesque aesthetic. The first volume of the Adam brothers' *Works* (1773) cited Kedleston Hall, designed by Robert in 1761, as an outstanding example of movement in architecture.

Adam also applied the concept of movement to his interiors by contrasting room sizes and decorative schemes. His style of decoration, described by Pevsner as 'Classical Rococo', drew on Roman 'grotesque' stucco decoration, the very style that had inspired Michelangelo and Raphael.

One of the most complete of Adam's commissions is Saltram House in Devon, which still has all of the original decor, plasterwork and furnishings. It is one of Britain's best preserved examples of an early Georgian house.

Robert Adam had a huge influence on American architecture when the United States was first developing its own style. In Post-Revolutionary America – politically independent, but culturally tied to England – Adam's stylistically influence flourished, via his friend Clérisseau's connection with Thomas Jefferson.

The Adam style would even reach Russia, via a young Brit called Charles Cameron. Having read his book about Roman *thermae*, Catherine the Great summoned Charles Cameron to Russia to reconstruct her summer residence in Tsarskoe Selo. Of all her country residences this was the one that she preferred.

Having moved away from the heavy, rather dour classical country house that had had so much success in England, Adam felt he could congratulate himself:

*'The massive entablature… the ponderous compartment ceiling… the tabernacle frame, almost the only species of ornament… formerly known in this country are now universally exploded. In their place we have adopted a beautiful variety, gracefully formed, delicately enriched and arranged with propriety and skill.'*

# The Grand Tour

The Grand Tour of Europe was an open-air finishing school for men of the nobility in the 17th and 18th centuries. Richard Lassels, a Catholic priest, is credited with introducing the term: he classified travel as a means of moral and political education. The tour could last from several months to a few years.

The first stop was Paris, where the 'Milord' might learn to speak French, dance and fence. Then, it was on to Geneva or across the Alps. If you were wealthy enough you would be carried over the most difficult terrain by servants. You might then go on to Turin, Venice or Milan, and would certainly visit the art treasures of Florence.

After the discovery of Herculaneum and Pompeii, both sites joined the itinerary, along with an ascent of Mount Vesuvius for the more adventurous. On your return, you might build in some study time at the universities in Munich or Heidelberg or visit Holland and Flanders. The ruins of ancient Rome were the highlight. For architects they were a school in themselves, particularly with a knowledgeable guide.

The French draughtsman, antiquary, and artist Charles-Louis Clérisseau befriended Robert Adam in Florence in 1755, and became a mentor to a generation of architectural students. Rome was a honeypot for Europe's cultural elite, and many brought back treasures – a Venetian view by Canaletto or a portrait of themselves by Pompeo Batoni. There were, in reality, few great masters to be had. Most collectors were happy to commission copies of Renaissance or Baroque masterpieces, many of which have ended up in English country houses.

**BELOW** While the majority of their schoolfriends were pottering around Herculaneum and Pompeii, the more adventurous could be seen climbing the slopes of Vesuvius as part of the Grand Tour

# Digging for Victory

Sometimes, bemused visitors to Stowe Landscape Gardens ask where all the flowers are. It's true there are scarcely any to be seen. There never were intended to be. Richard Temple's early 18th-century park in the heart of England is not a mere garden – it is a political and cultural statement. The Buckinghamshire garden is an argument conducted through the landscape, a monument to one family's 'defence' of political liberty and the ideals of human virtue. Patriotic, moral and uplifting, the messages built into the landscape were meant to be read like an allegory. This world-famous creation, the first garden in history ever to warrant a guidebook, would influence European garden design from Sweden to Germany, France and Poland.

A landscape garden in 18th century England was as much about architecture and sculpture as planting and landscape. The 'ideal' vista was a pastoral one: trees were planted in naturalistic clumps and sometimes thousands of tonnes of earth were shifted to create 'naturally' lilting hills and vales.

Stowe's spectacular gardens were initially laid out in 1713 as a relatively straightforward expression of the Temple family's love of art, literature and gardens. Richard Temple, later Viscount Cobham, created an idealized vision of nature, with spectacular views and vast open spaces sweeping to distant arches, temples and other 'eye-catchers' as they were called. Stowe is huge, all 560 acres of it, and everywhere are pathways, new lakes and secret corners waiting to be discovered.

As gardens go, it is also an architectural feast. Temples, man-made

lakes, Palladian bridges and monuments all contributed to a refined representation of an 'Arcadia', modelled on ideas of Greek antiquity. The work was done by many of the most famous figures of the day, including the architects John Vanbrugh, William and James Kent and the sculptor John Michael Rysbrack. Lancelot 'Capability' Brown arrived at Stowe in 1741 and made his name there.

Even then, Stowe was a story, a stage set: the little valley below the house is 'the Elysian fields' of classical mythology; a dammed stream is the River Styx. Every corner told a new tale – of British history, of

**ABOVE** Stowe House: the south facade is by Adam and Thomas Pitt: at 460 feet (140m) long, nearly every room could take advantage of the vista

**RIGHT** The country's best architects designed Stowe's garden monuments, from Vanbrugh to Kent and Gibbs

**BELOW** Stowe's Palladian Bridge, designed to be used by horse-drawn carriages. It may have been by James Gibbs, designer of the Radcliffe Camera in Oxford

friendship, even of Temple's favourite dog, a greyhound. Its messages were not always subtle, either. At one point, a statue of Caroline Princess of Wales (later George II's queen) was placed to face a gilded statue of the Venus de Medici, an overt piece of flattery. Princess and goddess looked at each other as equals.

Temple, who came from a family of prominent (Whig) liberals, would soon fall out with the monarchy, and Caroline's statue would be turned away from the Venus. In 1733 Cobham also fell out with the prime minister, Sir Robert Walpole, whom he regarded as corrupt. Extraordinarily, the viscount turned to his garden as a way of speaking out. Stowe's landscape became a hotbed of oppositional politics. Before long, an artificial ruin, the 'Temple of Modern Virtue', faced an intact 'Temple of Ancient Virtue' across a wooded glade. The 'Modern' temple housed a headless torso, rumoured to be that of Walpole. The message was clear: 18th century Britain was in a state of moral decay, compared to the virtue and honour of classical antiquity.

Eventually, Viscount Cobham's moralizing itself came under attack. It happened in the worst possible way – by mocking his precious garden. The jester was none other than the notorious rake and libertine Sir Francis Dashwood, who lived little more than 20 miles away from Stowe. At first, it seems to have been a case of one-upmanship. If Stowe had an elongated Octagon Lake, then West Wycombe should have one too. If Stowe

had a glamorous Rotondo mounted on a knoll, with a shining gold statue of Venus at its centre – the embodiment of classical virtue – then West Wycombe must have its own version.

But Dashwood was actually poking fun at Temple, with an extended built satire. Whereas Stowe's murals and monuments and the inscriptions in its 'Garden of Love' warned young men to beware the dangers of sensual indulgence, Dashwood's garden advertised decadence and the pursuit of earthly pleasures. The park to the north of the house became a tribute to male lust, in the form of the god Bacchus. Dashwood scored a cultural triumph by securing the services of the antiquarian Nicholas Revett, newly-returned from an expedition to the coast of Asia Minor. He designed a reproduction of the Temple of Bacchus at Teos in Turkey, which was the first re-creation of a specific Greek monument in England.

Meanwhile, the monument to Venus on the south side was absolutely notorious in its day, an architectural in-joke that was later dismantled by Dashwood's embarrassed descendants. The temple itself was innocent enough, but it was preceded by a grassy mound shaped expressly to represent, as the contemporary journalist John Wilkes put it, 'the ... entrance by which we all come into the world.' A small statue of Mercury still stands by the now dilapidated mound.

Mercury was yet another symbol of the competition between the gardens. At Stowe a statue of Mercury conducted the

souls of chosen mortals across the River Styx to the heavenly Elysian Fields, while at West Wycombe he led the visitor into temptation. The West Wycombe statue also refers to the racy contemporary joke that 'after Venus comes mercury'. (The highly dangerous 'cure' for syphilis at the time was liquid mercury.)

As the rivalry became more personal, the garden wars became more pointed. When Dashwood ousted Temple as Lord Lieutenant of Buckinghamshire, he remodelled his lake in the shape of a swan – the county emblem. Then as a riposte to Stowe's Temple of Concord and Victory, a celebration of British success in the Seven Years War, Dashwood had Nicholas Revett throw a comical little 'pepperbox' bridge across his river, implying that all the 'magnificent' victory had done was secure a ready supply of pepper.

Stowe had a sad end. The 2nd Duke ran up huge debts in the 19th century, living at the Great Western Hotel at Paddington and gambling away his inheritance. There was an enormous sale in 1848 lasting 40 days. The house became a public school. Ironically, the place now resembled the grand ruins that the British so loved in Greece or Italy, its forlorn decay recorded in the paintings of John Piper. In 1989 it was handed over to the National Trust, and a restoration programme is now under way. And in the hot sun of an early summer evening, the Elysian Fields seem almost as magical as they did in Stowe's extraordinary heyday.

**RIGHT** Follies: the Temple of Music at Dashwood's gardens in West Wycombe is modelled on the Temple of Vesta, Rome and was used as a theatre

# The Democratic Ideal

There aren't that many top politicians who have also been architects. But as we all know, almost anything can happen in America and on the cusp of the 18th century this was especially true.

All of a sudden, America needed buildings. Lots of them. Two factors would associate Neoclassicism so closely with the founding of the fledgling state that the style would eventually be called 'Federal'. Firstly, the former British colony was painfully aware of its cultural inferiority to Europe; secondly, American thinking was permeated by that buzzword, 'democracy'. Desperate to rid themselves of autocratic England, Americans chose to be ruled by a Senate. In symbolic terms, anything at all classical held overtones of this high ideal.

The most important figure in the early history of America's built environment was Thomas Jefferson, one-time American Ambassador to France and Governor of Virginia. The new nation needed to establish its own identity, and Jefferson was sure he knew how, because he was passionate about architecture. To this day America owes its solid, immutable architectural metaphor, the idea that classical, Roman ideals underpin the harmonious coexistence of the individual and the State, to Jefferson. He ensured that these ideals would have a physical – architectural – expression. As a result classicism, and rationalism, are enduring themes in American architecture.

But it is for his own house outside Charlottesville, Monticello, that Jefferson is best remembered. In a country where public architecture had more or less been represented by domestic houses built big, Neoclassicism was a novelty. So much so that Monticello has been depicted on the back of the $2 bill as well as the nickel. Here, as Lord Burlington had done at Chiswick, the enthusiast built his own Greek idyll and lived the life of an independent farmer. Monticello (1771–82) is quintessentially Georgian – which in America was called Colonial – its façade reputedly taken from the only copy of Palladio's *Quattro Libri* in the United States.

In a sense, Monticello is a marker, a comma in a sentence that begins with an America happy with the English Palladian

**ABOVE** Monticello: author of the American Declaration of Independence Thomas Jefferson helped associate the neo-Palladian style with Enlightenment ideals of liberty and justice

**RIGHT** Jefferson's Rotunda for the University of Virginia was inspired by Rome's Pantheon

and Robert Adam. The sentence ends with America accepting a full-blown, revolutionary and democratic Federal style. By 1811 Jefferson was telling the Society of Artists in Philadelphia that a new Greece was growing 'in the woods of America'.

What had happened? Like so many, Jefferson loved the Maison Carée at Nîmes. When he lived in France in 1785 he admitted

gazing at it for hours: 'like a lover at his mistress'. So when the University of Virginia, the first state university in the United States, was established, Jefferson decided to send home plans modelled after his favourite building. Clérisseau acted as his assistant.

And when George Washington decided that a new capital should be built, it was Jefferson who sketched out the first grids.

# ROMANTIC LEANINGS

It was Adam's friend, the artist Piranesi, who gave voice to this idea: 'Out of fear,' he wrote, 'pleasure springs.' What did he mean?

**I**n *The Analysis of Beauty* in 1753, the artist Hogarth proposed that there should be a training of the eye, as well as the brain, in a gentleman's education. His analysis was that the eye could be 'fix-d' to a point that offends it. It could be 'led', it could be 'employed' (for example in examining the folds of material in a piece of material), it could be 'entertained', or it could be 'in play'. The eye found uniformity 'disagreeable'.

The classical ideals of rationality and of order, so visible in the architecture of an Adam, would soon be competing with new ones of raw beauty and the 'sublime'. It had its beginnings with landscape. The mid-century interest in Greece brought with it the desire for an ideal wilderness, an Arcadia which could be imported wholesale. In Lord Lyttelton's Doric temple at Hagley Park (1758) you could sit out and look at a natural landscape which he called his 'Vale of Tempe'.

**ABOVE** Symbol of a marriage: Castle Ward in Northern Ireland – building began in 1762 for a classical front. Inside, the saloons on the man's side of the house were Palladian in style

**RIGHT** Lady Anne Ward, soon to leave her husband, insisted her side of the house be Gothick. Her apartments on the west side have pointed doors and elaborate plaster vaulting

Tempe is a rugged part of Thessaly, with a deep and dangerous gorge, celebrated by the ancient poets as the wilderness haunt of Apollo and the Muses. Gradually, 18th-century travellers and writers like William Gilpin helped Britain to elaborate the story: the pastoral, Arcadian ideal became a wilder romantic crush on nature. The thrilling, dangerous mountains of the Lake District were the new Greece.

With the Picturesque came the new aesthetic and cultural strands of Celticism and the Gothic. Ruins became fascinating, not because of what they once were, but precisely because of what they meant as ruins: *memento mori*. Gilpin famously suggested that 'a mallet judiciously used' might improve Tintern Abbey's gables, which were still too intact.

But not everyone could agree on the new style. In one instance, a husband and wife had a serious difference. When Bernard Ward rebuilt Castle Ward, in County Down, he decided on the Palladian style. But his wife, Lady Anne, wanted to adopt the fashionable new 'Gothick', the first phase of the Gothic revival. So they decided to have one façade of each. The Gothick façade was essentially a lacquer painted on a shell, and that seems to have been a metaphor for their marriage. Lord and Lady Ward parted not long after the house was finished.

# Modesty Blaise

**ABOVE** Old England? Nestling in the west of England, Blaise Hamlet is actually a picturesque invention of the 19th century, designed by John Nash

**LEFT** The stone half-hipped roof of Vine Cottage. Lattice-leaded casements and a dovecote set into the gable make this very cute indeed

Tucked away on a country estate near Bristol is a tiny, but hugely influential group of cottages. John Nash, the most fashionable architect of the Regency period, is famed for his metropolitan terraces and country houses and for the remarkable Royal Pavilion at Brighton. Yet no place, the architect was once heard to say, ever gave him more pleasure to build than humble little Blaise Hamlet.

Nine cottages sit, casually grouped, on an irregular but immaculate village green. A monumental village pump and a sundial, neatly and determinedly off-centre, are the focal point of the idyll. Each of the quaint rubble-walled buildings has a dormer window and casements. Some of the tall, Tudor-style chimneys are alike, most have hipped roofs and all the cottages are on a similar scale. But apart from that, each is completely different. Some have a fetching bonnet of thatch; others are roofed with pantiles or stone. One or two have arched 'Gothic' windows, others have a narrow 'Maltese cross'. All the gables and dormers are at different heights, and no one profile is the same as the other. Why? Because the 'antique' perfection you see at Blaise did not grow up, unbidden, over centuries of honest toil. What you see at Blaise is not in any way real. It is 'The Picturesque'. In this carefully constructed vision of an ideal rural England, asymmetry is all: difference is everything.

Built between 1810 and 1811, this group of cottages was intended for retired workers from Quaker banker John Harford's country estate. Dovecotes, arched nooks, comfortable porches and oversized brick chimneys make these rustic dwellings, most of them in rough stone, perfect models of whimsy: they each have cutesy names like 'Sweetbriar', 'Vine' and 'Dial'. The cottages do not open on to the green; in fact they seem to turn their faces modestly away from each other. People say that this was to discourage idle gossip. Who knows? What is certainly true is that Harford took great interest in every aspect of the village for his old retainers, even

writing to Nash to query details about the placing of coppers and ovens in the kitchens. Oak Cottage is especially rustic, with a thatched roof, an open bay with a tree support and a fitted bench. Look closely, and you'll see that Double Cottage's white gables double as a dovecote.

The grounds of the wider estate, based around the 'Gothick' folly of Blaise Castle, were completely redesigned for Harford by Humphry Repton. In Britain, so many of the romantic, secluded landscapes we think of as 'wild' are entire concoctions, completely man-made. Repton, in his usual manner, cut out wooded glens and added mossy outcrops of rock and winding paths that ran down to a tree-lined gorge.

As Repton himself described it:

*'A deep ravine crosses the road, and seemed at first to render hopeless all attempt to make any approach except that thro' the village of Henbury. By cutting away the face of the rock in some places and by taking advantage of the natural projections and recesses to make the necessary curvatures, carriages now pass this tremendous chasm with perfect ease.'*

Why was the earth moved in this profligate fashion? By creating a manufactured, circuitous route through the estate, Repton obliged travellers to pass by 'all the wonders of nature', and also managed to give the impression that his patron's home, Blaise Castle House (designed by Robert Mylne) and its church were set deep in the country – emphasizing the amount of land Harford owned. In fact, they are only a few yards from the village, and very close indeed to Bristol.

How many artless, 'historic' or 'vernacular', picturesque English villages – or European ones, for that matter – have been created in this way? A surprising number. The best-known example in England was created in the 1730s by Robert Walpole at New Houghton. He built a group of cottages at his impressive gates, straddling a long, formal street. Marie Antoinette's Petit Hameau at the Petit Trianon, designed by Richard Mique in 1785 with the help of painter Hubert Robert, is probably the most famous of these romanticized creations.

So in practical terms, was all this artifice worthwhile? No matter how

prettified the image, rural cottage life in the 19th century was rarely idyllic. Starvation was not uncommon. According to the agricultural author, Arthur Young, most labourers had to work 'like negroes and did not live so well as the inhabitants of the poor house'. Real rural cottages were usually tiny hovels. People were dismissive of the rural poor, like the writer John Loudon:

*'The part acted by the cottager in the great drama of life, although important when viewed collectively, is nevertheless... barely discernible.'*

George Morland's paintings chronicle the crude dwellings and ragged children that were the frequent reality of the country. For Harland's 'old retainers', having decent sanitation and the facility to cook and to draw water must have been bliss. Even earth closets were rarities. Thanks to Nash and patron, at Blaise every cottage had its privy, its copper and its oven.

This quiet little village was enormously influential, in Britain and abroad. The village's aesthetic descendants – now with drives, security alarms and double garages – are still being built today.

# The Committee of Taste

Architecture is mostly a sensible art. Yet occasionally, a wild flight of fantasy takes wing. The castle of Neuschwanstein in Bavaria, for example, which inspired Walt Disney's immense, if saccharine, creativity. King Ludwig II, said to be so beautiful that maidens swooned when he entered the room, was himself inspired to create the castle by Wagner's swan king in the opera *Lohengrin*.

Ludwig wasn't alone in embracing this elaborate fakery. Horace Walpole was the author of the first 'Gothic' novel, *The Castle of Otranto*, in 1762 – a manuscript he pretended had been 'rediscovered' lurking in the library of an ancient Catholic family. He set a trend for the lurid novel that is still alive today. Unlike many others who had done the Grand Tour, young Walpole was so wildly enthused by what he saw that he decided to resurrect the medieval British past.

**RIGHT** Strawberry Hill in Twickenham, London. Walpole and his friends called themselves 'The Committee of Taste' and set out to define the Gothick style

**BELOW** The exterior was relatively plain, but on the inside, the rooms are 'sharawaggi' – a word invented by the colourful Walpole. A peculiarly English folly

Walpole, who never married (as the great design writer Bevis Hillier once said: 'He was what the 18th century calls "a dilettante'", the 19th "an exquisite", and the 20th "a homosexual"'), devoted much of his life to a strange house in London named Strawberry Hill – and to the creation of a picturesque taste we now know as the Gothick.

Some of the group's designs were pure copies – something then considered perfectly normal. Today we often value 'concept' and originality over an actual artefact: an artist has to have come up with something first, or else it isn't worth anything. This way of thinking was alien to 18th-century culture. What mattered was the craft of making – and being able to actually own and use something of beauty.

The gilded and ribbed plaster ceiling in Strawberry Hill's Great North Bedchamber was copied from a room at The Vyne, his friend John Chute's mainly Tudor ancestral home in Hampshire. Where the imaginative Walpole did score a 'first' – not that he would have thought of it like that – was in recycling ancient stylistic influences in an imaginative way. At Strawberry Hill, the Westminster tomb of William Dudley, bishop of Durham, became an elaborate chimney-piece.

Walpole wasn't alone – far from it. Most Georgian architects could turn their hand to the Gothic when asked. When Walpole could afford their services he asked in professionals, such as James Essex and James Wyatt. Even the great Robert Adam was involved, designing the ceiling and chimney-piece in the Round Drawing Room.

Wyatt was a pretty awful architect, in practical terms. In that sense at least he was a good pairing for the precious, indeed glorious William Beckford. Beckford, a sugar trade heir, was the author of another, particularly groan-worthy gothic fantasy novel, *Vathek*. They designed the remarkable fantasy of Fonthill Abbey near Bath between 1795 and 1807, developing the picturesque potential of medieval revival architecture and causing a public stir by adding towers and spires to Fonthill's irregular, darkly looming silhouettes. Having bankrupted the fabulously wealthy Beckford, Fonthill promptly fell down.

Yet the massive interest that these two 'Gothick' experiments prompted would have its fruit in the next century, with a full-blown Gothic revival. Walpole, one of the world's most endearing letter-writers and popularizers, was also one of the great British taste-makers. In the next century, the future George IV would let his own imagination run riot, just as Walpole had.

The Indo-Saracen domes and minarets of the Prince Regent's Brighton Pavilion are a fantasy of Empire. Inside, the architect John Nash had fun mixing the exotic – gilded dragons, lotus-shaped chandeliers, carved palm trees and imitation bamboo staircases – with standard English eccentricity.

# THE AGE OF EMPIRE

When Victoria came to the throne most people lived and worked in the countryside and Britain was still a series of towns and small villages: you would travel between them by stage coach. But the periodic Chartist riots gave rise to real concern that British workers would emulate their French counterparts and stage a revolution. A series of Acts broadened the social and economic base of the electorate, and by 1884 nearly all householders and even lodgers were entitled to vote. Most importantly for architecture, the new ways of living would soon demand the creation of new forms, workhouses being the most obvious example. In the new era, there would be town halls, schools, libraries, hospitals, hotels. Victorian architects needed to invent and re-invent the shopping arcade, the department store, the railway station, just as designers had to somehow deal with the new technologies – the gas lamp, the telephone, the automobile.

The Royal Albert Hall sums up style tensions in Victorian Britain. Renaissance-inspired, it was built by an engineer but styled by an architect. A modern extension shows that classical building skills still exist today

# THE HYPERACTIVE CENTURY

It was the century of build, build, build; the century of style after style. Take a cross-section of what was built in London, then the world's largest city, between 1800 and 1900. The diversity is overwhelming. It ranges from Nash's precise, white stuccoed 'Regency' style to vast Greek temples, strange Neo-Byzantine churches, 'Venetian' factory buildings and 'Queen Anne'-style mansions.

**W**hy should the state of 19th century British architecture matter so much in comparison with the rest of the world? It mattered because Britain at that time was a powerhouse of both industrial innovation and political might. Like the self-help writer Samuel Smiles, optimistic Victorians believed that the Industrial Revolution would allow the 'conquest of Nature' as well as 'the betterment of the species'. By 1820, when George IV came to the throne, a broad sea of red marked the map of empire: the huge dynamism of

Britain's building programme reflected this avid sense of exploration. Through its fast-expanding empire Britain's architecture would affect the world.

But what forms could be used to express this extraordinary financial and geopolitical might? It was a question that disturbed the era's architects more than most. It led to a furious mid-century debate that destroyed entire careers. How could such a modern, urbanized and advanced society find beauty and above all, a new identity in built form?

The century began with Europe at war.

# Key Dates

**1800** Parliamentary union of Great Britain and Ireland.

**1804** Napoleon declares himself Emperor.

**1805** Battle of Trafalgar – Nelson's victory and death.

**1807** Slave trade abolished in British Empire.

**1811** George III is declared insane.

**1812** Napoleon's retreat from Moscow.

**1814** Stephenson's steam locomotive.

**1815** Battle of Waterloo.

**1831** Darwin's voyage on *The Beagle*.

**1837** Queen Victoria ascends the throne. Dickens, *Oliver Twist*. Thomas Carlyle, *The French Revolution*.

**1840** Penny post established in UK.

**1842** New Chartist riots.

**1843** Colonization of Africa.

**1844** Factory Act restricts working hours for women and children.

**1845** Potato famine in Ireland; boom in railway building speculation.

**1846** Ruskin, *Modern Painters II*.

**1848** Revolutions throughout Europe; discovery of nuggets in California starts 'The Gold Rush'; Marx and Engels, *Communist Manifesto*.

**1851** Great Exhibition in Hyde Park; Religious Census; Mayhew London, *Labour and the London Poor*.

**1852** New Houses of Parliament open.

**1854** Britain and France declare war against Russia and begin Crimean war.

**1857** Indian 'Mutiny'.

**1858** 'Big Ben' is installed in the Houses of Parliament clock tower; India 'transferred' to the British Crown.

**1859** Charles Darwin, *On the Origin of Species*.

**1861** American civil war begins. Emancipation of serfs in Russia; Italy united under King Victor Emmanuel; Hans Christian Andersen, *Fairytales*.

**1863** Polish rising against Russian occupation; opening of the first underground railway in London.

**1865** Assassination of Abraham Lincoln; Lister develops antiseptic surgery; Leo Tolstoy, *War and Peace*; Lewis Carrol, *Alice's Adventures in Wonderland*.

**1867** Russia sells Alaska to America.

**1869** Suez canal opened; J.S. Mill, *The Subjection of Women* (written in 1860); Matthew Arnold, *Culture and Anarchy*.

**1870** French declare war against Prussia – and are heavily defeated; Paris occupied.

**1875** Disraeli buys Suez Canal shares, gaining a controlling interest for Britain; Anthony Trollope, *The Way We Live Now*.

**1876** Queen Victoria declared Empress of India; Bell invents the telephone.

**1877** Henry James, *The American*; Zola, *L'Assommoir*; phonograph invented by Edison.

**1878** University of London admits women to degrees; electric street lighting in London.

**1879** Henrik Ibsen, *A Doll's House*; George Meredith, *The Egoist*; Henry James, *Daisy Miller*.

**1880** First Anglo-Boer war in South Africa; Education Act in Britain makes schooling compulsory to age of ten.

**1881** The Natural History Museum is opened, London; President Garfield of the USA and Tsar Alexander II of Russia are assassinated.

**1884** In Britain, the franchise is extended by the Third Reform Bill; first *Oxford English Dictionary*.

**1885** Radio waves are discovered; internal combustion engine invented.

**1886** Daimler produces first motor car.

**1888** George Eastman develops the Kodak camera; English vet John Dunlop patents the pneumatic tyre; Jack the Ripper murders in London.

**1889** Eiffel Tower built for the Paris Centennial Exposition; Coca-Cola developed in Atlanta; 10,000 dockers strike in London.

**1893** First motor cars built by Karl Benz in Germany and Henry Ford in the USA; Alexander Graham Bell makes the first long-distance telephone call; Whitcome Judson patents the zip fastener; Independent Labour Party founded in Britain.

**1894** Manchester Ship Canal opens.

**1895** X-rays discovered; first radio broadcast by Marconi; the very first moving images displayed by French cinematographer.

**1896** Wireless telegraphy invented.

**1898** Second Anglo-Boer War begins; Henry James, *The Turn of the Screw*.

**1900** Freud's *Interpretation of Dreams*; Einstein's *General Theory of Relativity*.

**1901** Queen Victoria dies – the Edwardian period begins.

**RIGHT** Caryatids bloom in the centre of a modern city: New St Pancras Church, its ladies a little short in the waist compared to those on the Acropolis

**LEFT** Greece re-discovered, and transported to 19th-century London in the form of the British Museum in Bloomsbury. Thousands of treasures are inside, but what of the building?

Britain, a nation obsessed with tradition, hierarchy and class, was constantly looking over its shoulder to France and the threat of revolution. On the other hand, ever since Napoleon had become emperor in 1804 he had started to invest his capital, Paris, with a dignity and grandeur that Britain coveted. France's Empire style was characterized by imposing public works. In 1806 two triumphal arches were begun: the Arc de Triomphe du Carrousel, designed by Percier and Fontaine and the Arc de Triomphe de l'Étoile,

completed by Blouet to Chalgrin's design. Neoclassical monuments like Napoleon's Église de la Madeleine, inspired by the Roman Maison Carrée at Nîmes, made a self-confident statement of greatness.

It wasn't just the French who had drawn on the past to create statement architecture. The Prussians were also exploring their own notions of nationhood, and as German archaeologists returned from Greece and the Middle East with a series of treasures, including the Ishtar Gate from the ancient

city of Babylon, the Neoclassical was re-interpreted with authority. In Berlin, this new self-confidence showed in buildings such as Karl Friedrich Schinkel's Neue Wache guardhouse of 1816, his Schauspielhaus of 1819 (see p.149), and the severely beautiful Altes Museum of 1823. Then there was von Klenze's Glyptothek in Munich, with its extraordinary interior vaulting and his Walhalla, near Regensburg – modelled on, but not a slavish copy of, the Parthenon. All of these buildings, and others, had translated the

architecture of ancient Greece into a distinctively Germanic form.

The ultimate French defeat at Waterloo in 1815 had a salutary effect on British building. If Napoleon's Paris was the new ancient Rome, why then, Britain would be the new ancient Greece. Almost immediately, in 1816, the epoch of grand new statement buildings began. St Pancras New Church, designed by the father and son team William and Henry Inwood, was the first Greek Revival church in Britain. It was also the most expensive to go up in London since the rebuilding of St Paul's. The building, which still stands, is genuinely extraordinary. A scholarly adaptation of the Acropolis temple known as the Erechtheion, its porticos are supported by caryatids, an exotic sight on the filthy Euston Road.

The British had been among the first to adopt the new wave of Neoclassicism pioneered by James 'Athenian' Stuart. Was it enough for the British to follow slavishly where the Continent had led? Was the bombastic Neoclassicism in vogue on the Continent really the right way for Britain to express its own individuality? At first, the Grecian Revival was the ultimate in fashionable good taste; but as the new century found its feet a more jingoistic spirit was soon in the air.

Britain's new Athenian assertiveness sometimes strayed into the realms of the overblown. Robert Smirke's first Grecian design was a severe new opera house in Covent Garden. The architect then rushed to create something as impressive as the Altes Museum for the British capital. His design for

# Greek Revival

Northumberland's Belsay Castle was the first country house in Britain to be modelled entirely on Greek examples. Built from 1807 by Sir Charles Monck (Middleton), it is modelled on the earliest and plainest of the classical orders of architecture, the Doric. The interior's simple plan is based on Graeco-Roman buildings: rooms grouped around a columned courtyard. The style had its adherents well into the 19th century, Sir Robert Smirke's Opera House being just one major example. Edinburgh in particular was to stay late at the Graeco-Roman party, becoming known as the 'Athens of the North' thanks to Thomas Hamilton's Royal High School (1825) and the work of Alexander 'Greek' Thomson (1817–75), whose terraced housing and Greek-style churches were interpreted in his own very individual style. Far from studying ancient Greek examples, Thomson never left his native land once.

### ● ST PANCRAS NEW CHURCH
Two thousand, two hundred and twenty-two years after the original temple on the Acropolis in Athens, a new Temple of Erechtheion was built in Bloomsbury. The original guards the grave of Cecrops, the first king of Athens. Here too, caryatids guard the crypt. Its tower, which is capped with a finial and cross, ascends in

diminishing octagons. It is another take on that winning formula, the evocative Tower of the Winds (see p.130).

The ladies are unfortunately a little bit stubbier than sculptor John Charles Felix Rossi intended them to be – they had to be cut down slightly at the waist after a miscalculation. Internally, the church is a great flat-ceilinged hall meant for preaching, with low, straight galleries. Although the building cost a fortune – £89,296 – its interior was originally plain, even the windows. They have now been replaced by stained glass. The high altar, designed by Charles Holden, was installed in 1912.

### ● THE BRITISH MUSEUM
The much-admired Royal Academician Sir John Soane had already criticized Robert Smirke's Greek Revivalist work for the new Covent Garden Opera House. Although it was impressive at first sight, the Opera House showed the speed with which it had been constructed – in particular, its portico was out of scale with the side and rear elevations of the building. Soane was censured by the Royal Academy for criticizing a fellow architect: perversely, the publicity made Greek Revival suddenly all the rage.

The British Museum's 44 Ionic columns are based on those of the temple of Athena Polias at Priene in Asia Minor, the ruins of which had been put on show at the Berlin Museum in 1895–9. As a public space, it is the ultimate patrician statement; significantly, the allegorical Richard Westmacott sculptures

commissioned for the vast pediment are called *The Progress of Civilization*. Civilization, in Smirke's terms, was Greek. It was emphatically not industrial Britain.

### ● TRAFALGAR – THE COLUMN
Even Nelson's Column had to be designed by someone. The job was given to architect William Railton in 1838 and it was built by the firm Peto & Grissell. The top of the Corinthian column is capped with bronze acanthus leaves cast from British cannons. The square pedestal is decorated with four bronze panels cast from captured French guns, depicting Nelson's four great victories. John Carew's 'Trafalgar' panel, all five tons of it, took five melted-down mortars and one 32-pound cannon to cast. The four huge lions at the base were reputed to be made from captured cannons of the French fleet.

Sir Charles Barry was put in charge of the overall architecture of Trafalgar Square, a dreadful stop-start process dominated by bureaucracy and money shortages. Barry specialized in tact and determination; he must have needed it. In 1844, lack of funds left even the work on the column suspended. *The Times* fulminated: 'Thus is everything in this country done; we never complete anything properly in the first instance.' The square was not finally finished until 1845.

The sandstone statue itself by E.H. Baily was described by a visiting Frenchman, Hippolyte Taine, as 'that hideous Nelson, planted on his column like a rat impaled on the end of a stick'.

LEFT A joint effort: Buckingham Palace was set to be a Nash disaster. Instead, the clever Sir Aston Webb made a good fist of the façade, although critics weren't happy

BELOW Karl Friedrich Schinkel's Greek Revival Neues Schauspielhaus or new theatre, redesigned between 1818 and 1821, and now known as the Konzerthaus Berlin

the British Museum in 1825 turned Bloomsbury into the world's largest building site. The result was rather overbearing.

While Schinkel's great genius was his finely-tuned sense of scale and proportion, Smirke's monumental museum shouted just that little too loudly, as if determined to drown out all its Continental cousins. A Parthenon with extensions, the British Museum was not just grand and monumental, but forbidding.

It was two other important buildings that helped wreck the reputation of the Neoclassicists. The first was John Nash's attempt to convert Buckingham House into a palace that was truly fit for a king. Neither Nash nor the new monarch George IV were known for keeping tabs on their purses.

Unfortunately, when it came to Buckingham Palace, Nash not only got it badly wrong in terms of design but he also started pouring money down the drain. Parliament gave him £250,000 but he spent nearly three times that – at least £600,000. The architect, who was then 73 years old, at one stage even pulled down his newly-built

palace wings in full public view and started again. So when George IV died in 1830, Nash was promptly sacked. The job of clearing up the rubble went to the cheaper Edward Blore, although what we see today is a new principal façade by Sir Aston Webb in Beaux-Arts mode: the Continental architecture of the Belle Époque.

But it was the creation of London's Trafalgar Square that really helped turn the tide against Neoclassicism. A suitable site had been cleared. When William Wilkins won the commission to design the new National Gallery in 1832, the first building to dominate the razed site, he was asked to design it in a Classical style.

Sad to say, nobody liked it – in fact, it was a disaster (see pp.152–3). The theatrically-minded Wilkins set a rather comical dome over the portico and turrets over the end pavilions. John Summerson, the critic, described them as 'like the clock and the vases on a mantelpiece, only less useful'. It was too small, its proportions were wrong – and it blocked the view of St Martin-in-the-Fields. The building was a notable failure.

# Colour and Classicism

Until James Stuart and Nicholas Revett went to Athens in 1751 and began to draw what was left of its ancient remains, very few European architects had any accurate knowledge of classical Greek building. Stuart and Revett's book, *The Antiquities of Athens,* published in 1762, not only helped clear this fog, but launched the first waves of a Greek revival on to an unsuspecting world.

The greatest herald and champion of Neoclassicism was the hugely influential German aesthetic historian Johann Winckelmann. In his *Gedanken,* published in 1755, he proclaimed:

*'The only way for us to become great, yes, inimitable, if it is possible, is in the imitation of the Greeks.'*

**RIGHT** Nashville Tennessee's full-scale reproduction of the Parthenon completed in the 1920s uses colour: a tasteful blue and red picked out on the frieze. It also houses a full-size reproduction of the Athena Parthenos statue: quite a sight

**BELOW** The delicate Cirque d'Hiver in Paris, Jacques-Ignace Hittorff's response to the colour debate. It is still operating as a circus

His book also set in stone the idea that Greek classical architecture was characterized by 'noble simplicity and quiet grandeur' (*edle Einfalt und stille Größe*).

These ideas left a permanent mark on the European mind, as well as on its landscape. Kant, Goethe, Walter Pater and Lessing were fervent admirers. Winckelmann and his followers launched a tidal wave of Neoclassical architecture that swept right across the continent and then on around the world.

By 1840, London had the National Gallery; the British Museum; the Theatre Royal; Covent Garden; and the General Post Office. At the same time, Edinburgh transformed itself into 'The Athens of the North (see box, p.147). The fledgling United States also took the Neoclassical idiom to heart, albeit in a quirky and characteristically individual way, with its folksy, American corncob additions to the style. Benjamin Latrobe's work on the United States Capitol and the Bank of Pennsylvania and Robert Mills' Washington Monument are some of the outstanding public examples. Further north, the centre of Helsinki is strongly Neoclassical to this day.

This was all well and good. But Winckelmann was wrong about ancient Greek architecture in one important respect. It was not always 'noble simplicity and quiet grandeur', its plain marble façades an invitation to quiet contemplation and

respect. On the contrary, much of it had been painted in the most riotous colours.

As pioneering archaeologists like Cockerell, von Steckelberg and Haller excavated more and more of the classical Greek cityscape during the first decades of the new century, the evidence became irrefutable. The Greeks had wallowed in colour: not just their public buildings, but their statuary, their homes and just about anything else that would take paint was treated to an enthusiastic coat. Brilliant yellows, deep reds and acid greens had all jostled for attention on the ancient façades.

As the news spread, many architects found it at first unbelievable and then shocking. It was something to be whispered in dark corners. Evangelical exponents of the bright white Neoclassical style were extremely unimpressed by the idea that the serene ancient buildings they strove to emulate had in fact been marred – as they saw it – by colours that would not have looked out of place daubed on the walls of a child's bedroom.

But there was at least one notable

exception to the general dismay: Jacques-Ignace Hittorff. A French public architect of Prussian origin, Hittorff (1792–1867) adopted the idea of using colour in his work with unabashed glee. In 1822, his friend François-Christian Gau exhibited *Les Antiquités de la Nubie ou Monuments inédits du bord du Nil.* To Hittorff, these coloured studies of Egyptian monuments were a revelation.

Two years later, Hittorff married the daughter of architect Jean-Baptiste Le Père, a member of Bonaparte's 1798 expedition to Egypt. Hittorff's enthusiasm for colour in buildings was reinforced by his father-in-law's accomplished drawings of ancient Egyptian architecture which, in almost every single case, featured bright colours and striking polychromatic murals.

A taste for colour in classically-inspired buildings never really took off in Britain, although a later generation of Gothicists ramped up the colour spectrum. Even in statuary, the British were conservative. When John Gibson gave a touch of colour to his 'Tinted Venus' in 1851, the *Athenaeum* magazine denounced it. She was 'a naked impudent English woman'.

But in Paris, Hittorff was appointed Government Architect in 1830. His works include the church of Saint-Vincent-de-Paul (1830–44) and the riotous confection of the Cirque d'Hiver, which was completed in eight short months. It opened as the Cirque Napoléon in 1852 and its cheerful 20-sided interior was immortalized in works by Toulouse-Lautrec and Edgar Degas. Newly renovated, it still operates as a circus today.

**ABOVE** Hittorff's fountain in the Place de la Concorde, Paris, which was restored recently. It features a colourful throng of exotic and exuberant sea gods and mermen

Hittorff also designed the two richly-coloured fountains in the Place de la Concorde (1832–40); the Circus of the Empress; the Gare du Nord (1861–3); many cafés and restaurants along the Champs-Élysées; and the houses that form a circle around the Place de l'Étoile. He also remodelled the Bois de Boulogne.

However, his many enemies despised his enthusiastic use of colour. They gave him the derogatory, not to say racist, nickname 'The Prussian'. But he set a long-lasting trend because many modern architects habitually use colour in their work. So the colourful Prussian, blue or not, had the last laugh.

# The National Gallery 'Disgrace'

William Wilkins wasn't the first, and surely won't be the last, architect to fall foul of a public relations disaster. But in this case, it was pretty much of his own making. The handsome James Gibbs church of St Martin-in-the-Fields stood on the north edge of what would soon become the new Trafalgar Square, planned as an architectural monument to Nelson's victory. After Nash's clearance of the medieval muddle around it, the church stood proud, and London liked what it saw. When Wilkins revealed his designs for the new National Gallery, it drew unfavourable comparisons with the popular Gibbs masterpiece. Critics described his design as 'incoherent' and by no means grand enough. And why was it blocking the new vista of St Martin's?

Wilkins was aggrieved: why such a fuss about a church no-one had even noticed before? No blushing violet, he had only just been prevented from obscuring Gibbs' structure completely. The Cambridge man decided to strike back with his own pamphlet. But its arrogant tone struck a sour note. Wilkins claimed that St Martin's should be subordinate to his own, far better building. 'Only the layman would think St Martin's a fine piece of architecture', he wrote, describing its pediment as being 'of prodigious, unnecessary and unexampled height' – a Gothic spire on a Greek church. His argument didn't go down well. The pamphlet ended with a phrase which tempted fate: 'I may be vain, and I shall

certainly be called so.' The hoardings went up and the building went ahead, to a continual chorus of disapproval.

In Parliament, there were complaints about the haphazard nature of the commissioning process for important public buildings. After all, the budget was continually being cut. Would it fall victim to the British disease – compromise? Said one critic: 'It will become another national blunder... erected in one reign to be abandoned in the next.' Other voices chimed in, saying that the £50,000 allotted by Parliament was ridiculous, that this gallery would be too small. Even worse, it would look too mean.

In truth, Wilkins was being asked to do the impossible. The Treasury was penny-pinching all the way, ordering him to reuse the Corinthian columns from the Prince Regent's out-of-favour Carlton House, along with some of the sculpture left over from the building of Marble Arch. Luckily for Wilkins, he came from a theatrical background, where old flats and scenery were constantly reused to stage new plays. Still, who knows how many compromises he had to make when he was 'making do' with these architectural cast-offs?

Even the very entrance to the building, a plan for a grand set of steps, was unceremoniously scrapped in the name of cost. Bizarrely, besides finding room for not just the National Gallery but the Royal Academy as well, the architect was forced to provide soldiers with access routes through the building. Their barracks were behind the site.

To add to the problems, when the new gallery was finally finished it was evidently too small for its purpose. Admittedly, Wilkins' decision to raise the entire building to 12 feet above street level helped make up for the lack of presence. To this day, it is one of the few buildings in the world to feel more impressive as you leave than when you arrived. Emerging visitors are given a dramatic, engaging, actor's-eye view of the square, which must have been

ABOVE Why did they only build two storeys? The commissioners being stingy, the National Gallery was too small as soon as it was built

what the theatrically-minded architect had planned all along. But that didn't stop the press and the cultural establishment hating the new gallery. The Illustrated London News claimed (that St Martin's):

*'is admired by everyone possessed of any taste and now has the advantage of standing in contrast with the National Gallery, a building which no one of any taste can admire at all.'*

It's ironic, given its history and design pedigree, that the architecturally-minded Prince Charles later chose to go into battle to defend this particular building.

However, another style had been waiting in the wings, ever since the architectural antics of William Beckford and Horace Walpole. Wilkins was even

LEFT Gibbs' radical St Martin-in-the-Fields of 1720, combining a classical portico with a steeple and influences from Wren to Rome, via Palladio. It had been hidden by all the medieval muddle around it, until Nash's clearance opened the area up

proficient in it. Because a lot of his professional career had been spent in the quiet cloisters of Britain's ancient university colleges he had developed a deep interest in medieval architecture. This was not the cute, high jinks style of Horace Walpole. It was more like the seriously academic, study-based interest of his friend, John Chute. A stylistic battle would soon rear its Janus-like head all over Britain. The struggle was between Neoclassicism on the one hand and a rediscovery of a native architecture on the other: one that harked back not to Rome but to steadfast Durham, not to Athens but to the choirs of Canterbury. Which would win out? One thing was for certain: The 'Gothick' was about to get serious – and drop its 'k'.

**RIGHT** The vista to Nelson's column: Wilkins certainly knew how to make the most of a theatrical view. Trafalgar Square actually slopes down towards Whitehall and the Houses of Parliament

# BRITAIN'S BATTLE OF THE STYLES

At the very height of the Empire, a young and inexperienced Queen, Victoria, acceded to the British throne. 'Tradition' – in other words a romanticized vision of the past – would come to have a crucial, symbolic role for both society and state. In Victorian England the higher worlds of religion, literature and architecture were an escape route for the soul and the imagination. Britain averted its eyes from industrial unrest, poverty and the despoliation of the countryside, preferring to dwell on the idealized past. Sir Walter Scott's historical novels were hugely popular. Poems like 'Idylls of the King' by Tennyson glorified Arthurian romance. The art of the time, particularly that of the Pre-Raphaelites, also had a dressing-up box of historic themes. With this fascination came a renewed interest in Britain's often glorious medieval architecture, and its heritage of magnificent cathedrals like Winchester and Wells.

This 'Battle of the Styles' would soon be subjected to a crucial test. In October 1834, a raging fire broke out in the Palace of Westminster. Huge crowds thronged the bridges to watch as the old Parliament, scorned by many as the seat of endemic corruption, burned almost to the ground. Two labourers, one of them an ex-convict, had been working since dawn at the House of Lords. Their task had been to burn two cart-loads of tallies – the notched wooden rods that were used for keeping the national accounts. Twice, a boy was sent to tell the men

that there was too much smoke coming from the stoves. Twice, he was told to go away – only in much rounder terms. By four o'clock in the afternoon the House of Lords was ablaze from end to end. The first fire engine arrived within the hour – which was far too late. Just as had happened with St Paul's Cathedral centuries before, it was as if Britain had a new opportunity, by Act of God.

The sight was momentous: travellers on the Brighton coach could see the blaze as they came into London. Hundreds of excited faces, fanned hot by the flames, watched from the

**ABOVE** The Palace of Westminster, also known as the Houses of Parliament, seen from the Thames. Its towers (Victoria Tower is in the foreground) are asymmetrical and of different heights

**LEFT** The Gothic style goes to war: Marochetti's handsome 1860 statue of Richard The Lionheart sits patriotically outside Barry's Gothic building, its nine-light window a copy of Westminster Hall's

**RIGHT** The opposing style: Greek Revival. This is Decimus Burton's dignified Athenaeum Club, a gentlemen's club on London's Pall Mall

banks. One of those faces was that of the 39-year-old Charles Barry. In his later oil painting, the artist J.M.W. Turner recorded the conflagration in great Impressionist swirls of smoky watercolour. A huge tower of flame stretches up into the sky over the Thames and you can see that some people have even taken to the river in boats, risking the burning coals of debris.

For years, MPs had complained bitterly about Parliament's unruly jumble of buildings, heaped up over the centuries. Among them, nevertheless, was many a gem of medieval architecture. Amazingly, much of the best survived the blaze.

In every civilization, architecture dresses the dramas of the age. The entire British Empire was controlled from that one

building. Britain now had the opportunity to express its deepest values, and its status as a world power, in stone.

It was the architectural job of the century, and Barry and every other architect in the country knew it. So did the politicians. Sir Edward Cust, an MP and former soldier, was first into print, complaining of the 'mortification' felt about Nash's (Neoclassical) Buckingham Palace and Wilkins' National Gallery. Contemporary architects were arrogant to a man, he complained: 'Men, whom the very circumstances of their position have already made mannerists, and induced them to despise the altering taste of the time.' It was strong stuff.

The ultimate decision on the design was taken by Prime Minister Robert Peel. It was

his first term as Prime Minister. Who knows? He might have been thinking of the mess that was the National Gallery. Maybe he wanted to deflect the mounting head of political steam that was the Reform movement. Or perhaps, with William Wordsworth's magnificent poem 'Tintern Abbey' newly popular, he was gripped by the Gothic leanings of the Romantics.

As the influential historian Thomas Carlyle was constantly arguing, Britain had a desperate need for 'some sort of King, made in the image of God'. Peel felt that political stability would be sustained if Britain had an unassailable, glamorous and popular leader, someone who could persuade the restive people of the virtues of obedience, duty, good behaviour and hard work. This was his opportunity to clothe the tiny and rather unimpressive young Victoria in architectural pomp and circumstance. Perhaps a home-grown, medieval or Tudor style would evoke romantic images of a time when another woman, Elizabeth I, had made Britain one of the world's most formidable powers? Yet there was general surprise when Peel announced not just a competition, but an aesthetic decision. There would be no discussion. The design was to be either 'the Gothic' or 'Elizabethan'. Drawings were to be submitted in less than five months.

There was public furore. Accusations of corruption flew. Public letters, notably from William Hamilton, friend to Lord Elgin, decried the fact that 'Gothic barbarism' was to triumph. Until this point, the Gothic style had been a bit of a plaything, used for garden follies and romantic country houses. Gradually, through the Oxford Movement, it had been gaining ground in church and university buildings, but it was simply not thought appropriate for formal government buildings. The very principles of civic government and law came to Britain via the Romans from the ancient Greeks, and those aesthetic values were associated with Britain's institutions. But Peel had mettle. In a speech of 1832 he said:

*'I have never been the decided supporter of any band of partisans, but have always thought it better to look steadily at the peculiar circumstances of the times in which we live.'*

The Prime Minister held true to that integrity now. The Gothic would fit the times. The glorious past would be used to validate the

enthusiastic sailor, the highly cultured A.W.N. Pugin was a magnificent draughtsman. He was also slightly mad. It was the madness of the brilliant: his mother described him as a 'universal genius'. Known for turning up at business meetings in a sailor's smock and even, horror of horrors, with sacking tied over his boots, Pugin was nothing if not an original. A passionate Catholic, he sought an architecture that would link the Anglo-Saxon world with its Christian medieval roots rather than the pagan past of either ancient Greece or Rome. Without Barry to champion his cause, Pugin, a natural outsider in convention-ridden Victorian England, would never have won the competition. (Indeed, a design he submitted separately failed.)

Barry was more than competent, but the job before him was vast. While he had in fact made a study of German Gothic, his interest was nothing to that of his new colleague. The young Pugin had diligently recorded, noted, drawn, discussed and studied hundreds of Britain's native medieval buildings. Not to put too fine a point on it, he was a man obsessed.

What did 'Gothic' really mean? Asymmetry, varied silhouettes, tracery and the lancet arch, and the use of local stone are all key characteristics. The term also came to imply a greater exploitation of colour and ornament. Crucially, Gothic revival design meant abandoning the clean, geometrically rigorous, enclosed space of the classical idiom, in favour of 'free plans'.

Full of mad enthusiasms, Pugin was rarely on top of his finances. Following the failure of an early business and a spell in a debtor's prison, he had set off on a Gothic tour of Britain. Railing against the 'monster of architectural depravity' James Wyatt for his insensitive restoration of Hereford Cathedral, Pugin was becoming more and more fevered in his obsession. To a friend who sent him a Cheddar cheese, he wrote, only half in jest: 'Although not strictly Gothic in its present shape, it may be daily rendered more so by cutting it into four, which will make a quatrefoil.'

He also admired the finest French Gothic, as at Notre-Dame, Sainte-Chapelle or Chartres. And what style wouldn't succeed with the fiery Pugin on its side? He believed

exciting, but somehow frightening – because the pace of technological change was so extreme – present realities of Victorian Britain. The stage was set for a new, and yet more dramatic architecture – one that had been forged at home.

On the face of it, though, it looked as if

Charles Barry was chancing his arm if he entered the competition. Best known as a classicist, he was more obviously at home with the Italianate idiom. But Barry had a wild card – a former set designer named Augustus Welby Northmore Pugin.

Architect, designer, theorist and

that Gothic architecture was the product of a purer society. It was the true architecture, driven by God's will on earth.

The strongest argument in the Gothic's favour was surely Barry's inspired design for Parliament itself. Ever the pragmatist, Barry had taken the best that both styles had to offer – and instead of 'Gothic' dark corridors, nooks and crannies, had planned a series of wide, uniform spaces within an intricately detailed exterior. Despite his 'exquisite details', as Pugin cracked to Barry, the proposal was 'all Grecian sir; Tudor details on a classic body'. The difficulty of the site and the many different functions of the Palace made the plan a particularly difficult job. With the new gas lighting, heating, sanitation and ventilation technologies, this would be the most technologically advanced public building in the world.

Barry's choice of the Perpendicular style gave the effect he wanted – 'grandeur of outline' – and chimed well with Henry VII's chapel, that famously sumptuous example of

genuine late Perpendicular. Crucially, Peel would have been able to see from Pugin's drawings that the design was absolutely soaked in rich symbolism, creating a space that would underline the 'Great' in Great Britain. The symbolism was planned at both a spatial and a decorative level. The immense Royal Gallery, for instance, is half as long again as the Lords Chamber. Heraldic emblems, meanwhile, would be everywhere. This was particularly true of the Tudor rose, the VR – Victoria Regina – monogram, and the portcullis emblem that Barry took from the old palace. The grandeur of the place and the opportunities it gave for elaborate ceremony would have been important to Peel and the Commissioners.

Ninety-seven competitors had entered

**ABOVE RIGHT** St George's Roman Catholic Cathedral, where lack of funds prevented Pugin's full plans from being built. It also suffered bomb damage in World War II

**BOTTOM RIGHT** Glass windows in St George's Roman Catholic Cathedral, Southwark. Many other Pugin interiors have suffered from stylistic purges

# Gothic and Decoration

● **VIOLLET-LE-DUC**

In France, a parallel movement was emerging. While Pugin and his architect father were on Gothic study holidays, Eugène-Emmanuel Viollet-le-Duc was literally piecing the crumbling Gothic buildings back together.

In 1839 Viollet-le-Duc was put in charge of the restoration of La Madeleine at Vézelay, the first building to be restored by a modern state commission. In a distinguished career this revivalist restored Notre Dame de Paris, the cathedral at Amiens and the fortifications at Carcassonne, but he is remembered today as a theorist who bridged the gulf between the 19th and 20th centuries. Viollet-le-Duc saw the real potential of cast iron, the first new building material since the Romans. He insisted that modern technology should be used openly and 'honestly'. Pugin would also aspire to this ideal of architectural honesty, and over time, the concept would become central to 20th century Modernism.

● **AUGUSTUS PUGIN (1812–52)**

Pugin was one of those people who live life hard, and die young. By 1844 he had had two wives and

six children. He also had a reputation for being rude. Favourite quote: 'There is nothing worth living for but Christian Architecture and a boat.' He once hired two nurses to look after two sick seamen – and then promptly bought the cottages to house them in.

Emphatically tidy, he would frequently tear up his plans, as he would do with any correspondence, and throw them away. Contemporary descriptions of his behaviour sound like some of the symptoms of manic depression. At the age of 40 he went insane. The fact that he had been prescribed mercury for an eye problem suggests that he might have had syphilis. Whether this is true or not, the mercury was enough to kill him.

● **LORD PALMERSTON'S VICTORY**

The 'Battle of the Styles' never truly ended. The key building in all the rumpus was the Foreign Office, which needed to be completely rebuilt. Decimus Burton's scheme of 1836 came to naught, as did many other architects' proposals. Then in 1856 an international competition was held and a 'Second Empire' proposal won.

After a change of government, the Gothicist Sir George Gilbert Scott was appointed, but Lord Palmerston, famous for his abrasive style and his 'gunboat diplomacy', threw out both his Gothic design and a later Italo-Byzantine suggestion, to ardent debate in Parliament. Eventually, Scott gave in and polished up his Neo-Renaissance proposal.

the competition to design the new Palace, only six of them in the Elizabethan style. Competition was stiff, to say the least. With 91 Gothic designs to choose from, one wonders how Peel and his advisers could possibly have made their choice. Perhaps it was made for them when they saw the profusion of detailed drawings that Pugin had prepared. As it was, Barry and Pugin emerged victorious, becoming the chief architects of Victorian England. But Pugin could not stop there. Barry was then asked to supply drawings of all the fixtures and fittings in the building so that detailed price estimates could be made. He turned again to the enthusiastic Pugin, who produced them at record speed. As a measure of his industry, it is said that he produced over 2,000 drawings for the House of Lords alone.

With Parliament won, could Gothic now become the official style of Victorian England? The 18th century's playful flirting with the 'Gothick', had been inspired by the combination of horror and romance in Gothic novels like *The Castle of Otranto* (1765) and the wistful ruin-mongering of the Picturesque movement. It had been a bit of a laugh, really: some cod-historicism and some fairy-tale stuff like mock Chinese, or 'Hindoo'. It had all the substance of a

cardboard cut-out. But properly researched fervent medievalism was a different matter. Gothic was now a 'moral' style, and the flirtation was becoming a passion.

The Houses of Parliament are not so much a Parliament as a theatre of state. Charles Barry designed the overall layout and form of the building, while Pugin provided the external decoration and the interiors. Their task was to create an overwhelming visual image of an ordered, rooted, hierarchical and unassailable monarchy nestling in the bosom of the most powerful nation on earth. They did so by creating several thousand detailed drawings and devoting the last part of their working lives to the vast edifice. Contemporary observers often saw Charles Barry climbing over the scaffolding, with the mercurial Pugin shouting and laughing at his side. The families of both men would later attribute their deaths to overwork.

The self-consciously historical, rich decoration of the building was full of allusions to the national past. There were Arthurian frescoes in the Robing Room, Tudor portraits in the Prince's Chamber, ribbed and compartmented wooden ceilings and walls with gilded carvings, pierced inscriptions and mouldings, as well as painted panels. In all this, the historicist Pugin was invaluable, not just because of his own talents, but because of a past life as a designer of jewellery, metalwork and building ornament. His contacts were good; even so, they had to search out and in some cases train a new school of craftsmen to rebuild the palace. Just like today, these skills, once created, were in high demand.

Barry had thought the building would cost £725,000 and take six years. In fact, the job would take a full 30 years and cost over £2m. Both architects worried constantly about the scale of the task. Pugin's lifelong friend John Hardman, his only assistant, was responsible for the metalwork and Pugin also persuaded him to begin producing stained glass. His specialist firm makes craft glass to this day. Hardman made the throne in the House of Lords from gilded wood, with inlaid enamel and rock crystals.

John Crace, meanwhile, was the head of a well-known firm of decorators in London. Both Crace's and Pugin's fathers had worked for George IV on the Brighton Pavilion. The talented Crace created the elaborate painted ceiling panels, the canopy above the throne and much of the other decorative painting.

Barry's symmetrical axial plan was an example of a type of layout design that had existed since the Renaissance, thus provoking Pugin's amused comment that the building had a 'Classic body'. Most medieval buildings, by contrast, are examples of additive planning or 'organic' growth; the sort of asymmetry that the new Gothicists valued. Barry laid out his new Palace of Westminster along a 720-feet-long (220m) axis. At one end were all of the 'royal' rooms: the Robing Room, the Prince's Chamber and the Royal Gallery, and at the other the House of Commons. Between them is the House of Lords, and they are all separated by lobbies. The government benches, facing those of the opposition parties, are the direct descendants of the pews in the converted medieval chapel that the Commons occupied until the Great Fire.

The entire plan demonstrates exactly the way that British 'oppositional' politics works, and is a physical expression of Britain's history. The monarch cannot even enter the House of Commons without invitation.

# A VERY PERSONAL FEUD

The 'Triumphal Arch' at London's Hyde Park Corner is a mute testament to one of the fiercest feuds in the history of architecture. The conflict began when the ubiquitous John Nash took on the quiet but clever Decimus, the youngest (10th) son of a wealthy Scottish property developer, James Burton. Already working in Nash's studio was Auguste Pugin. He too had a brilliant son.

**D**id the 'Battle of the Styles' – pitting the Gothic against the Greek – have a less pious, more personal dimension? Perhaps so, when that 'brilliant son' was Augustus Welby Northmore Pugin. It seems that in the mild-mannered figure of Decimus Burton the artist might well have imagined a deadly enemy.

Pugin's father was a remarkably talented artist/draughtsman, but he stayed poor all his life. Nash soon promoted Burton – whose father financed lots of the architect's major schemes – but Pugin senior stayed at the drawing board. Meanwhile Pugin junior, for all his brilliance, had already had one business fail spectacularly. He'd even seen time in a debtor's prison. The struggling Augustus might well have resented the boy Decimus, who thanks to his developer-builder father, seemed to have been born with an architectural silver spoon in his mouth.

By contrast with Pugin, the path of

Decimus Burton's life was strewn with gifts. Learning his trade on Nash's terraces around Regent's Park, Burton had patrons and commissions aplenty. His commissions were extremely high profile, probably to Pugin's annoyance. Burton was only 18 when his wealthy father gave him his first, fat individual job – to design a grand villa in the new Regent's Park, on the fringes of Nash's new picturesque, artificial lake. The Holme – which is still there – would be his father's London residence. To

Pugin, who worked harder than ten men, Decimus' easy ascent up the greasy pole of success must have had a bitter taste.

Decimus' father, James Burton, was certainly the right man to know. Time and again, he bailed Nash out on major projects. He also had dazzling society contacts like the top scientist Humphrey Davy, who duly commissioned a Decimus house. Decimus went on to design buildings for Regent's Park's new zoo, as well as highly prestigious clubs like the Athenaeum, which followed the ultra-fashionable Greek style. But the building that confirmed Decimus' career as a society architect was a commission for a ceremonial screen and arch for Hyde Park. His handsome Ionic screen had a large Roman arch at the centre, linked by colonnades to two side arches. It was faced by an elaborate 'Roman' arch. Although he had been forced to make the triumphal arch far bigger than he had wanted, Hyde Park corner was his. Decimus Burton had definitely arrived.

By all accounts success hadn't gone to his head. Burton was modest, polite and endearing. The building committee of the Athenaeum was ecstatic. Not only with the Club but also with the architect's courteous and efficient management of the contract: 'The Club at large as well as the public must be satisfied at his professional skill and the beauty of his Architectural Designs…'

Before Peel's decision in favour of the Gothic style, it must have seemed as if the whole of London would soon look like a city from classical antiquity. But if Burton, and the rest of the Neo-Cons felt secure, they were severely mistaken. The tide was turning, and Burton, of all architects, was to see his reputation swept away.

As we saw earlier, Sir Edward Cust had complained of the 'mortifications' of modern architecture. But then a former pupil of the fashionable society architect Decimus Burton had decided to publish a riposte to Cust. Anonymously, he had argued that the Neo-Greek knowledge developed over the last decades was a positive, not a negative, legacy. The Gothic, he had argued, 'was sullen and to itself'. Antiquity was associated with all that was best, all that was educated, and all that was

rational and proper in a civilized society. Would it be allowed to blossom, or 'be doomed to crouch and wither in the groinings, vaultings, tracery, pointed roof and flying buttresses of a Gothic building?'

Far from being seen as 'sullen', though, Gothic was beginning to be enthusiastically taken up by Victorian England. Buoyed up by his new Parliamentary success, Pugin charged. He wrote an inflammatory public letter to Burton in 1835.

'*Sir. As… you have directed a virulent attack on that most noble style of architecture termed Gothic, I feel I should ill become my station as a jealous professor of its styles, were I to remain silent.*'

He sneered at architecture that was, he said,

'*… in vogue about 2,000 years ago, among nations whose climate, religion, government and manners were totally dissimilar to our own… I trust fully that Anglo-Greek will shortly cease to exist, except in those buildings erected in the last few years, whose slight constructions give great hope for their speedy decay – a result most fervently wished for.*'

Suddenly, it was Pugin who was showered with commissions, which he undertook in a great fever, at one point complaining happily: 'I am almost worked to death.' As Pugin's star rose, Burton's fell almost as fast, accelerated by a series of increasingly savage personal attacks.

Suddenly, Burton was a laughing stock. To ram home his ideological superiority, Pugin would soon denounce the architecture of Greece as 'heathen' and 'sinful'. Pugin self-published his book *Contrasts* in 1836; no publisher would touch it, it was so vitriolic. Championing the medieval forms of the country's Catholic past, he entitled the final chapter 'The Wretched State of Architecture at the Present Day'. It caused a sensation: Pugin was attacking Burton personally. In a frontispiece dedicated to 'The Trade', he wrote:

'*Places and Situations: A Young Man just set up as an Architect wants a Partner who can give him a Few Hints; an Architect has a Vacancy in his Office for 1 pupil, Talent of No Consequence…*'

The illustration, under the heading 'Designs Done in This Style', showed Burton's triumphal arch at Hyde Park.

Almost overnight, the decade's most

fashionable architect had become its most scorned. Burton had been calumnized by a rival of whom he'd scarcely heard. Worse, his work had been seized on as 'heathen'. Was Burton an architectural Antichrist? His career would never recover. His designs for the Foreign and Commonwealth Office remained on paper. He built the beautifully sensuous Palm House at Kew, and was dammed with faint praise as the person who'd 'assisted' engineer and ironmaster Richard Turner. When he designed a 'Gothic' church in Tunbridge Wells, it was widely ridiculed for being coarsely detailed. His good name more or less lost, Decimus Burton retired, hurt, to Tunbridge Wells and the margins of architectural history.

**BELOW** Burton always had a delicate touch. He worked with ironmaster Richard Turner on the Palm House at Kew, pre-dating the Crystal Palace by three years

**ABOVE LEFT** Pugin's one-off tiles for St Augustine's Priory Church. The process was manual, except for the few machines used to prepare the heavy clay

**ABOVE** Pugin was nothing if not a perfectionist, designing every detail. He revived the medieval craft of encaustic tile-making that had disappeared with the dissolution of the monasteries

# The Arc de Triomphe

The Arc de Triomphe was, like Decimus Burton's English version (see below right) inspired by the Arch of Titus (see p.51) near the Forum in Rome, with its skilful sculptural reliefs that proclaimed victory after the sack of Jerusalem.

Commissioned in 1806 by Emperor Napoleon I after his victory at Austerlitz, the arch is so vast that by 1810 it was still unfinished. When Napoleon entered Paris from the west with his new bride Archduchess Marie-Louise of Austria, he had to have a wooden mock-up made. The architect, Jean Chalgrin, died in 1811, not long before the Battle of Waterloo scotched Napoleon's dreams of world domination. In 1825 George IV decided to outdo Napoleon, and commissioned Burton to create a screen entrance for Buckingham Palace, along with an arch. Burton's instinct was to stick to the restraint of the original in Rome, but in that he was thwarted.

Nevertheless, Napoleon's more ornamental arch was, until 1982, the tallest in the world. It stands 165 feet (49.5 metres) high. A slightly larger arch was built in Pyongyang, North Korea in 1982, for the 70th birthday of Kim Il-Sung. It stands 200 feet (60 metres) high and 164 feet (50 metres) wide.

**ABOVE RIGHT** Napoleon's Arc de Triomphe at the end of the Champs Elysées. Burton's arch was moved to Hyde Park Corner in 1883, so now both are besieged by traffic

**BOTTOM RIGHT** The Wellington Arch, now topped by the largest bronze in Europe, the Quadriga, by Adrian Jones (1912), with the angel of peace in a chariot

**BELOW** Pyongyang, North Korea. Now the world's tallest, this arch commemorates victory over the Japanese. Each of its 25,500 granite blocks is said to celebrate Kim Il-Sung's days on earth

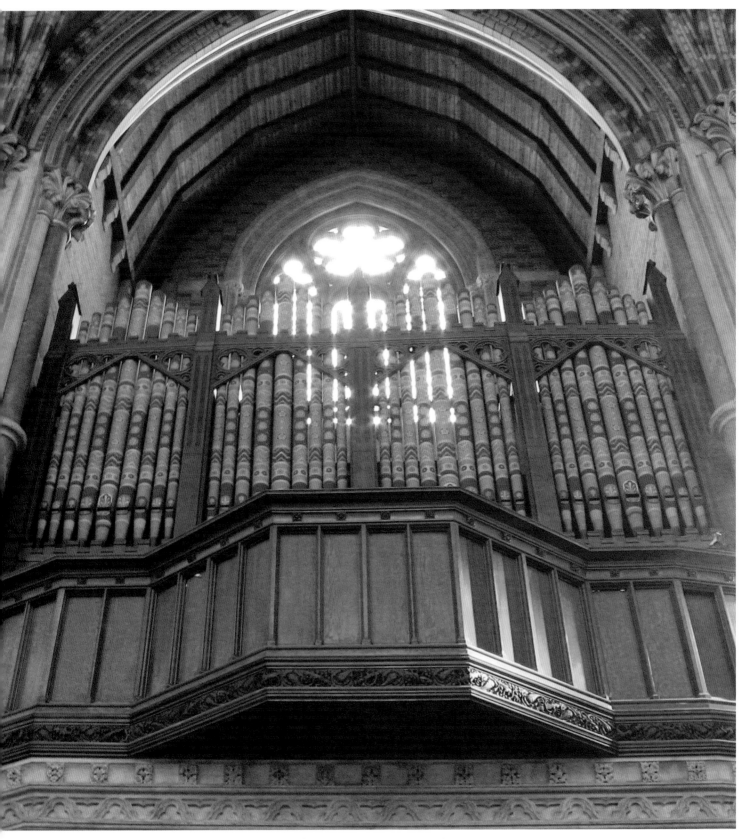

# NEW MEDIEVALISM

Ornate, mysterious, elaborate. All of these words and plenty of others – like 'industrial', or 'muscular' – can be used to describe the architecture of the Victorian age. To some, it is bleak, overbearing, cluttered, or simply ugly. But like it or not, the Victorians had certainly achieved one thing – originality. No longer was every public building a copy of either the Parthenon or the Maison Carrée.

The continued success of Gothic revivalism after Pugin's early death can be largely put down to the intervention of one man. Art critic, thinker and author, John Ruskin is possibly better known now as the sponsor and promoter of the Pre-Raphaelite Brotherhood. However, his influence on both architectural thinking and politics was immense. His book *Seven Lamps of Architecture*, published in 1849, inspired generations of architects. A medievalist and a famously moving speaker, Ruskin was a passionate advocate of the Gothic. For him, beauty was inseparable from virtue. The colourful medieval architecture of Venice was the foundation of all Ruskin's architectural theorizing.

To Ruskin, art and architecture were serious, moral concerns. In art, he praised the accurate representation of nature above all things. It followed that the Gothic, with its lavish naturalistic decoration, was better than contrived classicism. He passionately rejected

**ABOVE** The new medievalists wanted a lyrical effect that harked back to the Middle Ages. Here, the cloister of New College, founded to educate priests after the depredations of the Black Death

**LEFT** Keble College is a riot of polychrome brick that has divided opinion at Oxford University for over a century. Here, the organ in the Chapel

**ABOVE** The trefoil is found in glass, tracery and ironwork of all ages. In the Gothic style, it was less rounded, like medieval heraldic emblems

**RIGHT** Gothic revival in Cambridge. The University towns had been a cauldron for the development of the 'new' style

# Marginalia

In Britain, the Gothic Revival went through a number of different phases: the romantic, when architects were trying to get back to the spirit of the Middle Ages, the antiquarian, when the aim was to meticulously and accurately perfect the form and detail, and the eclectic, when architects began to feel free to improvise.

### ● IRON RAILINGS
Were iron railings always painted black? No: various colours have been found on historic ironwork. Humphrey Repton would sometimes recommend a 'bronze' finish, made by powdering copper or gold dust on a green ground. In the first half of the 19th century so called 'invisible' greens (they would blend into a background of foliage) were used for fences, gates, railings and garden furniture. Green was used throughout the mid-Victorian period, but dark blue, red

and chocolate brown were also popular.

### ● THE LIFE OF JOHN RUSKIN
Ruskin was an art critic and writer who had a strong effect on nineteenth century romanticism in both art and architecture.

The highly-charged moral influence of this author/aesthete cannot be underestimated. His scandals are more famous today; the non-consummation of his marriage and his later love for the 10-year-old Rose La Touche. In his later writing he turned to politics and social theory, and was a huge spur to the founding of both the Labour Party and the environmental movement.

### ● ARCHITECTURAL TERRACOTTA
Architects from Alfred Waterhouse to Karl Friedrich Schinkel used terracotta. The façade of Waterhouse's Natural History Museum in London positively writhes with monkeys, snakes, fish and wolves, all carved by craftsmen. The colour of the material varies with the source of the clay: the bright red you sometimes see comes from Ruabon (North Wales) clay. London clay is pale pink or neutral. Terracotta was cheap and light, and suited to mass-production techniques. However, polluted Victorian London was not the best place to use the material, which is difficult to keep clean in a smoky city. Its popularity as a material soon gave way to faience, or glazed terracotta, which was often used by architects such as Cass Gilbert and Louis Sullivan in the United States.

**ABOVE** The Natural History Museum, London: a cathedral to the radical new enquiring spirit of the century that discovered dinosaurs and Charles Darwin, with his theory on the origin of species the mechanization and the standardization that came with mass production. Almost as important to Ruskin, though, were the human values he felt medieval Gothic represented. Creativity was close to God: Gothic architecture had always employed creative craftsmen, and it was therefore the only moral choice.

Stone carving by hand had to be done by true craftsmen, and the work involved real creative expression being put into a building. Ruskin believed that this creativity, along with a closer connection with nature, brought people closer to God. Much as Pugin had done, John Ruskin passionately argued the case for Gothic public and government buildings, and he did it with great success.

The physician Sir Henry Acland, who introduced the new study of natural science into Oxford University, was Ruskin's personal friend. When he instigated the new Oxford University Museum of Natural History it was with Ruskin's collaboration. It would be built as a model of modern Gothic, they decided. Unfortunately, when Ruskin's ideas were put into practice, he often despised the results.

Designed by the Irish architects Thomas Newenham Deane and Benjamin Woodward, and built between 1855 and 1860, this little gem of a building has a large square court at its centre. Its dramatic glass roof is supported by cast-iron pillars, which divide the court into three aisles. Stone-columned cloistered

arcades run around the ground and first floors of the building, each of the columns being made from a different British stone. There is delicate ornamentation everywhere: the iron pillars are decorated with naturalistic leaves and branches.

Poor Ruskin: even Acland's homage displeased him. Since the publication of his essay 'The Stones of Venice', Britain had covered itself with the strapped coloured brickwork of the Doges' 14th century palace. He railed against the spate of copying, even when, as here, it was with the best of intentions. The situation in Oxford wasn't helped by a certain amount of political infighting. The Irish freehand stone carvers

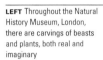

**LEFT** Throughout the Natural History Museum, London, there are carvings of beasts and plants, both real and imaginary

**BELOW** Carved up: Ruskin got more than he bargained for in the form of the mischievous O'Shea brothers, craftsmen brought over from Ireland

O'Shea and Whelan had been specially chosen for the project. Three brothers and a cousin, they were the skilled craftsmen that Ruskin felt were essential for building in the true, creatively enterprising Gothic spirit. However, the O'Sheas were far too irreverent for Ruskin's liking. When money ran out and the University Congregation refused to pay any more for the carving, the brothers offered to work for free. The only problem was that James O'Shea proceeded to carve excellent caricatures of the Congregation on to the building, in the form of parrots and owls.

Whether Ruskin approved or not, the Gothic revival was now in full spate, and the results couldn't have been more different from the Greek revivalism movement of a few decades earlier. In some cases, the legacy is a questionable one. 'Ornamentation is the

principal part of architecture', Ruskin had said, and Victorian architects took him at his word.

William Butterfield, for instance, whose churches and particularly his university buildings like that for Keble College Oxford, have divided critics and public ever since the key stones were laid. Are they ugly, or are they simply 'muscular', as some critics described them? Butterfield took Ruskin's theories about colour in buildings to a logical conclusion. His strident colour schemes are the result of what's called 'constructional' or 'permanent' polychromy – the patterns and colours being the result of using differently-coloured bricks and stones. All Saints, Margaret Street, his massive church built in a bohemian slum off Regent Street between 1850 and 1859, shocked the critics, who saw in it '[a] deliberate preference of ugliness'.

While some buildings may be failures, we have Gothic revivalism to thank for many marvellous examples, like G.E. Street's Law Courts (1870–2) and Alfred Waterhouse's Natural History Museum. And yes, they are original. Sir George Gilbert Scott's Midland Grand Hotel, begun in 1862 to front St Pancras Station, borrows to some extent from the Cloth Hall at Ypres and from Italianate rhythms when it comes to the pacing of the windows (see p.179). Other than that, it is highly individual. As he himself said: 'I almost originated it.'

In America, terminally split from Britain and in the throes of a Beaux-Arts resurgence, the Gothic style remained an alien import. The few inroads it made were in church architecture, like St Patrick's cathedral in New York. It also won hearts at a folk level. Gingerbread tracery – a so-called 'Carpenter

LEFT The Mammal Gallery of the Oxford University Museum of Natural History, a hymn to the mysteries of nature. It was built in honour of John Ruskin's theories

BELOW Canada adopts Gothic, at Notre Dame de Montréal. The interior, of 1872 to 1879, was designed by Victor Bourgeau and the stonemason John Redpath

Gothic' that would have had Pugin and Ruskin running away screaming – was part of a picturesque reaction to the monumental 'Greek' towns spreading out in a mantle of pure white over the once wild West.

In Canada, however, it was a different story. The Revival was taken completely to heart, only falling out of favour in the 1930s. It had one crucial difference: like Barry's Parliament, the simpler Canadian interpretation still values Georgian levels of symmetry. Canada's first major Gothic Revival structure, Notre-Dame de Montréal, was not only the largest church in North America but was imitated throughout Canada and the USA.

If there was now a direct link between contemporary Gothic architecture and morality, Ruskin wasn't happy with it. He wrote:

*'The Greek could stay in his triglyph burrow and be at peace, but the work of the Gothic heart is fretwork still, and it can neither rest in, nor from, its labour, but must pass on, sleeplessly, until its love of change shall be pacified for ever.'*

Nothing was going to measure up, in the restless Ruskin's view, to the stones of Venice.

**RIGHT** The drama of neo-Gothic. St Patrick's, New York, still holds its own against the monsters of the sky

# FULL SWING

So what of the famous new technologies of world-conquering Britain? As the pioneer of industrialization, Britain's great migrations into the city had happened early. The rapid development of new cities brought different ways of coping with urbanization. The new metropolis would need new building forms, like the railway station. The very fact that trains existed made new demands on civic architecture – clocks and clock towers were needed, for instance. Meanwhile, hundreds of new town halls, libraries, hospitals, hotels and department stores gave architects massive opportunities to work in the new Gothic style. In previous centuries only churches and fortresses would have given them the chance to create so much on such a scale.

**B**ut strangely, it was in other parts of the world that the new wonder material, cast iron, would be used to best effect. Let Thomas Telford and Isambard Kingdom Brunel use iron as much as they like: it was not going to be allowed to influence architects without a struggle. Cheaper than stone and more resilient, iron had distinct advantages as a building material. It could be prefabricated in bulk and shipped to a building site ready-made. It was also hugely flexible when it came to design: at the Prince Regent's Royal Pavilion, John Nash had used it openly for ceilings and columns – especially in the kitchen, where he installed two great palm trees, complete with copper leaves, as columns. It was a marvellous novelty, but hardly something to be taken seriously.

Cast iron was being tentatively introduced into major public buildings – the British Museum, for instance, has concealed cast-iron beams. But in the main, architects would do as Smirke had done, and conceal it under a sheath of facing stone.

François-Joseph Bélanger built the first full iron-and-glass dome over the Halle aux Blés, not far from the Louvre in Paris. He modestly described it as 'a new conception for the first time in this genre, which gives Europe the idea'. Another outstanding Paris building showed how new technology could

**RIGHT** Telford's beautiful Menai Straits suspension bridge of 1826, linking Anglesey in North Wales to the mainland. Sixteen huge chain cables suspended from the limestone towers hold up the span

**LEFT** Surrealist Gothic: a bridge between the old world and the new? Spanish architect Genaro Palacios designed this church for the Philippines and it may have been prefabricated by Gustave Eiffel

**RIGHT** Paris' Bibliothèque Sainte-Geneviève. Labrouste was there every day for seven years, designing every detail right down to the inkwells

convert effortlessly into fine architecture. Far from concealing iron, the Bibliothèque Sainte-Geneviève, an elegant library in the 5th arrondissement designed by Henri Labrouste (1842), uses it as a decorative feature. Labrouste's delicate ribbing of open-work barrel arches in the interior is inspired by the book bindings. Now much admired, Labrouste was ridiculed by his peers for using this upstart, vulgar material in a supposedly serious building.

Other nations were by no means so hide-bound with respect to architectural tradition. The extraordinary church of San Sebastian in the old district of Manila in the Philippines is the world's only Neo-Gothic church, made entirely of steel. Although Filipino artist Lorenzo Rocha painted the interior walls and ceiling to resemble marble and jasper, the rust-streaked exterior is plainly made of a steel frame and panels. The choice of steel was apparently determined by an exasperated parish priest, who was looking for a church

**RIGHT** Paddington Station opened in 1854 and was designed by Isambard Kingdom Brunel. The glazed roof is carried by three arches, each 699 feet (213m) long

that was both fire- and earthquake-proof. The prefabricated parts of the church are said to have been initially designed by Gustave Eiffel.

By contrast, Britain's most daring adventures with iron were in its new railway stations. New roof trusses, like the so-called sickle girder and the hinged arch, allowed the creation of vast vaulted spaces. The second Paddington station reached a width of 242 feet (74 metres) with its triple span roof. But it was only in an industrial context that engineers unselfconciously exploited the obvious potential of iron.

Engineer Jesse Hartley's dignified warehouse scheme at Albert Dock, Liverpool, occupying seven acres next to the River Mersey, has now been rescued from an era of industrial decline and rehabilitated as a leisure area of shops, restaurants and an art gallery. The first British structure devised entirely in iron, brick and stone, Albert Dock was no less than a small industrial town when it was built. It had its own rhythm of daily activities and a structure determined by the work itself – storing and transporting spices, sugar and other commodities. Albert Dock in many ways represents the pure, muscular energy of Victorian enterprise. Here, there were no lofty ideals of building as an expression of a religious or a secular ideal. Yet Hartley's buildings are still handsome: the iron-framed structures are quirkily but happily mounted on massive, cast-iron Doric columns. Today, the buildings still seem honest, but at the same time somehow heroic.

Albert Dock uses hundreds of thousands of neat, uniform, red bricks. Like the production of glass, mass brick production was perfected in this era of total invention. The simplest

Inside the Menier factory, the cast iron columns spread their skirts. The cross-bracing pattern of the outside is repeated on the decorative floor

**ABOVE** Architect Jules Saulnier made the iron frame bracing part of the decoration in the Menier Chocolate Factory, Noisiel, France. It was built in 1872

**RIGHT** Truly a Gothic pile: Tyntesfield, near Bristol, was one of the Victorian country houses that embraced technological innovation, with early forms of showers

mechanical process imaginable – extruding a mix through a rectangular die and then slicing the result into units with a cutting wire – replaced the labour-intensive tradition of hand-moulding that had existed for 3,000 years.

It wasn't just bricks. When the inventor and arms manufacturer William Armstrong created a huge new country house, Cragside, near Newcastle, in 1864, he also built a hydroelectric turbine to power a revolutionary hydraulic lift, electric lighting and even a turning kitchen spit. New Gothic piles like the vast mansion built on a guano fortune – Tyntesfield, near Bristol – had working showers. Steam heating systems began to appear, an innovation not seen since the days of Ancient Rome. Gas lighting came to

London at the start of the century, blackening many a building and burning down yet more. Electric lighting – also initially dangerous – arrived by its end, as did telephones and mechanical ventilation systems.

The water closet was another famously useful invention, demonstrating that there was a better way than chamber pots and open pits. George Jennings installed the first-ever public toilets at the Great Exhibition, in 1851. Built for the same event, the famous Crystal Palace was the high point of Victorian building technology (see p.176).

It might have been condemned by Ruskin – he thought it the very model of mechanical dehumanization in design – but the palace was hugely popular with the general public. In France, Napoleon III demanded that Jacques Hittorff give him a building as good as Paxton's. Hittorff was only too happy to oblige, yet these new building types made many uneasy, including Napoleon III who rejected his ambitious design as 'too difficult'.

Most of these techniques had been evolved to span great spaces in factories, or to support machinery in textile mills. The result was that their potential was largely ignored

when it came to other sorts of buildings: they were associated with engineering, rather than with architectural skills. However, while some manufacturers scarcely considered aesthetics, to

others architecture was crucial. Some attempted to humanize design by making it playful. The Menier Chocolate Factory at Noisel-sur-Marne (1871–2) by Jules Saulnier does not apologize for its structural inventiveness. Its pretty iron skeleton is wrapped around it like a ribbon: it is used simultaneously as support structure and decoration. The building is also, incidentally, highly energy-efficient. It stands across a river, and the water that flowed through the arches between its stone piers was used to drive the factory's machinery.

But in Britain, 'serious' architects were reluctant to use these 'base' materials. Oriel Chambers in Liverpool was one of the few buildings in the UK to openly express the new frame construction that was now possible. Designed by Peter Ellis in 1865, the building's stone piers held iron panels, each with a plate-glass oriel window. But its simplified forms and large windows were controversial in Victorian Britain. It was described as 'a great abortion' and 'an agglomeration of great glass bubbles'. The Gothic lobby was the new

**ABOVE** Belgium's King Leopold II commissioned the so-called 'Iron Church', a domed glasshouse, as the royal chapel at Laeken. It was the first time this type of building had been treated so seriously

**LEFT** Crystal Palace: revolutionary technology employed over an incredibly short space of time

orthodoxy: real buildings didn't use iron, they didn't let in lots of light, and they had to be highly ornamented. The disheartened Ellis abandoned architecture altogether.

So change came creeping slowly, but the new technologies would eventually come into their own: the advantages of using them were so self-evident. By 1870 iron and glass could be used to cover an entire street, protecting shoppers from the elements, as the Galleria Vittorio Emanuele proved in Milan. The Paris store Bon Marche used the skills of Gustave Eiffel – who would later design the world-beating tower – in 1876, creating an airy, open and dramatic interior for its new department store.

In Belgium King Leopold II commissioned a truly magnificent series of garden buildings with an 'Iron Church'. Leopold's beautiful Royal Greenhouses designed by Alphonse Balat covered 270,000 square feet. Across the Atlantic, in Chicago, meanwhile, a quiet revolution was gaining ground. A totally new building type, the office, was stretching taller using the radical new iron frames. American city architecture would soon lead the world.

**RIGHT** The Galleria Vittorio Emanuele: thoroughly urban elegance in an arcade whose two arms meet in an octagonal central space, topped with an impressive dome

# Lifts and Escalators

Picture the scene: a balmy day in autumn, 1854. Britain's Queen Victoria has travelled by train with her children to visit the latest in high technology – William Armstrong's dock gates at Grimsby. They are powered by water pressure from a specially built 300ft high tower. She laughs and claps as her children are rushed up into the air on a hydraulic lift. Just a few short years beforehand such lifts didn't exist, and neither did the railway tracks that had conveyed the royal party to Grimsby.

Lifts supported by a rope over some kind of pulley have been in use throughout the history of human ingenuity. For example, a lift carried firewood to the top of the lighthouse on the island of Pharos at Alexandria, around 300BC. The young farmer's son, Elisha Graves Otis, didn't

invent the steam-powered 'elevators' that carried freight. His first great contribution was to invent a safety back-up system that would work if the hoisting cable broke; an automatic brake would stop the platform from falling. His second stroke of genius was to realize that 'elevators' had the potential to carry passengers.

Otis got the impresario P.T. Barnum to whip up a crowd at the Crystal Palace exhibition in 1853 and then stunned the throng by ordering an axeman to cut the rope. The platform fell only a few inches – what showmanship! – before coming to a halt. By 1857, the first commercial passenger elevators were in use in department stores in New York. Otis' invention would transform the cityscapes of New York and then the world by making high buildings workable.

In 1899 another new method of travelling between floors was invented by Charles D. Seeberger. It took its name from the elevator and the Latin word for stairs, *scala,* and so the escalator was born, taking first prize at the Paris Exhibition of 1900.

# The Crystal Palace

The Crystal Palace was an architectural anomaly. It was not designed by an architect or even an engineer, but by a gardener. Joseph Paxton had already built impressive, lightweight palm and lily houses in the beautiful gardens of Chatsworth House in Derbyshire in the 1840s. Prime Minister Benjamin Disraeli described the one Paxton now went on to build in the centre of Hyde Park as 'an enchanted pile'.

Created to house the Great Exhibition of 1851, the structure was a symphony in wrought iron and sheet glass. Designed to be put up in the smallest amount of time by only semi-skilled workers, its genius was twofold. Firstly, it stripped everything down to the essentials of space, light and air. In the context of the elaborate architecture of the time, this in itself was a great leap of the imagination.

Secondly, it was technically brilliant. Paxton's standardized, prefabricated parts meant that it could be ready in less than five months. This pointed the way to a new way of building and foreshadowed the great glazed spaces of the late 20th century. Over a century later, Richard Rogers' Lloyd's Building (see p.240) in the City of London had a central atrium that quoted directly from Paxton's design.

Longer than the Palace of Versailles, and higher than Westminster Abbey, the Crystal Palace was a sensation. So was the exhibition itself. Even the intensely serious Charlotte Brontë admitted to going six times. Yet without any roots in history, with no cultural precedents at all, Paxton's achievement was in a sense ignored. It wasn't really thought of as a building; more a gigantic house of glass cards. The rumour that Paxton had designed it in a few stolen minutes – doodling when he was supposed to be in an official meeting – didn't help people take it seriously. John Ruskin dismissed it as 'a huge greenhouse'.

Paxton had studied nature at source. Observing that the giant water lilies he was cultivating at Chatsworth – brought back from the Amazon by plant hunters – were 'a natural feat of engineering', he tested the idea by floating his young daughter Annie on one leaf. When he built a greenhouse to house a giant lily, he patterned the

structure after the lily leaves themselves, with mutually reinforcing ribs and cross-ribs. Paxton reasoned that a building too could be constructed with a vascular system supporting a stretched skin – the skin being the newly-invented plate glass.

The Crystal Palace used 300,000 sheets of glass and was put together from millions of prefabricated units. Paxton and railroad engineer Peter Barlow devised nodes at the intersections which allowed them to slot in the support columns. The glass was hung from fastenings. This follows exactly the same principles as the curtain walls of modern buildings. The other impressive aspect of the design is its multi-functionality. Economy of design was everything: Paxton's hollow pillar supports doubled as drain pipes. A special rafter, designed as an external gutter, also acted as a runnel: the workers installed the glass as they moved along, lifting it out of specially-designed trolleys. In the high, arched central transept, where girders and trusses didn't provide enough stability, slender diagonal rods were installed in a radiating pattern.

Closing ranks against the untutored Paxton, some critics – including the Institution of Civil Engineers – gloomily predicted that the glass would break in a storm, or that the building's raised

walkways would collapse under the weight of spectators. To test its strength, 300 of the workmen were asked to run and jump in the upper galleries all at the same time. The building hardly quivered. The Palace, which was only ever meant to be a temporary structure, was an overwhelming success. Six million people visited the exhibition.

'Truly it was astonishing, a fairy scene. Many cried, and all felt touched and impressed with devotional feelings. It was the happiest, proudest day in my life, and I can think of nothing else,' wrote Queen Victoria in her diary.

The huge structure, enclosing 19 acres, took just 20 weeks to build, and cost a modest £79,800. At one stage the proud gardener reported seeing two columns and three girders put up by two men in 16 minutes... Paxton's influence on modern design and construction is clear. The original drawings for his great masterpiece are now in the Victoria & Albert Museum. What had started out as a brief doodle became one of the most influential buildings in the history of architecture.

# The Eiffel Tower

*'There is an attractive element in the colossal... What visitor is insensitive before [the Pyramids]? And what is the source of this admiration if not the immensity of the effort and the grandeur of the result? The Tower will be the tallest structure ever built by man. Will it not be grand in its own right?'*

Gustave Eiffel

The Eiffel Tower became the world's tallest structure when it was completed in 1889. At just under 1,000 feet (300m) it was a revolutionary construction that celebrated the new iron-clad language of industrial civilization: a potent symbol of the modern France. It seems ironic, given its iconic status now, but when Eiffel's plan was first mooted, there was widespread opposition to the idea of a giant tower dominating the heart of Paris.

The tower was built as the grand entrance arch for the 1889 Exposition Universelle, which celebrated the centenary of the French Revolution. Alexandre Gustave Eiffel was assisted by engineers Maurice Koechlin and Emile Nouguier, along with the architect Stephen Sauvestre. Essentially, the structure was straightforward. Four tapering, curved, lattice-girder piers, rising from an immensely broad 125 square metre base, meet at the top. They are laced together at two levels by connecting girders. The tower's architectural language was its very structural logic: even at the end of the 19th century, this was a genuinely revolutionary aesthetic. Once it was up, more French voices rose in anger against it. A petition of 300 names, including Guy de Maupassant, Émile Zola, Charles Garnier (architect of the Opéra Garnier), and Dumas the Younger – was presented to the city government in protest at its construction.

*'We, the writers, painters, sculptors, architects and lovers of the beauty of Paris, do protest with all our vigour and all our indignation, in the name of French taste... against the useless and monstrous Eiffel Tower.'*

Nature lovers, meanwhile, worried that it would interfere with the flight of birds over Paris. But the Eiffel Tower was admired by artists Rousseau and Chagall, among others.

Eiffel, who ran his own international firm, was the leading European authority on the aerodynamics of high frames. The curve of the tower's base pylons was so precisely calculated that the bending and shearing forces of the wind were progressively transformed into forces of compression. Such was Eiffel's engineering wizardry that even in gales his tower never sways more than 6 inches (15cm), on a bad day.

The novelist Guy de Maupassant, who claimed to hate the tower, reportedly ate there every day. Asked why, he replied that it was the one place in Paris you could not see it. The tower is now the most visited structure in the world.

**BELOW** Each of the 18,000 iron pieces used were made to an accurancy of a tenth of a millimetre in Eiffel's factory at Levallois-Perret outside Paris

**LEFT** Eiffel's structure is an engineering triumph, prefabricated to save time on site. Two-thirds of the 2,500,000 rivets used were put in at the factory

# BRICK PALACES

This is how George Weerth, a young German on holiday in England, described Bradford in an article that he wrote for a German newspaper in 1846.

*'Every other factory town in England is a paradise in comparison to this hole. In Manchester the air lies like lead upon you; in Birmingham it is just as if you were sitting with your nose in a stove pipe; in Leeds you have to cough with the dust and the stink as if you had swallowed a pound of Cayenne pepper in one go – but you can put up with all that. In Bradford, however, you think you have been lodged with the devil incarnate. If anyone wants to feel how a poor sinner is tormented in Purgatory, let him travel to Bradford.'*

**T**itus Salt, the wool mill owner, obviously agreed. Salt upped and left Bradford because he was so disgusted by the pollution. The new Victorian prosperity had a rotten armpit. Overcrowding wasn't the only problem – so was the rapid destruction of the countryside.

Ruskin, in despair, envisaged a 20th-century England 'set as thick with chimneys as the masts stand on the docks of Liverpool,' with 'no meadows… no trees, no gardens.'

According to the railway pioneer George Stephenson:

*'The strength of Britain lies in her iron and coal beds… The Lord Chancellor now sits on a bag of wool, but... he ought rather to sit on a bag of coals, although it might not prove so comfortable a seat.'*

Industry's drastic changes mattered – not least to the building industry, given the three-fold increase in the population. There were more men working in the building industry than there were in mines or quarries.

These were heady times. Queen Victoria even allowed her children to be hoisted into the air on one of William Armstrong's new steam-powered cranes, which would shortly come into use on building sites.

And, quite suddenly, with the advent of the railways buildings were transportable commodities. Yet the fear of social upheaval

was strong, putting a huge focus on home and hearth. Everybody, rich and poor, looked for a haven of peace in family life.

The ornamentation that Ruskin had recommended was also within the reach of all, through cheap mass-produced masonry, plaster and woodwork. The new canals and railways carried cast iron from Scotland, terracotta from the Midlands and slates from Wales. Local, vernacular materials became almost a thing of the past. The profusion of polychromatic brickwork used by enthusiastic builders on door-frames, windows and chimneys from Stirling to Portsmouth would have driven Ruskin to desperation and distraction – if he hadn't already retreated in horror to the Lake District.

One third of the houses in Britain today date from before the First World War, and the majority are Victorian. The railways meant that for the first time people had the option of living half in and half out of the city – by commuting. Thousands of the middle classes left the cities in search of cleaner air. Whole new suburbs like Ealing in west London, or

**LEFT** A London street of the 1870s. Developers could buy kits of parts: doors, window frames, plaster mouldings and embellish even quite humble dwellings

**ABOVE** The Midland Grand Hotel, now known as St Pancras Chambers, by Sir George Gilbert Scott 1868–77. Much disliked while Victorian Gothic was out of favour

north Oxford, were designed in a Gothicized high Victorian idiom. But for some idealists this wasn't enough. Nostalgia for clean air and the community values of the countryside and village fused with the idea of suburbia to create a new ideal – the garden suburb. The idea was heralded in the 1870s at Bedford Park (see p.189), a planned suburb designed by committed architects in an area that is now Chiswick, west London.

However, in the main, speculative builders weren't interested in architectural integrity. They often adopted different elements of various styles randomly – Romanesque, Italianate, Tudor, Elizabethan. A perfectly ordinary house could have half-timbered gables, filigree finials on the roof, towers and even medievalist overhanging windowed galleries.

Those in charge of architectural practices, meanwhile, weren't interested in ordinary housing. They had more than enough work to keep them busy: vast country houses were wanted by the new wealthy and large numbers of new churches and public buildings would make it easier to sustain a quiescent society. This was the beginning of the big architectural firms: they were called 'Plan Factories'. They were so busy that Sir George Gilbert Scott, who ran one of them, was sometimes unclear which of the new buildings appearing so rapidly on the skyline had been designed by his own firm.

To many socially aspiring Victorians simplicity was anathema: it implied poverty, not good taste. Domestic interiors were heavily cluttered with gimcracks and gewgaws. Popular favourites were dark, highly-ornamented fireplaces, covered with cheap pottery figures of Victoria and Albert. With the ready availability of pre-manufactured goods from catalogues, you could pick and mix your styles with gay abandon. The catalogues of firms like Hampton & Sons offered 'classical' or 'Gothic' doors, for instance, the classical alternative being available in polished pine with *carton-pierre* (a form of papier mâché) decoration. Elaborate decorative features like window heads were easily prefabricated using terracotta by companies like Houlton.

So, while on the outside houses became an utter muddle of jumbled styles, the same thing was happening in the cluttered front rooms of Britain. Something had to give.

# American Gothic

In Grant Wood's famous picture, two stoic American frontier archetypes stand gaunt. They are framed against another uniquely American structure: a simple, white wooden house with high pitched eaves. Painted in 1930, just before the Great Depression, Wood's painting was probably first intended as a satire, a critique of small-town American life. Even if it was meant to symbolize the hard-working yet narrow-minded ethics of the aspirational working class the picture has transcended that to become one of America's best-loved – and most-parodied – paintings.

The house was built sometime between 1881 and 1882 in Eldon, Iowa, a town with only 947 inhabitants. Wood, who taught sketching there, scribbled a drawing of the window and part of the house on the back of an envelope, before returning to his studio. There he painted his sister Nan and his dentist Dr B.H. McKeeby, the painting's grim-faced protagonists. The artist didn't say much about the meaning of the painting and what little he did say was contradictory. By one account he chose this house because its raw, Midwestern simplicity contrasted with the 'pretentiousness' of its arched, cross-paned window. The composition, with the straight-laced figures closely echoing the shape of the house, roof and windows, identifies the architectural values of 'American Gothic' with those of the American people. Thus did a medieval European architectural style – imitated in wood – come to symbolize the pioneering values of Middle America.

Whether Wood was mocking the determination of the owners to have this fanciful, upwardly-mobile ornamentation or honouring it, the 'American Gothic House' is now a tourist attraction where people come to be photographed with their own pitchfork and aprons, along with the sternest expression they can manage.

Where Gothic was being hotly debated in Britain and subjected to academic scrutiny, not least by John Ruskin and Augustus Pugin, American Gothic was a picturesque improvization, allowed to develop in its own quirky way. With cheaper, wooden-built houses the norm, the style was able to develop freely in the hands of carpenters and builders, rather than architects. It is sometimes called 'Carpenter Gothic'. Charm, along with straightforward practicality, was therefore what dictated the shape and form of these houses, churches and community halls.

In prosperous Europe, churches were almost invariably built in stone or brick. But in North America, given the cheapness and ready availability of timber, even churches were built with planks and nails. Yet this didn't stop the builders aiming high. In the tiny village of Skatin, tucked into the forests of British Columbia, Canada, lies a hidden Gothic treasure, inspired by pictures of the cathedrals of Chartres and St Denis in France.

The Church of the Holy Cross was built a century ago by some of BC's first Christians. The 17 people from the Skatin, Samahquam, and Douglas bands had no architectural plans and only rudimentary tools, yet the church's foundations are hand-hewn timbers set on giant stones dragged from the Lillooet River. The Skookumchuk reserve is so deep in the forest that the only roads are logging tracks, originally carved out by prospectors on the gold rush to the Cariboo. The three-spired church – sadly now threatened by damp – is an exciting anomaly in the

**BELOW** American Gothic: a controversial depiction of the pioneering spirit. Is Wood lampooning small-town values, or is he praising them?

**RIGHT** So famous and yet so tiny: this 'Carpenter Gothic' home is possibly the most familiar house in the USA

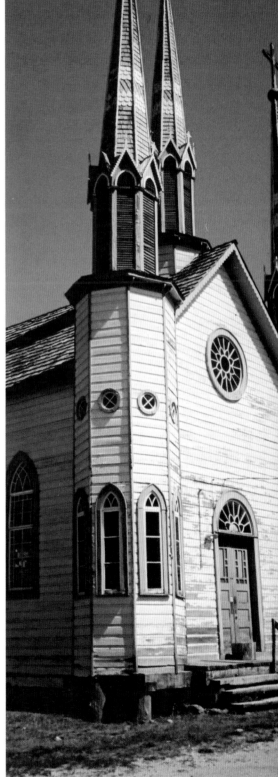

forest, and lovingly detailed, particularly on the interior.

ABOVE Lyndhurst, built near the Hudson River for the railroad baron Jay Gould, is a very elegant, almost languid take on the Gothic spirit. Its limestone was quarried at Sing Sing.

The architect/illustrator Alexander Jackson Davis was the first person to promote this kind of vernacular Gothic. He produced a pattern book, *Rural Residences,* begun in 1835. His most famous Gothic revival house, Lyndhurst (also known as the house of railroad tycoon Jay Gould) was designed in 1838. It has fanciful turrets and redundant chimneys worthy of the UK's earlier 'Gothick'. The gloomy, narrow-corridored interiors have won it a place in several movies along with the distinction of being the first representative of the generic term 'Hudson River Gothic'.

At least eight distinct post-classical domestic architectural styles developed in the United States from the 1830s. A by no means exhaustive list would include Gothic Revival, Italianate, Richardsonian Romanesque, Shingle and Colonial Revival – and then there was the home-grown 'Stick' style. All of them produced many handsome dwellings but in some of them all the styles were stirred up together into an impossible *pot pourri*. The American Queen Anne style is particularly intriguing, producing comfortably handsome designs. It followed the patterns being set by Norman Shaw in England, with half-timbers, hipped roofs and patterned masonry, but it added decorative elements of its own; particularly spindles used in friezes and balustrades and strong, often Italianate, porch posts. Intriguingly, by the 1880s some Queen Anne style houses were even being prefabricated and transported by rail across the United States. Yet there is one house and one house only that somehow symbolizes the quintessential American pioneer spirit. And its portrait hangs in the Art Institute of Chicago.

RIGHT The Church of the Holy Cross in Skookumchuk, British Columbia: an inspired creation with three spires to represent the Holy Trinity. Now in desperate need of conservation

# A WORLD OF EXCESS

From the 1850s onwards, the Victorians didn't simply look backwards into the past – they mined it, excavated it and exhibited it. Then they looked abroad for new sources, and started all over again. The word 'eclecticism' is used time and again to describe this enthusiastic free-for-all. In the Southwest, Bristol was so full of warehouse buildings using red, white and black bricks from a local brickpit that the style was referred to as 'Bristol Byzantine'. Perhaps the wealth of Victorian England had gone to their heads. Perhaps there was just too much money about.

Ideas, materials and even people travelled remarkably far and fast in the second half of the century, and it must have seemed that anything at all was possible. Gradually, even mainstream architects adopted a pick-and-mix attitude to stylistic norms. The results were appealing at their best but embarrassing when not.

A bewildering range of styles – Egyptian, Byzantine, Romanesque, Venetian Gothic, even Muslim Indian – hit the streets of Britain. John Francis Bentley's Westminster Cathedral (1895–1903) is a real surprise when you discover it in the best-hidden public square in all of London: a Byzantine-inspired squat cathedral, with alternating red-and-white brickwork and a Romanesque entrance.

The style fest was not limited to Britain. The Palais de Justice in Paris, rebuilt after fire destroyed portions of the structure in 1776, was a stepped chocolate cake, its roof like a Mesopotamian ziggurat.

The 'Free Style', as it came to be known, was at its lyrical best in the hands of figures like Richard Norman Shaw.

His New Scotland Yard breaks from stern granite into red brickwork; its catalogue of windows ranges from Elizabethan to Baroque. But whereas Shaw was a genius, the generality of buildings were created by lesser minds with a resultant hotchpotch of styles. Soon, 'baronial' would be mixed with Flemish influences, Doric columns with Egyptian pylons, domes with pointed arches. Enough.

**LEFT** Inside the 'Palais Garnier' in Paris. The stunning neo-Baroque building was part of Baron Haussmann and Napoleon III's rationalization plan for Paris

## The Opera House, Paris

Between 1850 and 1870 Napoleon III transformed Paris from an unhealthy, overcrowded and sometimes squalid medieval city into a modern capital of calm, broad boulevards; of squares, markets, public parks and spectacular modern buildings. Influenced by the palaces of the French and Italian Renaissance the Neo-Baroque Opera House, designed by Charles Garnier, would soon become known as the 'Palais Garnier'. It was completed in 1874. Garnier's great staircase, encircled by balconies and highly visible from below, became the most fashionable place in Paris to see and be seen – particularly where the wide, sweeping marble stairs join in the centre in a 'Y' shape. It's the inspiration behind the famous Gaston Leroux novel *The Phantom of the Opera*. The idea for the novel came from an incident in 1896, when one of the chandelier's counterweights fell, killing the unfortunate person underneath.

The only European building to compete with it in terms of absurdist grandeur is the eye-popping Victor Emmanuel II Monument in Rome, designed in 1884 and commonly known as 'the wedding cake'.

# THE ARTS AND CRAFTS MOVEMENT

It was time for a new design hero. Ruskin's personal life was in ruins: his wife Effie Gray had long since left him for a happier life with his one-time protégé John Everett Millais. There had been an embarrassing scandal and divorce. Worse, the famous thinker and great mind was losing his reason. Much of his later life was spent in strict seclusion in the Lake District. For 12 years, his last, he did not speak. Luckily, a new – and truly forceful – voice was about to be heard.

**P**assionate, determined and an indefatigable writer, lecturer and campaigner, William Morris was the right man in the right place at the right time. A 19th-century eco-warrior – one of his last campaigns was to halt the felling of the magnificent hornbeams of Epping Forest – he combined the spirit of a true romantic with the energy of a demon. Like Ruskin, he was adamant that modern society had lost its way.

Never one to sit back and let others do the work, Morris was above all a 'doer'. As a sulky 17-year-old heir to a City-made fortune, he visited the Great Exhibition. When he found the British goods wanting, he decided to design them himself. He loathed excess, he hated fakery and he detested bad design and production, from the ugliness of false veneers to the crudeness of the Victorians' harsh aniline dyes.

The new romantic – 'Topsy' to his friends, because of his unruly mass of black curls – had 'rescued' his sombrely-beautiful wife Jane Burden from a life of poverty. In 1859 he commissioned a friend, Philip Webb, to design a house for him that encapsulated all that he loved about the simple, solid domestic architecture of the Middle Ages. That house was Red House (above).

It was a key experience for the young 'Topsy', who was closely connected with the Pre-Raphaelites and had tried being both architect and artist. He had finally found his metier – design. Morris, 'Janey' and his artist-architect friends decorated ceilings and wallcoverings and sewed tapestries. They created a comfortable, cottage-style garden to suit a house that was dignified but somehow cute, old-looking but somehow new. Topsy discovered that his muscular, highly original designs – often inspired by simple, natural motifs like leaves, snails or flowers, had

**ABOVE** Red House, in Bexleyheath south of London. A comforting and comfortable medievalism, the site was chosen because it was once on the pilgrim route to Canterbury

commercial potential. And so 'The Firm' – Morris, Marshall, Faulkner and Company – came into being.

Britain was paying a bitter price for its wealth, its rampaging industrial might, Morris argued. To recapture the wholeness of pre-industrial life, he reasoned, taking Ruskin's ideas one step further, then society must take beauty seriously. In Morris' Utopian world view, every individual should be allowed creativity and fulfilment in their work, as he had been. Craft is noble, he taught; beauty is crucial; simplicity is good. Technology must be kept at arm's length.

*'But now only let the arts beautify our labour, and be widely spread, intelligent, well understood both by the maker and by the user… and there will be pretty much an end of dull work and its wearing slavery.'*

To the end of his life, Morris would take joy in making carpets, wallpapers, fabrics, and furniture. No detail was too small: he painstakingly revived forgotten vegetable

183

**LEFT** H. Baillie Scott's outstanding Arts and Crafts house moved away from the heavy look of much Victorian design. Scott believed that good houses had a soul

**RIGHT** Strong but simple lines characterize Blackwell, Baillie Scott often relying on the natural aesthetic of the stone itself for visual effect

**ABOVE** Morris' emphatic decorative designs such as this tile series became world-famous. 'Have nothing in your house that you do not know to be useful, or believe to be beautiful,' he once said

printing and dyeing techniques for indigo blue and madder red. When business wore him down, he would take to the loom, and weave for relaxation.

'Lord bless us, how nice it will be,' he wrote to a friend, 'when I can get back to my little patterns and dyeing, and the dear warp and weft at Hammersmith.'

*You look in your history books to see who built Westminster Abbey, who built St Sophia at Constantinople,'* he said in a lecture at a working men's club in 1877. *'And they tell you Henry III, Justinian The Emperor. Did they? Or, rather, [was it] men like you and me, handicraftsmen, who have left no names behind them, nothing but their work?'*

Morris's business success was worldwide, although to the end of his life it vexed him that he could not really crack the conundrum: people on low incomes wanted to imitate upper-class elegance. Yet mass methods produced crass results. The sad thing for Morris was that for all his efforts, most of his own, high-quality goods were out of the reach of all but the wealthy.

Still, his passions would also be felt across the Atlantic, in the American Craftsman movement, and in both Russia and Germany. Morris' romantic pragmatism would evolve into the full-blown Arts and Crafts movement – which aimed to reunite the designer and the craftsman with the act of creation – and its more febrile cousin, the Aesthetic movement.

Other designers like Arthur Mackmurdo and Norman Shaw took to this plainer, somehow more contented, vision of craftsmen-like spaces. There were many interpretations of the style, but all put 'honesty' high on the agenda. C.F.A. Voysey adopted a design ethic that was direct, workmanlike, or as the critics would put it, 'vernacular'. A plain plank door, topped by glazed panels, was one of his trademarks (much imitated, becoming the standard American Craftsman door in the 20th century). Voysey's white rough rendered walls and horizontal ribbon windows have something in common with Frank Lloyd Wright's early houses. Other Arts and Crafts architects like M.H. Baillie Scott took historical tradition more seriously and used 'Old English' models. Blackwell, a Lake District house designed between 1898 and 1900, even has a minstrel's gallery.

Love and care are given to every detail, down to the doorknobs and the locks. Charles and Henry Greene's Gamble House in Pasadena, California, now a National Historic landmark, is a perfect example. Its furnishings, light fixtures, windows and landscaping were designed by the brothers themselves, and then made up by local craftspeople. The Tiffany glass doors – where a spreading oak tree reaches across all three doors and up to the transom lights – were an exception. They were made in Tiffany's studios by Emile Lang.

The key thing about Arts and Crafts houses is their democratic foundations. Like Red House, they don't aspire to be grand. But neither do they ignore tradition. They aspire to be practical, solid, warm, creative, happy spaces in which a family can grow and learn.

Although the level of the individualistic craft skills in Red House was still beyond the reach of most ordinary folk, through his writings, Morris prompted a building revolution. A rash of plain, comfortable houses with opened-out spaces set a new design standard of clarity and comfort.

The Arts and Crafts movement's values of simplicity and honest use of materials inspired a whole new way of thinking about design and architecture. The De Stijl group in Holland, and eventually the German Bauhaus, would be inspired by Morris. They would in due time take a different, more philosophical route through the design process. A radical restructuring of the aesthetic motives behind design would end up as Modernism. To paraphrase another famous thinker's phrase, William Morris had proved that 'less' could definitely be 'more'.

# Artistic Colonies

Other countries besides Britain were reacting against the excesses of 19th century revisionism and ornament. As president of the Moscow Architectural Society, Konstantin Bykovskii complained:

'*The romanticism that embraced Europe in the first half of our century counterposed to classicism a fascination with the Middle Ages... Instead of imitating classical styles, architects attempted to reproduce other styles previously rejected. It is essential to orient oneself in all this material, to find a guiding thread that will finally bring us out of empty eclecticism.*'

In America a rugged simplicity began to emerge as a national style, with the influence of architects like Frank Lloyd Wright, while in Russia and Germany colonies of artists went back to mine their folk traditions.

The Arts and Crafts movement in Russia was centred on industrialist Savva Mamontov's country estate, Abramtsevo. It was already a haven for artists and writers, and when Mamontov inherited a railway engineering fortune in 1870 he decided to extend it into an artist's colony. The fanciful 'Teremok' bathhouse, a log cabin with a trapezoid roof designed by Ivan Ropet, recalls the heavy pitched roofs of British figures like Edwin Lutyens and C. Voysey. In the church of the Icon of the Saviour, built as a group effort in 1880, the decorative detail that dominated much of the Russian Revival style has gone. The building's outlines are simpler and cleaner. The design itself was loosely inspired by medieval buildings from towns like Novgorod and Pskov, with exaggerated contours, carved limestone details and curved segmented windows. Ceramic strips crown the drum of the cupola. The artistic ideals of the community, along with the veneration of vernacular models, were worlds away from the mainstream Beaux Arts approach fashionable in St Petersburg.

The colony founded in 1898 at Matildenhohe, Darmstadt (now Germany) was the brainchild of Grand Duke Ernst Ludwig of Hesse-Darmstadt. He wanted to consolidate the political status of his tiny city-state and boost its economy. Part of his plan was to launch a German equivalent of the Arts and Crafts movement.

A grandson of Queen Victoria, Ludwig was a firm believer in William Morris' determined attempt to counter 'ugly' mass production, especially when it came to architecture, furnishings and interior design. For both men, good art and design belonged in the home, not just in the gallery.

**BELOW** Viennese radicalism: Olbrich's remarkable Secession building is anti-history, and showed the way towards expressionism. The building was for alternative forms of art

In the summer of 1899 Ludwig invited internationally renowned Austrian architect Joseph Maria Olbrich, artist and interior designer Peter Behrens, sculptors Ludwig Habich and Rudolf Bosselt, graphic artists Paul Burck and Hans Christiansen, and interior designer and jeweller Patriz Huber to become the colony's seven founder members. Olbrich, the eldest, was already famous for his 1897 'Sezession' building, the headquarters of the Vienna

Secessionist movement he had helped found two years previously. The others were recent graduates, eager to make the same kind of international mark.

They got their chance in 1900, at the Great Exhibition in Paris. This featured 'Darmstadt rooms' designed and equipped down to the last detail by the Magnificent Seven. Heavily influenced by *Jugendstil* (Youth Style), the more geometric Austro-German take on French Art Nouveau, the 'Darmstadt look' was a runaway success.

In May 1901, the Matildenhohe group put on a joint exhibition. Together with the main exhibition space, Ernst Ludwig House, the eight purpose-built, fully equipped Art Nouveau houses dazzled the thousands who flocked to see them. Although it was Olbrich who designed the exteriors and the overall site plan, the interior furnishing and fittings of each house were the work of a different group member.

Olbrich's slightly classicist take on the exuberant curvilinear and natural forms of French Art Nouveau became the European

**LEFT** The dramatic wedding tower for Ludwig at Darmstadt. The bands of windows carrying around the corners of the building were to be influential in Modernism

**BELOW** The artist's colony at Abramtsevo built in traditional Russian styles, the culmination of which was the tiny Church of the Saviour Not Made by Human Hand

rage. Suburban living could be safely adventurous and reassuringly chic. Darmstadt proved it. But Darmstadt's triumph was shortlived. Internal dissent arose when some of Olbrich's colleagues tried to escape his shadow, leading to the colony's dissolution in 1902. Only Olbrich and Huber remained.

For Peter Behrens, who had started out as a painter, designing and building his own home at Darmstadt was to be a major turning point. He gave up painting for a life in design and architecture. Working for German manufacturing giant AEG he became the world's first designer of a coherent corporate identity. His designs for factory buildings, clocks and even street lamps became world famous. Behrens went on to teach both Walter Gropius and Le Corbusier and it can be argued that the seeds of Modernism were sown in the clean, modern lines of Darmstadt and *Jugendstil*.

Ludwig replaced the 'defectors' with new artists, and the Matildenhohe colony continued to flourish. In 1905, Olbrich started work on what would become Darmstadt's signature building: the Wedding Tower. It was intended as a gift to Ludwig on the occasion of his second marriage. Olbrich died of leukaemia in early 1908 before the building was completed, but the exhibitions of 1904, 1908 and 1914 were more successful than ever.

The colony lasted 15 years and employed 23 members. But the First World War put paid both to Darmstadt and Art Nouveau. At the war's end Germany became a republic and Grand Duke Ludwig lost his throne. Although he lived in Darmstadt for the rest of his life, caring for wounded veterans, the dream he had brought to reality seemed forever lost.

Miraculously, while the centre of Darmstadt had suffered the same Allied carpet bombing in WWII that had destroyed so many other German conurbations, most of Matildenhohe's buildings survived. Only two of its houses were lost. However, it very nearly succumbed to years of neglect, not to mention Germany's post-World War Two obsession with wiping away built reminders of the past and replacing them with new 'forward-looking' architecture.

# Utopias and Garden Cities

*'There are in reality not only, as is so constantly assumed, two alternatives – town life and country life – but a third alternative, in which all the advantages of the most energetic and active town life, with all the beauty and delight of the country, may be secured in perfect combination. Human society and the beauty of nature are meant to be enjoyed together.'*

Ebenezer Howard, 1898

As 19th-century industrialization continued apace, speculative builders in major British cities like Manchester, Leeds and Birmingham took advantage of the desperate need for new housing. They packed houses close together in ugly monotonous rows, frequently without introducing water supplies or sanitation. Industrial cities were not just cramped and horrible places to live; they were also prey to bouts of cholera and other diseases. It became evident that what cities of this size and complexity really needed was planning. Thankfully for the workers, a few manufacturers were ahead of their time.

In Germany there was Alfred Krupp at Essen, while in England it was Sir Titus Salt in Yorkshire and Lord Leverhulme at Port Sunlight. Their ideal towns for their workers had well-designed houses with shops and amenities close to the factories. These were the pioneers of the 'new towns' and 'garden cities' of the 20th century.

With over 200 factory chimneys continually churning out black, sulphurous smoke, the city of Bradford was the most polluted town in England. Its sewage was dumped directly into the River Beck. With a population that had gone from 13,000 to 104,000 in the space of 50 years, there were regular outbreaks of typhoid and cholera and life expectancy dropped to 18 years, the lowest in the country. Only 30 per cent of children born to textile workers reached the age of 15.

In 1853 the wool baron Sir Titus Salt, who had unsuccessfully campaigned for Bradford council to clean up the city's pollution, moved his entire manufacturing business away from the slums to the fresh air of Shipley. Naming his new community

**RIGHT** A campanile in the country? Saltaire, a vision of a healthy and morally uplifting industrial village for 3,000 mill workers. The tower is modelled on Venice's campanile

'Saltaire', by joining together his own name with that of the nearby river, he commissioned the local architects Lockwood and Mawson to build neat stone houses for his workers in an Italianate style – 850 in all. Fresh water and gas lighting was available to each house, along with an outside lavatory. The communal wash-houses had running water, and the new town had what we would even now think of as luxurious facilities: a hospital, a concert hall, a clubhouse, a reading room. There was also a park and a boathouse, along with almshouses for the aged and infirm.

*'My recollections are of well cared for houses, neat curtains regularly washed, well swept yards and frontages, all gleaming with white and yellow stone.*

*And much swilling of pavements,'* recalled Bert Thornton, who was born at Shirley Street in 1917.

Salt's mill was the largest and most modern in Europe. Noise was reduced by placing much machinery underground and large flues removed dust and dirt from the factory floor. A low-emitting burner was fitted to the mill chimney. The six-storey spinning shed was modelled on the architecture of Osborne House, Queen Victoria's Isle of Wight residence and the mill itself was based on an Italian Palazzo.

Robert Owen had proved that a clean, healthy industrial environment and a content workforce could still mean a viable business venture. However, Titus Salt was the first British manufacturer

whose philanthropic vision combined good working conditions with a healthy, cultured environment and a good quality of architecture. When he died, an estimated 100,000 people lined the streets to say their goodbyes.

When, a few decades later, soap manufacturer William Hesketh Lever created 'Port Sunlight', a similar model village, it was truly squeaky clean. It was named for the company's biggest brand of cleaning powder. Lever summed up his feelings on the subject of worker housing in the following words:

'At the ballot box we are certainly all equal. Have we not equal rights to the beauties of this world, to enjoy beautiful homes and beautiful surroundings? Are these conditions only for the well-to-do? The well-do-do should be those who work, and the ill-to-do those who do not work.'

By 1888, the Arts and Crafts movement was in full swing and across Britain the middle classes were on the move. In search of fresh air and greener spaces they peopled newly-created suburbs with high-specification villas inspired by William

Morris' ideals. The new worker village in Cheshire would emulate these high standards with an often Flemish-influenced Arts and Crafts ethic. According to former employee Andrew Knox, in his autobiography *Coming Clean*:

'The houses were of a greatly varied but harmonious and pleasant architecture, built seven to the acre compared with the then officially permitted maximum of forty-five. They all had baths and a private lavatory, though neither was standard in buildings at the time.'

It was a labour of love. Lever was highly involved in the planning himself, but he used nearly 30 different architects to build 800 houses, thereby ensuring each was slightly different in character. He had really thought about the implications of creating an entirely new village and some of his decisions would be much-lauded today.

A mix of local and more specialist talent was used when it came to the architecture, for instance. While an untried (and therefore cheaper) Edwin Lutyens designed much of Cornice Road, black-and-

white half-timbering specialists Grayson & Ould were also there in the mix.

Lever told his villagers that improving Port Sunlight was an exercise in profit sharing – except that he was the one in charge of the purse.

'It would not do you much good if you send it down your throats in the forms of bottles of whisky, bags of sweets or fat geese at Christmas... If you leave the money with me, I shall use it to provide for you everything that makes life pleasant.'

Needless to say, rent for the comfortable housing was deducted direct from the workers' pay packets. When Lever had a magnificent art gallery built there in memory of his wife, it was in a patrician Neoclassical style, not the mock English vernacular of the tiny terraces. It stands there like Lady Bountiful at a village fête.

It's too easy, though, to dismiss the efforts of these pioneer philanthropists as simply paternalistic. When it came to the most revolutionary housing concept of them all, the Garden City movement, the first directors of the Garden City Association were Lever and the Quaker cocoa refiners Joseph Rowntree and Edward Cadbury, who had also set up model villages to house their workers. All three demonstrated a huge personal commitment to improving the lot of 'ordinary people'.

Rowntree's various charitable foundations help the poor to this day. In the case of Lever, he campaigned for housing reform across Britain. He had been true to his word. He organized artistic and literary events and he had a swimming pool, a theatre, schools, pubs and games rooms built. 'Old and young cheered him when he visited the village,' confirms Knox. And to workers whose expectations might have otherwise been the instant slums of coal-mining South Wales or the Manchester mills, the clean, well-planned environments must have seemed like Utopia.

The pioneering socialist Robert Owen

had blazed Salt's trail at the town of New Lanark, Scotland, way back in 1786. Carrying his ideas to the extreme, and across the Atlantic, in 1826 Owen tried to create a second 'New Harmony' in Indiana. His town design was based on a vast central square with mixed housing and factories stretching out into its centre, much like Ledoux's 1775 Royal Saltworks in France. Money was banned, together with other commodities. The community was a notable failure. But Owen didn't give up easily and in 1841 he proposed the development of similar 'self-supporting Home Colonies' in England.

In the 1890s, fired up by the writings of William Morris, the architects of the newly-created London County Council applied the Arts and Crafts style to one of the best inner-city housing developments ever built: the Boundary Estate in London's Shoreditch.

Garden City pioneers like Sir Ebenezer Howard and the architects Sir Raymond Unwin and Barry Parker took the idea of urban planning much further, with a balance of residential and factory areas, agricultural land, public buildings and

**ABOVE** Bedford Park in West London. Artists and writers flocked to the new suburban development. Traditional steep roofs and dormers, tall chimneys and larger windows typified the red brick style

**RIGHT** Hampstead Garden Suburb, a tightly-packed but still friendly and comfortable little village-like enclave in the middle of urban north London

parks. Unlike Owen's square form, their overall design was not based on a purely geometric grid but on a refined and simplified medieval outline. The whole idea was to make their towns feel as natural and unplanned as possible, while still building to meet modern needs: civic space; roads; easily-accessed working areas. The concept was genuinely Utopian. Largely inspired by Morris' anarcho-communist dreamscapes in *News From Nowhere* (1891), one overriding notion was the idea that a community should hold its land in common. It was to be held in a kind of perpetual trust for the lessees, so if the price of land went up then they were able to share in the benefits.

Remarkably, the Garden City became reality at Letchworth Garden City in 1903. The experiment was followed by Hampstead Garden Suburb in 1907 and a further development at Hellerau in Germany in 1909. Much of the modern 20th-century urban environment worldwide, along with the very notion of town planning, green belts, and zoning, began in this small Hertfordshire town. Architecturally, with Unwin and Parker at the helm, a stalwart, low-cost but individualistic architecture had been achieved: handsome but homely. But the success of this Arts and Crafts-inspired idiom in England is what would hold Modernism at bay for much of the early part of the next century.

# THE 20TH CENTURY

When it comes to architectural styles, the Modern
Age is a roller-coaster ride of movements and
counter-movements. No sooner had one style
emerged than it was knocked down for the next.
The long list of 20th-century styles ranges from
Art Nouveau to Brutalism, from Modernism
to Deconstructivism.

New York: who can fail to
recognize it? The skyline of
Midtown Manhattan owes
much of its distinctiveness to
the audacious Art Deco
Chrysler Building of 1928–1930

# TUG-OF-WAR

The 20th century was defined by astonishing technological change, delivered at astounding speed. Its breathless, roller-coaster architecture reflected the unremitting shock of the new. A bewildering succession of architectural styles flickered and flourished, extinguishing and replacing one another with unprecedented rapidity.

One way of making sense of these movements and counter-movements is to look at the century as a tug-of-war between two impulses: the ferocious New Puritan beast that became known as Modernism and the fight of the old guard to hang on to tradition. Another way is to see it as a war of attrition – between a radical minimalism and the human desire for colour, warmth and decoration.

It was an ultra-decorative style that began both the century and the backlash against tradition. Before Modernism gained the architectural upper hand, Art Nouveau, its antithesis and immediate precursor, briefly charmed the developed world with a butterfly-like explosion of effusive grace. Characterized by flowing and highly-stylized lines and mostly floral and plant-inspired motifs, Art Nouveau was a movement for total design: buildings, fittings, furniture and even subway systems fell under its hectic spell.

For a single movement, it has a bewildering variety of names. Called Jugendstil in Germany and Stile Floreale or Stile Liberty in Italy, after the London department store Liberty & Co., Art Nouveau quickly spread across Europe.

It found two of its most brilliant expressions in Belgium and in Britain, where Charles Rennie Mackintosh's slightly sterner version at the Glasgow School of Art left the city a lasting legacy.

In Brussels, the leading talent of the new movement was Baron Victor Horta, whose Maison du Peuple was the first Belgian structure to have an iron and glass façade. The movement may have been romantic in spirit, but it was also highly technological. His Hotel Solvay, with its graceful spaces and bravura decorative ironwork, summed up the

**RIGHT** The butterfly wings of Art Nouveau: Jules Lavirotte's 1900 front door for an apartment building on Avenue Rapp, Paris. He also designed the Elysées Ceramic Hotel on the Avenue de Wagram

# Key Dates

**1900** The Gare d'Orsay, now the Musée d'Orsay, built in Paris by Victor Laloux.

**1901** Peter Behrens' house at Darmstadt is completed.

**1903** Josef Hoffman finishes the Moser House, Vienna; first silent movie, *The Great Train Robbery*.

**1904** New York subway opens.

**1905** Frank Lloyd Wright designs the Unity Temple, Oak Park, Illinois; Einstein's Theory of Relativity.

**1907** Gaudí completes the Casa Batlló, Barcelona.

**1908** Adolf Loos publishes his essay 'Ornament and Crime'.

**1912** Sinking of the *Titanic.*

**1913** Cass Gilbert completes Woolworth Building, New York.

**1914** World War I begins.

**1915** Le Corbusier finishes designs for Domino Houses.

**1916** De Stijl movement is founded in Holland.

**1919** Walter Gropius founds the Bauhaus in Weimar, Germany.

**1920** Erich Mendelsohn's Einstein Tower in Potsdam, Germany completed.

**1923** Le Corbusier publishes *Vers une architecture*.

**1927** Mies van der Rohe designs the Barcelona Pavilion.

**1930** William van Alen completes the Chrysler Building.

**1931** The Empire State Building succeeds the Chrysler Building as the tallest skyscraper in the world.

**1933** The Nazis force the Bauhaus to close.

**1937** Frank Lloyd Wright finishes Fallingwater.

**1939** World War II begins.

**1949** Charles and Ray Eames build the Eames House, Pacific Palisades, California.

**1951** Mies van der Rohe's Lake Shore Drive Apartments, Chicago.

**1955** Le Corbusier finishes his Notre-Dame-du-Haut chapel at Ronchamp, France; Disneyland opens.

**1958** Mies van der Rohe and Philip Johnson's Seagram Building, New York.

**1960** Lucio Costa and Oscar Niemeyer design Brasilia, Brazil's new capital.

**1967** Geodesic dome designed by Buckminster Fuller for Expo 67, Montreal.

**1969** First man on the Moon.

**1970** Construction begins on Sears Tower, Chicago.

**1973** World Trade Center by Minoru Yamasaki opens, New York.

**1977** Frank Gehry redesigns his house in Santa Monica, California.

**1984** Philip Johnson's AT&T Building, New York.

**1986** Lloyd's Building designed by Richard Rogers opens in London.

**1989** World Wide Web created.

**1991** Stansted Airport by Sir Norman Foster completed.

**1997** Guggenheim Museum, Bilbao finished by Frank Gehry.

**1998** Petronas Twin Towers, Kuala Lumpur, designed by Cesar Pelli – the world's new tallest building.

**1999** Daniel Libeskind completes the Jewish Museum, Berlin.

**LEFT AND RIGHT** Street lamp, or space alien? Station entrance, or UFO? Hector Guimard's designs for the Paris Metro were highly idiosyncratic, and inspired by nature

**BELOW** Highly decorative glass was the flavour of the age: it filtered the light into increasingly intricate interiors

**LEFT** Art Nouveau was very taken with the human form and the human face. This extraordinary adaptation of a caryatid is in Riga, Latvia

**ABOVE** The column as stalk and tendril: the main stair at the first Art Nouveau building in the world, Victor Horta's lavish house for Emile Tassel, Brussels, 1893

**LEFT** The sumptuous staircase of the Treppenhaus, Riga, decorated in extraordinary detail. The house was owned by the artist Janis Rozental and his Finnish wife Elli

**RIGHT** At the turn of the century there was a building boom in Riga, out of which the *Jugendstil* emerged as a dominant style

grace of Art Nouveau. Horta's work embodies the term artistry: his architecture is all light and form, written in curves.

Spanish Art Nouveau was represented by the *Modernisme* movement, whose most significant – and visionary – practitioner was Antoni Gaudí (see p.196): his Casa Batlló in Barcelona (1905–7) is a superb example of his extraordinary and individualistic style.

In Prague, having already created a legacy of inimitable posters that would go on to adorn a million student walls, Alfons Mucha covered the Theatre of Fine Arts and the Mayor's Office at the Municipal House with extravagant, overflowing murals. Melbourne, which suddenly found itself the capital of Australia in 1901, embraced Art Nouveau for the Sports Depot, the Conservatory of Music, the Melba Hall and the City Baths.

The Russian art magazine *Mir iskusstva* (World of Art) championed Art Nouveau so well that its influence was felt as far as Riga, where no fewer than 800 buildings went up in the curvilinear style. For a brief three years or so, Art Nouveau was all-dominant in fashionable Moscow, where Lev Kekushev's Mindovsky House is now the New Zealand Embassy. But it is Hector Guimard's Métro entrances, which flowered on the bustling streets of turn-of-the-century Paris, that are among the best-known and loved examples of Art Nouveau today.

The zephyrs of change were about to reach gale force. In Russia, after the First Revolution of 1905, the style was dismissed as an irrelevance. As the shadow of the First World War crept ever closer, the death knell sounded for the delicate excesses of Art Nouveau. Forget flowers; forget this bourgeois frippery. The new century would throw away the past. It would be about one thing, and one thing only: 'Progress'.

## Hector Guimard

Hector Guimard's work is possibly one of the most famous sights in one of Europe's greatest cities. And yet you are unlikely to be told much about the man who, in 1900, created the remarkable Art Nouveau entrances to the Métro. Guimard's rather Baudelarian flash of genius was to reconcile the intimidating new underworld technology with the daylight world of nature – with extraordinary Triffid-like lamps and glass roofs supported by a forest of vegetation. The inventive Frenchman tried to standardize his remarkable moulded iron forms, in order to restrict the cost. Some entrances are fan-shaped, with enclosed glass pavilions protecting the crowds from the weather: other, simpler versions have ornate curved balustrades. When the Nazis invaded Paris, Guimard and his Jewish wife fled into exile. He died lonely, unrecognized and virtually penniless, in New York in 1942.

**BELOW** By contrast, in the USA, the Beaux-Arts style was in full swing. Grand Central Terminal in New York, was a triumph of planning and engineering

# Grand Central Terminal New York

Early 20th century America was a nation obsessed with the railroad. Only a country such as this could have produced not one, but two of the world's most perfect railway stations. And only a society fixated with the notion of 'progress' would then have tried to knock both of them down again. Grand Central Terminal, unlike its 1911 peer Pennsylvania Station, only survived demolition in the 1960s after a petition to the Supreme Court. The exterior is modest, but once inside, this is a place that takes your breath away. Some say it is the largest train station in the world: it has 44 platforms, with 67 tracks running alongside them.

The Beaux-Arts style, a form of classicism imported into the United States via Paris, advocated 'speaking architecture'. The station's cathedral-like, monumental concourse is a homage to travel. A barrel-vaulted ceiling slopes down to giant arched windows that create wide arcs of streaming natural light from on high: the sense of drama and excitement is palpable. The central globe clock, its four faces made from pure opal worth some $20m, must be the most famous meeting place in the world. In 1947, over 65 million people, 40 per cent of the population of the United States, travelled through Grand Central Station. Today it averages 500,000 visitors a day.

The name Grand Central Terminal replaced Grand Central Station in 1913, but many still use the original term.

# Antoni Gaudí (1852–1926)

*'Gaudí is the most significant artist of Art Nouveau... the only genius that this movement has really produced.'*

Nikolaus Pevsner,
*Pioneers of Modern Design*

Antoni Gaudí is a mysterious figure in the history of architecture, mainly because his work defies any absolute categorization. When he left Barcelona's Higher School of Architecture the principal, Elies Rogent, wondered aloud: 'I don't know whether we have given the qualification to a madman or a genius.'

As a young man, Gaudí saw medievalism as the true route to follow. His work reflects this, for in it the ideals of William Morris meet Art Nouveau – via what can only be described as the mystical. Gaudí's buildings also seem to possess a God-given ability to defy the laws of gravity. They bring hundreds of thousands of tourists to the great Catalan city of Barcelona, where his most famous projects include the Palau Güell, the remarkable, mountain-like Casa Milà, now a World Heritage Site, and the astonishing Sagrada Família, still unfinished to this day.

Pass by Casa Batlló (1905–7) on the top

**LEFT** Casa Batlló, Gaudí's most obviously Art Nouveau building. The original local name for it was 'the house of bones', and it does have a strong skeletal quality

**FAR LEFT** The dramatic shape of Barcelona's great, unfinished Catholic cathedral, the Sagrada, covered with astonishing, almost surrealistic, sculpture

**BELOW** The scaly, undulating roof of Casa Batlló. Ceramic tiling has a long heritage in Spanish architecture and, in this at least, Gaudi was following tradition

**ABOVE** The forms are more convoluted, but in some ways the Sagrada Família's ceiling is reminiscent of medieval fan vaults. Gaudi composed these forms using fractal geometry

Gaudí has managed to transform these elements into something else – the bones of a building that almost seems alive. His deliberately organic structure becomes a witty homage to palaeontology and the sacred power of Nature.

What is surprising is that 19th century Barcelona was so forward-thinking as to commission architecture this unsettling, this revolutionary. Perhaps it is because Gaudí's style manages to be both avant-garde and traditional, referring back as it does to Spanish Plateresque and North African vernacular. His Parc Güell (1900–14) is dream-like, bordering on the surreal, and would not look out of place in a painting by Salvador Dalí. There are also strong Expressionist elements to his work. Gaudí's buildings are often loosely described as 'organic', a term that Einstein would one day use when he described the Potsdam Tower to the young Erich Mendelsohn.

Was Gaudí actually responding to the theories of Charles Darwin in his remarkable buildings? The son of sons and daughters of coppersmiths, Gaudí suffered from rheumatism as a child. He spent much time on his own. His twin obsessions were Geometry and Nature: instead of going to class, he preferred to stare at the sea. Beautiful drawings of minute sea organisms and protozoa by the great biologist and Darwinian thinker Ernst Haeckel were first published at that time, and it seems reasonable to think they were an influence. The bell towers of the Sagrada look as much like a bell-shaped sea creature as a flower. Peepholes at the Casa Calvert are exactly like the strange sea protozoa Haeckel named 'radiolarians'.

The Casa Milà, where the apartments look like tumble-down cave dwellings carved out of rock, is known locally as 'La Pedrera', or the stone quarry, because it looks so elemental. As the young Gaudí reasoned in his diary:

*'Nature does not produce anything that is monochrome or uniform in colour; neither vegetation nor in geology, nor in topography nor in the animal kingdom. We are obliged to colour an architectural piece – colouring that will perhaps disappear when the hand of time gives it another colour that is more befitting and precise for something old.'*

deck of a double-decker bus and instead of a red-tiled roof-line, as you would expect, you see a colourful dinosaur spine sweeping down from the sky. The town house's extraordinary balconies resemble skulls; its pillars are not unlike bones. At street level, the stone masonry undulates unmistakably like a dinosaur's skeleton. Yet

If any of Gaudí's buildings are a riposte to Darwin, then it's the Temple de la Sagrada Família. It will show, said Gaudí, 'the religious realities of present and future life... man's origin, his end'.

Still the subject of huge controversy within Spain, the story of the Sagrada is an astonishing one. The interior will one day be a sculpted forest, with porphyry columns and spreading stone leaves inspired by the city's glorious plane trees. Each façade is uniquely sculpted: the unfinished south façade, the Gloria, will be the building's high point. Begun in 1882, it is hoped that the Sagrada will be completed in 2026. Gaudí used to joke: 'My client is not in a hurry.'

Described by George Orwell as 'one of the most hideous buildings in the world', the Temple has had a chequered history. In the 1930s Spanish Civil War anarchists destroyed all the plans and models by burning down the workshops and the crypt. Work didn't start again until the 1950s, to renewed controversy. Should it be left incomplete, as a mute homage to Gaudí? Or did the architect intend this to be, like Cologne Cathedral, a project built on by successive generations?

With the original plans lost, Barcelona will have to complete much of this masterpiece by instinct and guesswork. This is causing yet more argument – as has the decision to use modern techniques and computer-aided design. Arguments rage over whether Gaudí's original design or a more modest version should complete the whole. More recently, the Spanish Government announced that a high-speed train tunnel will be built directly underneath the principal façade, to howls of protest.

Almost as dedicated a nationalist as he was a fervent Christian, the architect was determined that this church should be for the ordinary Catalan people. Stonecutters, their wives and girlfriends, and most of the residents of the nearby 'people's quarter' were photographed and cast, becoming forever part of the façade. King Solomon was modelled on an eccentric local ragman, who was well known for shouting out in the streets in Latin: *'Ipso facto: Amicus Plato sed magis amica veritas!'*

FAR LEFT The Guell park in Barcelona

LEFT The Astorga episcopal palace, León

RIGHT A celebration of the glories of nature: the Sagrada's Nativity façade, the first finished, celebrates the Christian principles of faith, hope and charity

(It is obvious: to me Plato is dear, but truth is dearer still!).

To illustrate the traumatic biblical tale of the Massacre of the Innocents, casts of babies were made from still-born infants at the Santa Cruz hospital, where the director was one of Gaudí's friends. For the Roman soldier he found a tavern waiter, whose features and six-foot body were perfect because he was from the ancient Roman colony of Tarragona. As they dressed the waiter's feet in Roman-style sandals, they discovered he had six toes on each foot. Gaudí's principal sculptor, Juan Matamala, wanted to hide them. 'No!,' Gaudí is said to have exclaimed. 'It is absolutely necessary to have them the way they are! It is an anomaly – just as it is to kill young children.' One wonders what the poor waiter thought of it all.

The young photographer on the project, Ricardo Opisso, was traumatized: he would be used as a photographer one day and on the next be cast as a 'herald angel'. On one occasion, Opisso recalled glumly: 'I became the executioner of all those birds on the façade.' The birds were given chloroform, then the photographer had to fan their wings out prettily and deliver them to the sculptors' workshop.

The last 12 years of Gaudí's life were devoted entirely to the Sagrada: it was his obsession. When the money ran out he went from door to door to collect subscriptions so that he could continue his beloved creation.

In 1926, the great architect was run over by a tram on the Gran Via as he went to 'say a few words to Mary'. He was 74. All that was found in his worn-out jacket, which was held together with pins, were a few hazelnuts, a piece of paper and a Gospel. As a young man he had inhabited high society: now, he was mistaken for a tramp and was taken to a pauper's hospital. He died three days later. But his legacy has made Barcelona a vital stopover on any Grand Tour of the world's greatest – and most emotive – architecture.

LEFT Detail of the colourful trencadis, a Catalan type of mosaic, on the 'dragon' roof at Casa Batlló. The cross is said to symbolize St George killing the dragon

# America Reaches for the Sky

*'A skyscraper is a boast in glass and steel.'*

Mason Cooley

Can you measure a man's ego by the size of building he puts up? In the 'Roaring Twenties' architects William Van Alen and H. Craig Severance were commissioned to design a towering building at 40 Wall Street, in Manhattan's financial district.

In 1928 Van Alen left the partnership amid much bitterness. He took his dramatic blueprint uptown, to design a new skyscraper, one that would fulfil even a millionaire's most self-aggrandizing dreams. The bullish Walter Chrysler, the self-made head of the motor car manufacturer Chrysler, accepted Van Alen's plans and began to work with him on the designs, with glee. They started to build on New York's Lexington Avenue, refusing to tell anyone the height of the new 'scraper. What followed was a dog-eat-dog race – to build the tallest building in the world.

Severance hatched a secret plan to add a lantern and a flagpole to 40 Wall Street. When Chrysler found out, he had Van Alen build the entire stainless steel spire destined for the Chrysler Building in secret in the elevator shaft, the stainless steel cladding hidden in five separate pieces. Once Severance's tower reached completion in November 1929, he hoisted up his own 185-foot (56m) spire and riveted it into place in just one and a half hours.

When it comes to building high, supremacy can be shortlived. Chrysler's Art Deco masterpiece was 1,046 feet (319m) high when it topped out, a statistic he could no longer keep under his trilby. But the very next year John Jacob Raskov of General Motors set out to trump Chrysler with the Empire State Building on Fifth Avenue. Taking unfair advantage of hindsight, Raskob had added an extra 17 stories to his original plan. He then stuck a 'hat' on top of his structure, including a dirigible mooring mast, so that the whole lot came in at 1,250 feet (381m). Perhaps the view from the top looked sweet to Raskob – with Chrysler's building 200 feet below him. But at least Van Alen and

Chrysler had had their year in the sun. Poor old 40 Wall Street, languishing far below its rivals, was the world's tallest building for little more than 90 minutes.

Until then, the tallest man-made structures in the world had been the great European cathedrals like Lincoln and Rouen, joined in 1889 by The Eiffel Tower. It was a new technique for mass producing steel – the Bessemer process, which converted pig-iron into steel by sending air through molten iron – that changed the game for good. When William Le Baron Jenney designed the 10-storey Home Insurance Building in Chicago in 1883–5, he used the new stronger and lighter material. Suddenly, the only way was up.

With land prices rising along with the demand for office and business space, the skyscraper was the obvious move. And if you had to choose one single phrase to sum up 20th-century design history, it would be the brief, but punchy: 'form follows function'. A young man who had worked with Jenney, Louis Sullivan, came up with that dictum – and was the first to develop an aesthetic for this radical new building form. A great writer and theorist, Sullivan was working a short 30 years after Charles Darwin published *On the Origin of Species*. Architectural form should also evolve organically, he felt. It should follow need, and adapt free from any allegiance to historic styles. Architects should clear their minds, and begin more or less from scratch. Sullivan's elegant 13-storey Guaranty Building in Buffalo (1894) combined rich detailing with the illusion of really soaring height: its lush façade is ornamented with plants that themselves seem to be evolving and mutating.

But the Chicago School was soon to be outgunned. Manhattan Island, built on solid granite and therefore perfect for high-rise, was expanding rapidly as a commercial and financial centre. Industrialists were flocking to the centre to share in its success, and land prices were shooting up as a result. The buildings soared ever higher, creating probably the most famous skyline in the modern world. Skyscrapers were a triumph over nature. For the first time, the United States had

**ABOVE** The Art Deco Chrysler, instantly recognizable. The corners are ornamented with replicas of the 1929 Chrysler radiator caps: the 'gargoyle' eagles of the 61st floor once graced the Chrysler hood

produced an architecture that could truly be called American.

The scrapers' deeply symbolic nature, meanwhile, was not lost on industrialists. The Chrysler Building was conceived as a gigantic mega-advertisement. Unlike any building before, it deployed imagery straight from the Art Deco consumerist catalogue. New York's building regulations asked for 'step-backs' to allow the sun to reach the streets far below. Van Alen had taken those zoning restrictions to a sculptural conclusion, creating the world's most rakish, ziggurat-style spire, with a sunburst pattern at the top. The building frame had stainless steel and aluminium symbolic 'need for speed' decoration, in

**ABOVE** The Empire State Building was the world's tallest building from 1931 to 1972

**ABOVE** New York's Twin Towers. The World Trade Center was the world's tallest building from 1972 to 1973. The terrible shock of 9/11 does not seem to have put the world off building skyscrapers

the form of 'hub cap' detailing and streamlined fins. At various points, metallic eagle 'gargoyles' protrude at the corners; at others, the wings of the 1926-model Chrysler radiator caps. It was architecture as brand. The interior was Egyptian, with lotus flower motifs everywhere, following the contemporary craze for Tutankhamun.

The skyscraper was also a place where miracles could happen. Iconic status was guaranteed even before King Kong apehandled Fay Wray around the Empire State Building. In 1945, a B-25 bomber, lost in fog, ploughed into it. Thirteen people died, but to great media excitement, the building stayed up. The new nation had produced certain proof of

its technological prowess. It was official: America was on top.

The World Trade Center, built 1966–73, was a revolutionary step forward in skyscraper design. To resist wind forces, many skyscrapers have a stiff core, cross walls and a braced outer skin, allowing the building to move slightly. The twin towers – again, the world's tallest – of the World Trade Center took this a stage further. Cages of steel columns, spaced just over a yard apart – so-called 'tubes' – took the gravity and wind loading. A state-of-the-art damping system, 11,000 of these in each building, helped minimize the wind's effect.

Yet what was most important about the WTC was neither its technology nor the

fact that architect Minoru Yamasaki's inspired space planning freed up 75 per cent of the floor area as rentable space, when the norm at the time was 62. It was its symbolic resonance. 1961, the year the design was announced, was also the year John F. Kennedy declared that America was planning to land a man on the moon.

Yamasaki idealistically declared: 'World trade means world peace... The World Trade Center is a living symbol of man's dedication to world peace.'

Built by the famous Rockefeller family, the Twin Towers could not escape the politics out of which they were born. Originally conceived as an economic tool to regenerate Lower Manhattan, they were recognizable all over the world: a symbol that said: 'America rules'. In the optimistic 1960s, American technological exhibitionism could not be escaped. And for a while, they were the tallest buildings on earth.

The towers were a triumph over nature, dominating the skyline in the same way that American military might would dominate world politics. Not everyone was pleased: the critic Lewis Mumford complained that the new generation of skyscrapers were: 'just glass-and-metal filing cabinets'. At the opening press conference the architect was asked: 'Why two 110-storey buildings? Why not one 220-storey building?' 'I didn't want to lose the human scale,' Yamasaki joked. The whole complex had 13.4 million square feet (1.24 million square metres) of office space. Ironically, Yamasaki himself was scared of heights.

On 11 September 2001, before the eyes of a shocked world, the extreme Islamist group al-Qaeda used two of the proudest technological achievements of the United States – the skyscraper and the aeroplane – against it. The natural forces of fire, gravity and momentum became murderous weapons: skyscrapers would never be viewed in the same way again.

If architecture is politics made form, then these vast buildings ultimately encapsulated the hubris and vulnerability of the West. But the empire is striking back: the 'Freedom Tower' will be 1,776 feet (541m) tall. The height was chosen to symbolize the year of American Independence.

# FORM AND FUNCTION

It may be true that while failure is an orphan, success has many fathers. But if one man can be said to have launched the new architectural wave, it was the American architect Louis Sullivan. In late 19th-century Chicago, technology, taste and economic forces collided to yield a new imperative.

A demand for new office space and factories in which large numbers of people could work efficiently in concert – at least, that was the theory – coincided with advances in steel and constructional technology. Suddenly it was possible to build high – really high. Dubbed 'the father of modernism', many credit Sullivan, a brilliant draughtsman and an ingenious designer, with the creation of the modern skyscraper. He certainly coined the famous aphorism 'form follows function'. By this he meant that the shape of a building or an object should be dictated by its intended purpose. That doesn't mean that they weren't decorative, though. Sullivan's buildings were urbane and elegant, often highly decorative. His Carson Scott Pirie store, Chicago, with its

lavish ironwork, and his Wainwright Building had restrained overtones of Art Nouveau.

'Form follows function' became the overriding credo of the new century. The aesthetics of a design, whether it was a teapot or a building, should be stripped down to its basic function. The idea was to be applied to architecture with what some came to feel was oppressive rigour.

As the new century climbed to its feet, the big debate was how architecture could meet the demands of the machine age. In a Europe that had seen millions die in the chaos and mud of the Western Front, both the war and the revolution in Russia were powerful catalysts. There was a widespread appetite for a new, rational sense of order.

The image of the machine set the public imagination on fire. The Modernists celebrated industrial artefacts like the car, the factory, the train or the ship. They were beautiful examples of plain, simple design integrity: things that worked, things that spoke of progress. The gleaming promise of the machine was soon transformed into a model for the new and positive future the world so desperately desired.

# NEW ARCHITECTURE

In 1900, mass production of the automobile had just begun. Most people lived and died within 30 miles of their place of birth. In Europe, only Finland allowed women the vote. But after 70 years of breathtaking advance in the new century, man would even walk on the moon.

**E**verything was on the move. Ever-faster steamships now shrank the oceans. Most magical of all was the fact that mankind's oldest fantasy had become reality – in 1911 the Wright Brothers took to the air. Humans could fly. Modernity meant change, but how should architecture respond? The Modernists were unhappy about working within a society that constantly looked over its shoulder to the past. Historicism hadn't yet solved society's problems and the avant-garde saw no reason why it would now. Many were also disgusted by what they saw as the excesses of Art Nouveau. It is worth remembering that ever since the Renaissance Western architecture had been locked into nostalgia, in one way or another. The mightiest monuments, from St Peter's Basilica in Rome to France's Palace of Versailles, still looked back to the supposed glories of former civilizations. In 1908, in a complete break with history, the Austrian architect Alfred Loos denounced all ornament as a 'crime'.

By contrast, the ideal of the machine meant moral virtue: honesty, simplicity and purity. The work of engineers like the American Albert Kahn (1869–1942), who had built hundreds of industrial assembly plants according to rational, ordered principles, showed the way forward. In Detroit Kahn had pioneered a new style of construction, where reinforced concrete replaced wood in factory walls, roofs and supports. This gave better fire protection and allowed large volumes of unobstructed interior. Ford's famous Model T assembly line had been perfected in a Kahn building, in 1909. So why not think big, think industrial? In 1923, the architect Le Corbusier made the new mechanistic priorities plain, saying: 'To create architecture is to put in order. Put what in order? Function and objects.'

In Europe, the seeds of dissent had already been sown by the iron masters of the 19th century. Gustave Eiffel may have been accused of crimes against aesthetics, but at least no-one could criticize his Eiffel Tower for being old-fashioned. From the beginning of the 20th century the architectural avant-garde decided to cut the ties with the past – forever.

After the 'covered chairleg' morality of the Victorian age, this was to be a time of true reforming, puritan zeal. The new utilitarian socialists of the Modern movement were in a sense the intellectual heirs to Morris and Ruskin. However, in the name of the machine, and of mass production, they would lay siege to craft ideals. The stylistic debate, like a clash of the Titans, was conducted well over the heads of most ordinary folk, but all this talking, thinking and theorizing was done in their name. Interspersed with the catastrophic

**LEFT** Kahn developed a new style of construction with reinforced concrete replacing wood in factory walls, roofs and supports. Factory man Henry Ford became interested

**BELOW** Albert Kahn was one of the new wave of German immigrants to America. This is his neo-Gothic Maccabees Building in Detroit

effects of two world wars, the new philosophies would eventually lead to a refocusing of architecture on to ordinary people, particularly their housing. Design needed to become democratic. What did society really *need*?

The architect, painter and sculptor Le Corbusier was to be the high priest of the new Modernism. Born in Switzerland, Charles Édouard Jeanneret adopted the name 'Le Corbusier', an abbreviated form of his grandfather's surname, in response to a short vogue in Paris. The name would become famous worldwide.

Le Corbusier wanted to change society's attitude towards design and aim for a new way of life. He believed that architecture could transform society.

*'Space and light and order. Those are the things that men need just as much as they need bread or a place to sleep'.*

Sunlight, fresh air and contact with nature were all at a premium. Continuing in a long line of theorists since Vitruvius and Leonardo da Vinci, Le Corbusier also placed a huge emphasis on grace and proportion in building,

devising his own system based on the golden ratio, the Fibonacci sequence and human measurements. He called it the Modulor, describing it as a 'range of harmonious measurements to suit the human scale, universally applicable to architecture and to mechanical things'.

With Le Corbusier at the stylistic helm the defining characteristics of Modernism would be simplicity, with opened-out interior spaces and mainly angular forms and, at least early on, a preoccupation with creating structures that were visually light. New materials, and techniques that included cantilever construction, helped make all that possible.

After working in the offices of the French architect Auguste Perret, a pioneer in using reinforced concrete, and Peter Behrens, a German who admired the engineer's ethic of mass production, logical design, and function over style, Corbusier produced the 'Maison Dom-Ino' plan of 1915. This concept was for a house that would be made of reinforced concrete and could therefore be mass produced. But it was also flexible: none of the internal walls were load-bearing, and so the interior could be changed by whoever lived in it.

The message was that architecture could be as efficient as a factory assembly line and so would solve the chronic housing problems of industrialized cities. Soon, Le Corbusier was developing ideas for standardized housing types like the Maison Citrohan, which was built and sponsored by the French car manufacturer.

The play on words is suggesting that the building industry should adopt the methods of the mass production automobile industry. Corbusier's 1923 book *Vers une architecture* (Towards an Architecture) is an impassioned manifesto. 'A house', Le Corbusier declared, 'is a machine for living in.'

Many people have interpreted Corbusier's love of the machine aesthetic as proof that he despised all things natural. The reverse is true: one of his 'five points of architecture' was to replace the footprint of the building with a garden on the roof. Convinced that a rationally planned city could be much better than the *ad hoc* 19th-century model, where the

**BELOW** Alvar Aalto's Finlandia Hall in Helsinki. Although it is a beautiful space, there were practical problems, including the Carrara marble cladding curving in the Finnish climate

ABOVE Spirit of the landscape: Corbusier's Notre-Dame-du-Haut takes its cue from the nearby Jura mountains. The upturned roof is concrete

poor lived in cramped, unnatural squalor, Le Corbusier was determined that his architecture would reintroduce nature and a healthy way of living into people's lives. The way of gaining the space to make gardens and parks was to build 'streets in the sky'.

Corbusier's first grand urban planning idea was the Ville Contemporaine of 1922. This proposed city of three million people would be divided into functional zones: 24 glass towers in the centre would form the commercial district, which would be separated from the industrial and residential areas by expansive green belts. Three years later he proposed pulling down large tracts of Paris, virtually the entire north bank of the Seine, to incorporate a mini version of the Ville Contemporaine. At the centre of the plan were hulking great 60-storey, cruciform skyscrapers built on steel frames and encased in huge curtain walls of glass. They would have a mix of offices and apartments (for the

rich) and be set within large, rectangular park-like green spaces. At the very centre was a huge transportation hub, which on different levels included depots for buses and trains, as well as highway intersections and, at the top, an airport. A pretty dotty scheme, and understandably, one that was ignored. More realistic was the Ville Radieuse, a scheme first published in 1933 to rehouse families from crumbling slums into clean, modern apartments. It was a happy Utopian vision in which long slab blocks were built on stilts in parkland: roads were raised, the pedestrian was all. A practical interpretation of these ideas was built at Roehampton in the United Kingdom in 1952, when Modernism became the official architecture of the British state.

By the 1930s, Le Corbusier was experimenting with glass curtain walls – most famously at the Salvation Army hostel in Paris (1933). The results, as so often with Le Corbusier, were less than perfect. 'The south-facing glass facade,' Matt Tyrnauer later reported for the magazine *Vanity Fair*, 'turned the un-air-conditioned dormitory into an *avant garde* toaster oven.'

## Be Different

The rigours of Modernism were not for everyone. In the 1920s United States, Albert Kahn, designer of the much-admired Ford Glass Plant in Dearborn (see p.203), dubbed Le Corbusier's work 'utterly stupid'. Architects who embraced the traditional Beaux-Arts type of classicism felt that a rigid language of white walls and flat roofs, large glass surfaces and horizontal windows was not enough. They also believed in a hierarchy of building types, with ceremonial or symbolic buildings being the most significant. In their view, different languages were needed to express different functions – and let's face it, to avoid being repetitive.

When it came to housing, British architects like Sir Edwin Lutyens were still designing Neo-Georgian or Arts and Crafts movement-inspired houses for those who could afford it. On the other hand, architects in the United States, like William Wurster with his Clark Beach House in Aptos, California, began exploring a new regionalism. The inspired Finn Alvar Aalto would do the same with his part-Modernist, part-vernacular house on the rim of a pine forest, the Villa Mairea in Noormarkku.

# Le Corbusier (1887–1965)

**BELOW AND RIGHT** The Villa Savoye internal spiral stair and main façade. Spare, beautiful, but impossible to live in

*'You employ stone, wood, concrete and with these materials you build houses and palaces. This is construction. Ingenuity is at work. But suddenly you touch my heart, you do me good. I am happy and I say: "This is beautiful". That is Architecture. Art enters in.'*

Charles Édouard Jeanneret (Le Corbusier)

Le Corbusier, the high priest of the Modern movement, is a troubling figure. We know he was an idealist. We also know he was an ardent self-publicist: one of the first architects to manipulate the media. He spent decades devoted to the ideals of creating and planning perfect modern housing and the perfect modern city. And he genuinely wanted to improve the lot of the ordinary man, woman and child by giving them affordable places to live that worked – efficiently – in a totally new way. Yet his work and ideas inspired brutal housing estates, where people could live and die alone and scared, never knowing the people who lived a few feet away.

Born in the Swiss Jura mountains, Charles Édouard Jeanneret worked all over the globe. He was destined to become one of the most famous and influential of a long line of architectural theoreticians that stretched back to Vitruvius. In his book *Vers une architecture* in 1923, he averred that 'a

house is a machine for living in'; just one of the phrases that have perplexed future generations of architects. The point, though, was that he was arguing not for a machine-like house, but rather for a truly efficient one. His worldwide reputation was immense: his dictum was 'Architecture – or Revolution'.

Jeanneret took the name Le Corbusier as a professional gambit. In practice, it was often abbreviated to 'Corbu', which in French means 'raven'. It well suited a man who, priest-like, invariably wore black suits and heavy, black-framed spectacles. This

artist–visionary would define a new language for architecture and, in time, a whole new dogma for cities. That language would celebrate, if not deify, technology.

His early structures reflected the play of light against simple geometric shapes: cones, pyramids and, particularly, rectangular planes. And as with any language, there were rules. Corbusier believed that a house should be supported on pillars in order to open up the ground underneath it. Façades should be unornamented and sculptural, with long window strips. When newly built, his houses were immaculate, beautiful and, depending on your point of view, either remotely stern or uniquely spiritual.

Open plan, with clear spaces and four strip windows as the only perforations in the façade, the Villa Savoye, for instance, is stubbornly simple. It was finished in 1929 and yet it still looks like a glamorous set for an expensive lifestyle commercial. Supported on implausibly slender pillars, the house is topped by a structure that could at first sight be a gas tower or the funnel of a steamship. A ramp leads up to the solarium, a bare sensual curve. The shapes allude to Cubism, to machines and steamship funnels, to classicism and to Roman courtyards. On the first floor the terrace is so large, the rooms so extensively glazed, that it is difficult to distinguish between interior and exterior. Yet the bedrooms are cramped.

From the moment you open the steel-framed front door, all is cleanliness and hygiene: a basin invites you to cleanse yourself of the outside world. 'What [modern man] wants is a monk's cell, well lit and well heated, with a corner from which he can look at the stars,' Corbusier said.

Yet the story of the Villa as a family home is a comic one. Corbusier was reluctant to allow the Savoyes any furniture – Madame was banned from introducing comfy sofas – and, more or less from day one, it leaked.

Le Corbusier had insisted, despite the Savoyes' misgivings, that his 'machine for living in' should have a flat roof, not a

pitched one. When it rained within a few days of the family moving in, young Roger Savoye's bedroom was inundated. He caught pneumonia – and had to spend a year recuperating in a Swiss sanatorium. Corbusier received a feverish letter from Mme Savoye six years later.

*'It's raining in the hall, it's raining on the ramp, and... what's more it's still raining in my bathroom, which floods in bad weather, as the water comes in through the skylight.'*

The architect promised to fix it, and consoled the perennially-damp Madame Savoye with the hardly reassuring fact that architectural critics the world over had praised her house.

During the war years, to his great shame, Le Corbusier collaborated with the Vichy regime. Like many architects in wartime he was mainly restricted to theorizing and took the opportunity to develop radical ideas on urban planning. In 1946, he was given a commission to design a 'vertical community' in Marseilles called the Unité d'habitation. Nearly 2,000 people were housed in 23 different types of split-level apartment, sharing internal streets, shops, a school and nursery, a crèche, a gym and an open-air theatre. It was 1952, and this, surely, was the brave new world. Today, it is popular with Marseilles' middle-classes, who are keen on facilities like the on-site swimming pool. There is, however, a very fast turnover.

Later buildings, like the soaring pilgrimage church of Notre-Dame-du-Haut,

Ronchamp (1950–4), illustrate the way Corbusier's work became increasingly spiritual. With his wife dead, he lived a monastic life between a small Paris apartment and a holiday home on the Mediterranean. On 27 August 1965, at the age of 78, Le Corbusier went for a swim against doctor's orders – and just kept on swimming towards the sunset. Bathers found his body the next morning.

His death rites were extraordinary. They were directed by author and French culture minister André Malraux from the heart of Paris, the courtyard of the Louvre. Homages came from every corner of the world. A Japanese TV channel broadcast the ceremony live and even one of Corbu's worst enemies, Salvador Dali, sent flowers. The Soviet Union sent an official tribute, as did US president, Lyndon B. Johnson. The Soviet message read: 'Modern architecture has lost its greatest master.'

**LEFT** The open deck on top of the Villa Savoye was intended as a space for exercise, although it could also be used for sunlounging. To the right is a funnel which gives you the feeling of being on a boat

**RIGHT** The Unité, meaning 'unit', in Marseilles. Corbusier called this the Cité Radieuse, or 'Radiant City'. The term the locals use for it translates as 'The Lunatic's House'

# ART DECO

The Modernist movement didn't quite sweep all before it. Colour – and riotous levels of decoration – were about to stage a comeback. Art Deco, Nouveau's sister movement and one of the world's most intense stylistic love affairs, would be just as flamboyant, but somehow more sassy.

**A** passion for things exotic was flooding through Europe, and particularly France, as the cultural elite discovered the art of Africa and Japan. Then came Egypt fever. On February 16 1923 the archaeologist Howard Carter got his first glimpse of the sarcophagus of Tutankhamun, in the Valley of the Kings. The world was plunged into total 'Tutmania'. As the 'Tutankhamun Rag' played out from the ballroom of the Winter Palace Hotel in Luxor, and the Folies Bergère began a titillating stage tableau called 'The Pleasures of the Nile', businessmen rushed to patent the names 'Tut', 'Ankh' and even 'Tut-tut'.

'Tomb Vogue Will Prolong Bobbed Hair', wrote the *New York Times* breathlessly. For a world depressed by the effects of war, Art Deco and its exotic imagery was like a permanent visual holiday. The sunburst motif became an Art Deco standard, used on the toes of shoes, on car radiator grilles, in the auditorium of the largest movie theatre in the world, New York's Radio City Music Hall, and most famously on the spire of the Chrysler Building. Materials like metal and glass, and the sharp angles that went with them, merged with a happy sense of decadence.

Also part of the alphabet were references to electrification and mechanization. Deco's sweeping motifs are bolder and brasher than the complex organic curves of Art Nouveau. Flat, geometric decoration was everywhere – along with a visual repertoire of frozen fountains, sunbursts, zigzags, and above all, colour. Buildings used stepped forms – the ziggurats of the Aztecs – and chevron patterns and the public languished in a fantasy world peopled with slave girls and unheard-of luxury, far away from the horrors of war.

Racy, luxurious and 'fast', Art Deco seemed to sum up a new spirit of youth and liberated sexuality. Nearly every area of art and design was swept up in the movement, from illustration to fine art, interior design to fabrics and fashion.

Finnish architect Eliel Saarinen had already bridged the gap between Art Nouveau and Art Deco with a confident stalwart of a building, Helsinki Railway Station (1906–14). Saarinen's railway station was flanked by monumental figures, as in ancient Egypt: the drama of the central curve at its entrance is distinctive Deco. America hugged the new aesthetic to its bosom.

Meanwhile, in England Rupert D'Oyly Carte chose this glamorous new approach, both for the interiors of Claridge's hotel and the new Savoy Theatre in 1929, where his designer Basil Ionides covered the walls in silver leaf. Nowadays the newly-restored theatre is quite the most decadent place to see panto in the entire world. D'Oyly Carte's brother-in-law, Viscount Bearsted, was redecorating Upton House, near Stratford in Warwickshire, at the time. The Queen Anne house holds something of a hidden surprise – a sumptuous Art Deco bathroom fit for a Pharaoh, with an opulent vaulted aluminium leaf ceiling and startling red columns. Look closely at the sink unit, and the ziggurat

**BELOW** Ground-breaking father: Eliel Saarinen's Helsinki Station was designed in 1909, a transition between Art Nouveau and Art Deco. His son would also become a great architect

**LEFT** The luminous ceiling of the Express Building, on London's Fleet Street. The ziggurat-type tower was designed by Owen Williams in 1932

**BELOW** The Deco buildings of South Beach, Miami, were once run down and mouldering. They have been saved by a concerted conservation campaign

influence is immediately obvious. P.G. Wodehouse had complained about the prison-like quality of the Great British bathroom. Upton (see p.210) was the country house exception that proved the rule.

Like the teen-focused 1950s, this was also a time of growing consumerism. One of the reasons for the style's rapid spread across the world was its pure adaptability, especially when it came to the new world of mass-consumer products. Before the war, cars were a luxury. By 1927, 15 million Model 'T' Fords had been sold.

For the first time, in both Canada and the United States, more people lived in cities than in small towns or rural areas. In America, land of the skyscraper, Deco's exuberant language quickly took on the angular shapes of a mega-metropolis, a concept that soon dominated America's view of itself – from Sullivan to Batman. All over the world, from Australia to Japan, India and Latin America, Art Deco was used to sell products and modernize buildings. New Zealanders even adopted traditional Maori motifs.

New Zealand is home to a surprisingly intact Art Deco jewel. On 3 February 1931 the town of Napier was levelled by an earthquake. When the town centre was rebuilt – some 40 square kilometres of today's Napier was under the sea before the earthquake – they used the new modern style. Although a few of those buildings were replaced with contemporary structures between the 1960s and 1980s, most of the centre remains intact: so much so that Napier is considered by many enthusiasts to be one of the world's two best preserved Art Deco sites. The other one is South Beach in Miami. Napier is the first cultural site in New Zealand to be nominated for UNESCO World Heritage Site status.

In fast-expanding America, Art Deco's spirit of naughty decadence became *de rigueur* for luxury hotels, as well as for the new cinemas springing up everywhere. The first colour movie came in 1922: by 1929, Warner Brothers had pre-emptively doused out the gloom of the Wall Street crash with the first all-colour, all-talking feature film, *On With the Show*, with Ethel Waters.

The Paramount Theatre in Oakland, California, is one of the most exciting results of the 'talkie' boom: a dream world of fantasy and escape. Its entrance lobby, 58 feet high, flatters its customers that they, too, are worthy of entering the palace of the Hollywood stars. Rare, luxurious materials and technological innovations are everywhere – Italian marble, Balinese rosewood, artificial light panels in audacious green.

Designed by San Francisco architect Timothy L. Pflueger and completed in late 1931, its extravagance flew in the face of the Depression era. The splendour of the auditorium is probably unmatched: gold walls are adorned with sculpted motifs from the Bible and mythology. Pflueger commissioned many artists to work on the Paramount, probably saving them from the gutter in the process. Its decadence even extends to a 'women's smoking room' in the basement. In 1931 few women smoked in public, so an elegant black-lacquered private room with remarkable murals by Charles Stafford Duncan was created on the lower level.

'It's the pictures that got small,' snarled Norma Desmond in *Sunset Boulevard*. Sadly, this old-time movie star has also had to fight with the ravages of time. Until recently, you could still go to the Paramount and enjoy a cocktail at the bar, while listening to Jimmy Riggs play 'The Mighty Wurlitzer' organ. Serenaded to your seat, you'd be treated to a newsreel, cartoon, previews and a movie classic – the full Monty, 1930s-style. Unfortunately, this magnificent piece of indulgent nostalgia didn't pull in enough visitors through the door, and the 'Movie Classics' series has been reluctantly suspended. At the time of writing, though, the theatre still runs tours on the first and third Saturdays of every month – go along.

In Britain, most of the great Deco picture palaces have been demolished – in the case of London's magnificent Regal, designed by F. Edward Jones, to make way for a chainstore shed. It was a different story in Europe, where optimism and self-indulgence were cut short by the Second World War.

But the brash confidence and faux internationalism of Art Deco had got under the skin of the United States. As designers and engineers began the century's quest for speed, the movement morphed into the useful Streamline style, prompted by the youthful nation's growing technological prowess. Flappers and King Tut bobs might go out of fashion, but in America the streamlined look would evolve into the brash pop culture we now know and either love or endure.

The Chrysler Airflow of 1934 came about when Chrysler Engineering's Carl Breer watched geese flying through the air in a 'V' flight pattern. Breer's wind tunnel tests, which showed that 'two box'-shaped cars didn't work aerodynamically, influenced not only the great American iconic designs like the Airstream Trailer, but even products that didn't need to be streamlined, like toasters.

By 1940, 89 per cent of American households had electricity installed. For those who could afford it the 20th century was yielding up personal luxuries unheard of only a few decades before – washing machines, telephones, toasters, cars... Electric clocks, sewing machines, radio sets and vacuum cleaners were all the rage, often in the new materials of aluminium or Bakelite. The seductive new look – heavily influenced by the emerging ideas of the International Style developing in Europe – emerged in some remarkable buildings across America, as well as places like Eaton's Seventh Floor in Toronto.

There was life in the old dog decoration yet. And as far away as India and the Philippines, Art Deco, in the form of its sweeping curves, had already become a spearhead for a new, modulated Modernism.

**ABOVE** Luxury lifestyle: the 17th century Upton House in Warwickshire, England has sumptuous Art Deco bathrooms, lined with silver leaf

**RIGHT** The famous Paramount in Oakland, California. No step was too grand, and no effort was spared in this homage to the power of Hollywood

# BAUHAUS

Walter Gropius and Ludwig Mies van der Rohe's stories are part of the Bauhaus, a German academy of design that became the powerhouse of the rationalist design movement. It has legendary status for design schools the world over. The monk-like 'Corbu' already knew Gropius and the priest-like Mies van der Rohe from working in the design office of the distinguished architect Peter Behrens.

**RIGHT** Expressionism ready to leap: the Potsdam Tower was designed for Einstein as a scientific laboratory and observatory, and its architectural style was just as forward-thinking

These European giants dominated the development of what, once translated to America, would become known as the International Style. What was it all about? The key to it all was Modernism's burning desire to reject history. The same radical simplification of form seen in the private houses that had been designed in Europe would soon become common in corporate America, along with glass, steel and concrete. Industrialized mass-production techniques should be used where possible: buildings were to be logical. Ornament was crime.

The name Bauhaus (building house) sounds simple, but in a stricken Germany full of millions made either poor or homeless by the catastrophe of the First World War, it was an emotive term. The movement took an ideological line, paring down design not simply for aesthetic reasons but also to fit the nation's tiny purse. The school produced schemes for prefabricated mass housing, exhibiting plans for low-cost but functional homes. Gropius was its director until 1928; Mies van der Rohe until Hitler came to power.

The International Style made no concessions to local tradition – because it was anti-tradition. Indifferent to location or climate, the International Style was its own thing. This boundary-less quality was seen as a strength at the time, symbolic of the new era. Naturally, Hitler despised it, because of its taint of true socialism. The Nazis denounced the functional, engineering-led school as a hotbed of decadence. The Bauhaus was closed and the Nazis began a massive building programme of their own, mainly in a historicist, Neoclassical style. Thus began a massive cultural diaspora. Thanks to Adolf Hitler, the Modern movement was about to go truly international.

At one stroke, Modernism became the new orthodoxy, the right versus the Nazi's Neoclassicist wrong. And as artists and architects fled, so did their ideas – to the United States, Britain and Russia. When Hitler drove Modernism out, he also scotched a brief northern European experiment called Expressionism.

Expressionism's significance lies in its stunning modernity, and its aspiration: creating buildings that are really expressive pieces of sculpture. We might think of the architectural works of Frank Gehry or Oscar Niemeyer as one-off eye-openers, we might even find them shocking, but their stylistic values do in fact have a heritage.

It is in Germany that we find the beginnings of Expressionist theory. As fine artists like Franz Marc and Vassily Kandinsky struggled to inspire emotion through abstract images rather than representational art, the buildings of Erich Mendelsohn, Hans Poelzig and Bruno Taut were doing the same thing in concrete. Hans Poelzig was a member of the Deutscher Werkbund (the German Work Federation), an influential association of architects, designers and industrialists which is now famous for its radical thinking. He renovated the Grosses Schauspielhaus (Great Theatre) in Berlin for the Weimar theatre impresario Max Reinhardt, decorating the ceiling with extraordinary stalactite- and stalagmite-like sculptural pendants and pillars. With their pierced 'windows', the remarkable rhythmic piers of stalactites were oddly reminiscent of the inside of the Colosseum. The theatre must have been a remarkable sight and is a great loss to Germany's architectural history: it was condemned and demolished in 1988.

Still standing, though, is Erich Mendelsohn's Einstein Tower. Built outside Potsdam between 1920 and 1921, the observatory was built for the cello-playing astrophysicist Erwin Finlay Freundlich. Freundlich needed an astronomical observatory to prove Einstein's Theory of Relativity. Built mostly in brick and then covered with plaster, the structure is still in use as a solar observatory today – although it is in constant need of repair. It was Mendelsohn's first building and his understanding of construction techniques was a little lacking.

Mendelsohn said its unique design came from some unknown urge, inspired by 'the mystique around Einstein's universe'. The story goes that when the bright-eyed young man at long last took the great physicist on a tour of the completed structure, eager to get a judgement on his masterpiece, Einstein said absolutely nothing.

Hours later, during a meeting with the building committee, Einstein whispered his one-word judgment: 'Organic'. And indeed, it does look alive, as if it is crouching within its landscape setting. With its height – which was actually purely functional, decided by the telescope inside – and its strange, undulating walls, it's been described as an 'ungainly

**RIGHT** The spiral staircase of the De La Warr Pavilion, Bexhill, a masterpiece of Modernist architecture in England

**BELOW** Cool white and sleek lines: the De La Warr Pavilion. Britain had not seen its like before the 1930s

spaceship'. Perhaps it looks a little more like a rather unfriendly amphibian.

And it was Erich Mendelsohn, driven out of mainland Europe by the Nazis, who was to create the UK's first building in the International Style, on the south coast. Up until then, Britain had been pretty slow to adopt the new style. Built in 1935, the De La Warr Pavilion at Bexhill-on-Sea was named after the 9th Earl De La Warr, a committed socialist and the town's mayor. He wanted an arts complex for the people, a place that would put Bexhill on the map. Mendelsohn and his partner on the project, Serge Chermayeff, were chosen not just for their streamlined, industrially-influenced designs, but for all that this modern style stood for – progressiveness and a real concern for ordinary people. Mendelsohn called his sleek, glamorous pavilion 'a horizontal skyscraper'.

Begun in 1935, the innovative structure had a welded steel frame construction. In the confusing arena of grand architectural labels, 'International Style', 'International Modern' and 'Modernism' are all attempts to describe what Mendelsohn and Chermayeff were doing. It was one of the very few Modernist buildings that the obdurately traditional British were to take to their hearts.

Wells Coates' dramatic Isokon Building in Lawn Road, Hampstead was built between 1933 and 1934 as an experiment in a different form of urban living. The Isokon company would design furniture for this new Modernist world and the building itself was to be the company's cauldron and testing ground.

The kitchens were small – no-one was expected to do any cooking, but if they did it would be in a large communal kitchen. A dumb waiter would then whisk their meals upstairs. Services like laundry and shoe-cleaning were provided on site. The building boasted a number of famous residents, including Agatha Christie and the famous architects Walter Gropius, Lázsló Moholy-Nagy, Marcel Breuer and (in the 1960s) James Stirling. A communal restaurant, the Isobar, set a style for living that would be much imitated in later decades the world over. The flats are nearer to Le Corbusier's efficient ideal of 'a machine for living in' than anything he himself produced. But brave new experiments are often derailed by circumstance. With the onset of war, Isokon foundered. The glamorous Grade 1 listed apartments are now owned by a housing association.

## Exodus

The architects driven out of Europe by the Nazis included:

Erich Mendelsohn
Walter Gropius
Marcel Breuer
Mies van der Rohe

Most of them ended up in the United States, at which point America, already growing in originality and innovation, took the undisputed lead in world architecture.

**LEFT** Design for living: the Isokon, for a while Agatha Christie's London home. Breuer designed and made his own kitchen in his small flat. It is still there

# The Word in Stone

*'For the commission to do a great building, I would have sold my soul like Faust. Now I had found my Mephistopheles. He seemed no less engaging than Goethe's.'*

Albert Speer.

In 1907, a 16-year-old school dropout and rebel decided that he wanted to direct his creativity into the art of architecture.

*'I myself knew that I should some day become an architect. To be sure, it was an incredibly hard road; [it] required a high-school degree. I had none of this. The fulfilment of my artistic dream seemed physically impossible.'*

Who was this architect manqué? A one-time painter and Viennese cartoonist, a bohemian called Adolf Hitler – whose other sombre story we know only too well.

In the 1930s, the image-obsessed future leader assembled around him a vast propaganda machine of photographers, artists and designers to fashion the 'new' Germany. Presentation was all. His skills as an orator would soon be magnified by

**LEFT** Schloss Wewelsburg, the Nazi Camelot: it was hoped that future generations would troop here to venerate the founders of the 1,000-year Reich, which in the event only lasted 12 years

searchlights and marching bands, billowing banners and fancy dress. To this day, our understanding of the architecture of the Third Reich is conditioned almost entirely by the propaganda Hitler wanted us to see, and modern-day Germany associates the 'classical' with guilt and tyranny.

But Hitler's ambitions for his architecture went much further than propaganda. His architectural sketches dated from the 1920s, when he couldn't possibly have hoped that the buildings they featured would ever be built. Hitler wanted to be the founder of a thousand-year Reich, a vision that went hand-in-hand with creating a built proclamation to the world. He called it 'the word in stone'.

Hitler saw the free-thinking ethos behind the Weimar Republic, like the architecture of Expressionism and the Bauhaus, as an object lesson in decadence and decline. So it was to two differing strands of architectural style that Nazism turned. The first was classicism and the second was a militarized version of German romanticism.

For Hitler, Rome meant power and laurel wreaths. Linking to Rome's imperial past would, he believed, associate both him and his regime with centuries of 'noble' emperors. It would also present the German people with a rationalist, cultured façade, a promise of a better civilization.

The untrained would-be empire builder needed an architect. At first Hitler learned at the knee of Paul Troost, who had worked with Peter Behrens: his was a severely puritan, pared-down form of classicism. Then the urbane, handsome and ambitious Albert Speer, a young architect and party member, was assigned to help Troost renovate the Chancellery in Berlin. Speer distinguished himself by adding the famous balcony from which Hitler later addressed the assembled crowds. However, as Speer records, Troost was Hitler's chief and much-trusted architect until he died in 1934.

*'For years he [Hitler] drove to the studio of Troost in his spare time in order to view the plans of new buildings. But the Führer did not occupy himself only with the overall plans; each single detail, each new material received his seal of approval, and much was improved through his fruitful suggestions. Those hours of joint planning, as the Führer often confesses, became hours of purest joy and the deepest feelings of happiness for him. They were relaxation of the purest kind, out of which he found new strength for other planning.'*

But Hitler's vast pre-war building programme needed more than just one architect. The 'wet-behind-the-ears' Albert Speer was easy to manipulate. Hitler produced pocket drawings specifying detail right down to the exact type of stone, which the compliant young Speer then dutifully refined and reproduced. When Troost died, Speer went on to become a member of Hitler's inner circle and his chosen architect. Neoclassicism was to play a key part in creating a template for the new Germany: Speer and Hitler even thought in terms of how heroic the ruins would one day appear.

One of Speer's first commissions as chief architect was to design the Zeppelintribüne – the Nuremberg parade grounds, well-known from Leni Riefenstahl's sinister films. Like so many Nazi creations, the outcome was grandiose, monumental and faintly ridiculous. Capable of holding 240,000 people, the Zeppelintribüne was based on a scaled-up version of the Pergamon Altar in Turkey, which was itself modelled on the Parthenon. Nothing new there, but at the 1934 Party rally, Speer surrounded the site with anti-aircraft searchlights, creating a 'Cathedral of Light' that symbolized soaring classical columns. The beams from 120 Army flak searchlights around the periphery of the field shot thousands of feet up into the night sky. The effect, by all accounts, was stunning.

Much of Hitler's architecture is dour, clumsy and out of proportion. Exceptions include the Pfeilerhalle, or Hall of Pillars, alongside the Zeppelintribüne, where a

soothing play of light caresseses the columns on sunny days. Then there was the Luitpoldhalle, scene of Nazi Party congresses, one of the most delicate buildings despite its size. First built in 1906 as an exhibition and events venue it was taken over by the Nazis in 1933. Albert Speer then had the building refaced with limestone slabs and a Nazi façade was added. The Luitpold Arena could hold over 150,000 Nazis and was the scene of SS and SA gatherings.

There was another strand to the Third Reich's aesthetic Ayran myth. Hitler, who had a traditional Alpine-style retreat on the Obersalzberg, above Berchtesgaden, had no objection to real Germanic architectural roots, but it was the second-most powerful man in Nazi Germany, Heinrich Himmler, who pushed this vernacular romanticism in the name of the Reich. Reichesführer-SS and head of the Gestapo, Himmler's main

historic interest was in Henry I of Saxony and the Ottonian Empire, a dynasty founded on incursions into the East, the territory of the Slavs. He wrote in the SS magazine *Das Schwarze Korps* (1941):

*'Through seven centuries, the castles of Allenstein, Heilsberg, Marienwerder and Neidenburg were just as much witnesses of well-fought conquest and most tenacious defence as they were symbols of higher German culture for all generations of the old "Ordensland" of East Prussia. The stones have not spoken in vain... the fields are German again.'*

These claims were meant to legitimize the German military drive to the East and hold up to the SS the image of a noble knight warrior race – an ideological projection designed to consolidate and enhance power.

The elite, knightly SS now needed a

**ABOVE** In 1933, the Luitpoldhalle was remodelled by the Nazis for party rallies, with up to 150,000 members turning up for ceremonies in the arena. These were crucial to Nazi myth-building

suitable base – a castle, in fact. Himmler's plans to reform the SS on the medieval knightly model were so advanced he had even created coats of arms for the most senior SS officers.

In 1934 Himmler signed a 100-year lease on Wewelsburg Castle in the Paderborn district of Germany. It had been built in 1603 on the site of earlier castles. A crypt in the basement was reserved for rituals and for the lying-in-state of SS leaders when they died. The castle was to be the hub of a vast housing complex that arced out in concentric circles across the landscape. In the meantime, alongside the castle was the smallest German concentration camp, Niederhagen. Out of 3,900 prisoners held there 1,285 died, according to the records.

grand colonnaded hall. For the facade alone, 350,000 cubic metres of granite was needed, an unheard of amount. By the time war broke out on 1 September 1939 the budgets for the German Stadium, the March Field and the Congress Hall had risen by over RM 28m.

The question of the extent of Speer's knowledge of the Nazi horrors was hotly debated after the Nuremberg trials. There is plenty of evidence that he knew exactly what was going on. For instance Heinz Schwarz, who was supervising the quarry operations and therefore in charge of the 'people problem', the euphemism for slave labour and mass extermination, told Speer that one prisoner could do the work of four civilians.

Whatever the answer, Speer certainly came under Hitler's spell. 'I am ashamed of it now,' he said, 'but at the time, I found him deeply exciting.' The architect claimed that, towards the end, he considered assassinating Hitler. Speer's name was found on a list of possible sympathisers drawn up by the conspirators of the 1944 July 20 plot. That list probably saved his life – although the conspirators followed his scribbled name with a question mark.

Well, Hitler got his ruins. On 2 January, 1945, the medieval centre of Nuremberg was systematically bombed (and then again a month later). About 90 per cent of the city was destroyed in a few hours. The United States Army blew up the large swastika on the top of the Zeppelintribüne, although they left the main structure standing; the Pfeilerhalle is a now a flat plinth; and the Luitpoldhalle was badly damaged in the bombing. Only a portion of the steps remains today.

In Berlin, where a horrifying 'hurricane of fire' was unleashed by the Allies on 1 May 1945, many of the buildings Hitler commissioned are either gone, or have been altered out of recognition. The vast Dietrich-Eckart-Bühne is known today as the Waldbühne, and is used for rock concerts. All insignia have been removed.

In 1937 Speer was put in charge of designing the entire Berlin cityscape, in a new infrastructure plan for the capital. The 32-year-old Speer, now with a growing group of architect-sympathisers to do his bidding, was also given authority to override the Mayor, Julius Lippert. By 1938 all Jewish council architects were 'excused' (*beurlaubt*).

The plan for Berlin now involved creating a vast triumphal north–south axis through Berlin, as suggested by Hitler. Dominated by monumental Neoclassical structures, at the southern end would be a huge triumphal arch that Speer had adapted from Hitler's drawings and a train station with a vast plaza. A smaller east–west axis would cross it, within which would be a redesigned Königsplatz, which would serve as a site for Nazi mass rallies, and a major housing programme. The aim: to trump Haussman's 19th century Paris, and compete with the imperial grandeur of ancient Rome.

Speer's German Stadium building was to hold 400,000 people. In its design, he was combining the horseshoe shape of the Roman circus and the Greek *propylaeum,* a

# Oscar Niemeyer (1907–2012)

**ABOVE** Niemeyer had the opportunity of an architect's lifetime in the form of the new city of Brasilia. Here, the Cultural Complex of the Republic

Oscar Niemeyer's perspective on life was completely different from that of many of those working elsewhere in modern architecture. He began life as a Modernist, but gradually forged an architectural style that was both unique and ahead of its time, a symbol of the colour and lust for life of his native Brazil. He once told a newspaper: 'Mine is an architecture of curves; the body of a woman, the sinuous rivers, the waves of the sea.'

Known largely for his large-scale projects throughout Brazil and Europe, Niemeyer was a baby architect when the august Le Corbusier came to Rio de Janeiro – on an airship. In 1936 Le Corbusier had arrived to work with Lúcio Costa on what became an international architectural landmark, the Ministry of Education and Health.

The great man was given an assistant to help him with drawings. 'Corbu', as he was known, was impressed by the young Brazilian's amazing draughtsmanship and took him under his wing. From that day on, Niemeyer retained another defining trait of the Modernists, who were often as much committed socialists as they were passionate architects. He was one of the few surviving champions of old-guard Communism, and counted Cuban leader Fidel Castro as a close personal friend.

'Corbu' was undoubtedly a great influence on Niemeyer, who went on to design a number of obviously Modernist houses. But some – including Niemeyer himself – argued that Corbusier was equally

217

influenced in return. Was the St Francis chapel at Pampulha, which broke all the rules with its radical, great wave-like concrete vaults, actually a model for the Ronchamp chapel, built six years later and arguably Le Corbusier's greatest building?

Niemeyer's own house at Canoas in Rio de Janeiro (1953) was a first stone cast at the stern Bauhaus box. An undulating white concrete roof peeked out from the forest, the roof mirrored by the shape of a pool below. Linking the two, a great boulder embedded in the terrace echoed the mountain landscape nearby.

'Your house is very beautiful, but it is not multipliable,' Walter Gropius told him sternly.

The young Brazilian simply didn't have the mass-production mindset natural to a European obsessed with finding ways of building cheap housing for the multitudes. Niemeyer protested – this was an individual house, designed specifically for its individual site.

'How can you repeat a house that has a definite environment, level curves where to settle, a light, a landscape. How can you build it over again?'

He explained later: 'It was not the imposition of the right angle which made me mad, but the obsessive concern of an architectonical purity, of structural logic, of the systematic campaign against the free and creative shape... it was contemporary architecture vanishing in its repeated glass cubes.'

When President Juscelino Kubitschek, Niemeyer's former client, was elected president he decided to change Brazil for ever. His slogan? 'Fifty years of progress in

**BELOW** The Museu Oscar Niemeyer in Curitiba is typically free-form as a building: a semi-surrealist confection in concrete. Niemeyer was still working at over 100 years of age

**ABOVE** Niemeyer's clean-limbed interior for his own house at Canoas. It is designed specifically to fit into its majestic natural site in the hills

five.' It was 1955. Turning up on the 49-year-old architect's doorstep, he declared:

*'Oscar, we are going to build the capital of Brazil. A modern capital – the most beautiful capital city in the world.'*

This was state reform by architecture, an optimistic Utopian dream. The very idea for a new capital was inspired by a century-old prophecy: a priest living in Turin had a vision that a new civilization would emerge somewhere between the 15th and 20th parallels. Kubitschek, or 'JK' to his followers, wanted nothing less than to create a new national identity, right there. With its broad avenues, well-defined living areas and revolutionary architecture, Brasilia would be the ideal city.

For his part, Niemeyer was being given the opportunity of a lifetime: to redesign an entire country's identity. The competition to design the urban master plan was won by his old friend Costa. A suitably visionary plan emerged – to plan the whole city in the form of a bird, with two outstretched wings.

An architectural staff of 60 designed most of the main buildings in two years –

and they were built in just 2,000 days. Time was just what they didn't have. Kubitschek had only a slight majority and there'd been a coup attempt even before he took power. There was scarcely a second to breathe, although Niemeyer did admit to the odd trip into the countryside to ogle the local girls.

*'I can see them [his colleagues] all now,'* he recalled in his memoirs. *'Hunched over their drawing boards, totally absorbed in their work, caught up in our great crusade to build Brasilia, come what may.'*

Sophisticated and idealistic, this completely modern 21st-century city, rising from the almost uninhabited highlands, would indeed transform Brazil's international image. And Brasilia does have a dream-like quality that somehow suits its visionary beginnings.

Niemeyer hated flying in planes, but he loved clouds, and would often dream of them on the long 550-mile drive from Rio. The influence seems most evident in his great Alvorada Palace (1956–8), the first major building of the new capital. Its three storeys and delicate white marble-clad columns, tapering top and bottom to a tiny point, reach up from behind a man-made lake. Described by Jean-Paul Sartre as 'a beautiful fan', the building looks as if it

could float right off the ground. But although incredibly light, dignified and delicate, its historical roots are rooted on terra firma – the long, lean layout of the traditional Brazilian vernacular farmhouses.

Another of the architect's egalitarian ideas can be seen at the long, low Palace of National Congress (1960). Guided up on two long ramps, the public could stroll along on the roof – and be literally on top of those who ruled them.

Sadly, this attempt at a democratic footprint did not last long. Fame didn't stop politics costing Niemeyer commissions and the military dictatorship that ruled Brazil from 1964 to 1985 was hostile. Facing investigations and threats, Niemeyer spent 18 years in exile, designing all the while – including the HQ of the French Communist Party in Paris, the Penang State Mosque in Malaysia and the campus of Constantine University in Algeria.

Niemeyer, who died at the age of 104, had never seen the need to make compromises. His imagination drove the construction of cathedrals, memorials, libraries, the stadium for Rio's amazing annual Carnival; indeed, young architects complain that the architecture of Brazil is only Niemeyer. This remained true even in his old age. He won the Pritzker Architectural Prize, the top award in the field, when he was 80. One of his most popular buildings, a giant, white disc seemingly floating above ocean waters that forms the Museum of Contemporary Art across Guanabara Bay was completed

**LEFT** Brasília's Cathedral-Basilica of Our Lady Aparecida. The Crown of Thorns re-interpreted by a spiritual, but aetheistic mind

**BELOW** The astounding landmark of the Contemporary Art Museum in the city of Niterói, across the bay from Rio. At 89, Niemeyer had fun: jutting 52 feet (16m) high on a promontory, his building looks like the Thunderbirds' Tracey Island

when he was a mere 88. Nowadays, people flock to have their wedding photographs taken in front of it.

The young Communist had done exactly what his great patron Kubitschek had asked him to do. He had created a new, modern and joyful image of Brazil, one that the Brazilian people believed in wholeheartedly. His great success was his immense popularity – perhaps born from the way he insisted on forcing rich and poor to interact. His buildings convey optimism and hope. One Niemeyer tower on the Rio beachfront, home to a business and law school, has no ocean views. According to Niemeyer, he knew that only the senior executives would get those top offices – so he made sure there were none.

# GOING UP IN THE WORLD

The Second World War finally achieved what the Modernists' reforming zeal alone had left untouched. A public sense of a break with the past was created by the legacy of slaughter from two world wars. Husbands, sons or even entire families were lost. In some villages, some local surnames would disappear entirely from the parish records, so many young men had been killed. The social upheaval was enormous: there was a sense that the world owed a huge debt to the ordinary, mainly working class, men and women, both civilian and military, who had given their lives. From this point on, public opinion would start to become a driving force in society. By the 1960s, the views of the masses were as important in forming tastes as those of the elite. Even from the time of the first conflict, whatever the actual reality within the Soviet Union, Fascist Italy, Nazi Germany and the liberal democracies, all governments claimed to be acting in the interest of the so-called 'common man'.

In 1930s 'Red Vienna' and Holland, worker housing had been built that would give inspiration to the rest of Europe. Estates had well-tended gardens and good-quality facilities were laced throughout. Vienna's Karl-Marx-Hof (1926–39) was a giant wall of worker housing which inspired the term 'worker fortress'. Nevertheless, there were playgrounds and gardens which were well-maintained, laundries, shops and open space. The kindergartens above all were held up as a model of the new social order.

In Britain in particular, where 200,000 homes had been destroyed and half a million seriously damaged by war-time bombs, a new philosophy was taking shape: of 'cradle to grave' socialism. The picture was made even more complicated by a half-finished slum clearance programme. 'Homes, health, education and social security, these are your birthright,' the Labour government's Minister of Health, Aneurin Bevan, told the electorate.

Faced with the housing problem in his own backyard, the austere evangelical

ABOVE Karl-Marx-Hof has 1,382 apartments and was designed for a population of 5,000. It was known as the 'street of the proletariat', but had good facilities such as kindergartens and laundries

Christian Sir Stafford Cripps – who was also Chancellor of the Exchequer – simply built a new estate in local Cotswold stone. It was in the tiny Oxfordshire village of Filkins. Tenants had generous-sized two- or three-bedroom houses in a traditional cottage style with strip gardens – and a communal playground and outdoor swimming pool to boot. But Cripps was a rich landowner: it was not practical to find patrons to build houses of such good quality the country over. Rich, Marxist philanthropists are generally thin on the ground.

The overwhelming focal point of architectural change was this: local authorities became vital patrons of architecture. This would have profound implications. An architecture driven by ideology and the bureaucrat would be whole worlds away from that driven by the patronage of individual princes and aristocrats.

As reconstruction began under Attlee's Labour government in 1945, the use of prefabricated elements, metal frames, concrete cladding – all of which were being viewed with real suspicion by the British – was adopted for housing developments and schools.

Park Hill in Sheffield, inspired by Le Corbusier's thinking, was the first estate of its kind in the UK. Many cities in Europe imitated its layout of flats, shops and other amenities. Concrete was to be the new wonder material, helping the UK build its way out of the war rubble. It was cheap and quick – and that was what mattered.

In France, Le Corbusier finally got the chance to put his urban theories into practice. The Unité d'habitation in Marseille (1952) had been three decades in coming. Seventeen storeys high and designed to house 1,600 people, the Unité incorporates various types of apartment, together with shops, clubs and meeting rooms: all connected by raised 'streets'. A different class of building from the mass housing that would soon be thrown up in Britain, there was even a hotel.

The very same year, the first blocks of the Alton estate were built. The Alton estate, much of it now listed, is set on the edge of London's Richmond Park. It's a homage to Le Corbusier's theories. The first block series, Alton East, is a mix of high-rise and low-rise housing, its towers carefully set amongst mature trees and parkland, just as Corbusier had imagined. However, its brightly coloured brickwork, painted window frames and wide bands of concrete on the exterior annoyed the hardline Modernist faction in the London County Council's Architects' Department.

Alton West, completed one year later, would return to Purist simplicity. The estates have been a far bigger success than many British counterparts, although you wouldn't think so to listen to the residents from the nearby suburbs. But Corbusier's wider planning is noticeably absent. If you go there, and feel like you've been there before, it's because the estate was the location for the dystopian film classic *Fahrenheit 451*.

Architects cared about detail and about planning: the technocrats didn't see why. Prominent Modernists wanted to develop a softer, 'humanist' Modernism, along the lines of the vernacular-friendly architecture of Jørn Utzon in Sweden, or the Halen Estate outside Berne. The scheme for the once-infamous Broadwater Farm estate in North London, scene of major riots in 1985, originally included shops, pub, launderette and dental and doctor's surgeries. All were cut as the first target of cost-savings. By the time it was built, all that was there at ground level were acres of unused car parks: a recipe for social disaster.

Ideologically, councils may have felt they were following Le Corbusier into an ideal future of 'streets in the sky'. Unfortunately, when it came to mass housing, few of the clod-hopping British interpretations of Corbusier's schemes had any of his sensitivity. And neither Park Hill – a 'concrete cliff' in one resident's opinion – nor places like Alison and Peter Smithson's 1972 Robin Hood Gardens in Poplar, London, were given the swimming pools, terraces and landscaped grounds of the 'Cité radieuse'. The bureaucrats failed to respond to the essential humanism behind Le Corbusier's thinking. A string of poorly conceived, badly-built estates have blighted British cities ever since.

In the United States the picture was little different. In 1961, American academic Jane Jacobs published *The Death and Life of Great American Cities*. Traditional neighbourhoods worked far better than modernist, planned estates, she said. Corbusier's 'streets in the sky' mean that when you look out of your window, you look out on to thin air. While Corbusier may have been a visionary thinker who believed that all modern man needed was 'a monk's cell, well lit and well heated, with a corner from which he can look at the stars,' the vast majority are not. People who live close together need to get to know each other, argued Jacobs and a raft of later academics. Shelter is not enough: what people need, above all, is a sense of community and safety – the 'eyes on the street'.

For ordinary people on modern estates, anonymity and isolation prevailed. Even Minoru Yamasaki's award-winning Pruitt-Igoe housing development in St Louis, Missouri, was knocked down after only 20 years.

Writer Tom Wolfe fulminated: 'The

**BELOW** Streets in the sky: the Park Hill Estate designed by Jack Lynn was built 1957–1961. Part of the estate, cresting a hill in Sheffield in the north of England, is now being redeveloped privately

**LEFT** The Trellick Tower shows how tastes can change. It is now a desirable address with young London cognoscenti, but does not appeal to families or the elderly

'*Cages au lapin*' – rabbit hutches. And the people in them were well and truly trapped.

There are moments in time where events and public opinion combine to tip the precarious balance on a controversial issue in a matter of days. In 1968, the same year that the Trellick Tower was built, there was one of those moments: a disastrous gas explosion in another London borough, Newham. The entire end of the Ronan Point tower block collapsed like a house of cards barely two months after the building had been occupied. Although 68-year-old Mrs Ivy Hodge had survived a brief visit to put the kettle on – lighting the gas with a match – five other people had died and 17 were injured. The relatively small explosion had caused a whole back section of concrete to blow out. A local architect, Sam Webb, discovered that the structure's joints were filled with newspaper, the walls resting on levelling bolts, two per panel, rather than on a continuous bed of mortar. The whole building was falling to pieces.

Now Modernists stood accused not only of creating ugly buildings that no-one except architects liked, but of actually putting people's lives at risk. The Trellick Tower would be the last of the Tower houses. Thus a block, the build quality of which would have appalled Le Corbusier and his colleagues, spelt out the death-knell to the British high-rise experiment.

Ronan Point was demolished. The Modernists had dreamed that their new architecture would help forge a better world for all. But the Dream, it seemed, was dead.

only people left trapped in worker housing today are those who don't work at all – and are on welfare.'

When Le Corbusier died in 1965, the backlash against Modernism was accelerating. In Britain alone over 1,850,000 flats had been built in the name of the Modern movement. A number of his 'Unité' had been built all over France, but they were not uniformly successful. One, at Briey-en-Forêt in northeast France, was abandoned after ten years. The painter Peter Doig describes discovering it, desolate and empty, in the 1990s.

'*You get this feeling you are coming across a spaceship which has just landed from another planet. When you walk through an urban environment, you take the strangeness of the architecture for granted.*'

The unearthly quality of the building, its very lack of tradition, was what was unsettling Doig. It seemed to have arrived, like a spaceship, from nowhere. That rootlessness was a problem even with a Corbusier design. Imitation would cause far bigger problems. By the 1980s, the *cités* of Paris, mass housing projects inspired by his theories, were social marginalization writ large. Reported crime in Paris seemingly rises by 10 per cent a year, with one crime affecting every sixth inhabitant. The problem is more than purely architectural, but without any connection to any social structures (sports clubs, churches), no historic grounding of any kind, the cités are home to a kind of anti-society. The only cultural frame of reference for these as structures is what became their popular name:

## The Tower of Terror

One British building above all symbolizes the great British public's hatred of Brutalism. The Trellick Tower was great tabloid newspaper fodder, with rapes in elevators, heroin addicts in the basement and squatters setting fire to the flats. Its reputation was so bad at one stage that urban myth had it that the architect, racked with guilt, had thrown himself off the roof of his 31-storey high tower. Great story, but untrue. The larger than life figure of Erno Goldfinger inspired Ian Fleming to create Goldfinger, one of his most energetic villains. The Hungarian émigré was a Marxist, a ladykiller and a bit of a bruiser. When others were questioning the wisdom of building so high, Goldfinger was having none of it. The man who once tried to sack one of his staff for smiling was not about to be put off by a little public opinion. 'I built skyscrapers for people to live in there and now they messed them up – disgusting.' It was his last commission. Today, the tower has become an urban icon, as Londoners become accustomed to high-rise and the 1960s take on the gilt of nostalgia.

### MONSTROUS CARBUNCLES?

Brutalism is now experiencing a major revival in Israel, where fortress-like security and strength is a stylistic must, especially for public buildings. And the Trellick Tower, once reviled across Britain, has suddenly become a trendy place to live. Exposed concrete is popular once more, now technology has moved on. UK television's Channel 4 has even run a programme called *I love carbuncles*.

# ENTER THE GLASS BOX

Mies van der Rohe liked to quote St Thomas Aquinas' saying: 'Reason is the first principle of all human work.' He was once asked by a student about the role of 'self-expression' in an architect's work. By way of reply, he asked her to write down her name. 'That's for self-expression,' he then declared. 'Now, we get to work.'

**H**is oft-quoted but cryptic aphorism, 'less is more', perfectly captures Van der Rohe's devotion to a pure, rationalist Modernism. Urban existence was complicated: rational solutions must be found. He'd first come up with his ambitious plan for glass skyscrapers as early as 1919. The steel frame of a building would be visible through acres of glass, like a skeleton barely concealed by a taut layer of skin. Not until the middle of the century did air-conditioning, heat-absorbing glass and cooler fluorescent lighting make his shining new ideas a technical possibility.

The Bauhaus was about to have its day. The self-educated Mies became head of the architecture school at Chicago, where he taught generations of students that architecture should communicate the meaning and significance of the culture in which it exists. His manufactured steel shapes, infilled with glass, resonated with Americans. They seemed like a natural progression of the 19th century Chicago School, but with added European sophistication. Walter Gropius was now installed at the Harvard Graduate School of Design and both he and Mies became American citizens in 1944. The classic 'Mies' look carries simplicity to extremes: features are cubic spaces, exposed structural steel and large expanses of glass. The strict symmetry was shown to advantage in projects like the famous Lake Shore Drive Apartments in Chicago. He hoped to create a new, easily imitable form of architecture that celebrated light, space and air. His architecture would be based on material honesty and structural integrity. The new style wasn't simply an aesthetic imperative. A huge new advantage was the speed of construction. Once a steel skeleton was up, prefabricated façade elements could be lifted into the right position by crane – and be welded in place on the spot.

By now, corporate America was keen to offer Mies the opportunity to build his pure glass cuboids on its expensive slices of real

**LEFT** Mies van der Rohe and Philip Johnson's Seagram Building, 1958, in New York is a building of pure form and genuine class. It spawned a host of poor imitations

**ABOVE** The Toronto-Dominion Centre, by Mies van der Rohe and Bregman & Hamann Architects. Six towers, covered in bronze-tinted glass and black painted steel

estate. His most celebrated tower was the headquarters for the whisky company Seagram. Completed in 1958, this 38-storey block was detailed in bronze, with its own plaza keeping the rest of New York at arm's length. The effect is impressive if emotionless, the epitome of 20th century corporate Modernism. His other buildings include the IBM Plaza in Chicago, and 1967's six-tower Toronto-Dominion Centre, with interiors fitted in black aluminum and travertine marble. In the clean-lined shopping mall below, Mies insisted that store fronts must conform to the glass panels and black aluminum that he specified. Even signage should be only white backlit letters within a black aluminium panel, in the specific type font he himself had designed.

Meanwhile, Le Corbusier, still living in France but in demand all over the world, loved Manhattan. He loved its newness, he loved its tall buildings. Above all, he loved its logic, a city planned to a rigid grid system. He had only one reservation, which he revealed on landing in New York City in 1935. The next day, a headline in the *Herald Tribune*

announced that the celebrated architect found American skyscrapers 'much too small'.

In 1947 he would get the chance to bring the International Style to First Avenue, with the new Secretariat for the United Nations. The only freestanding skyscraper in New York at 38 stories (544 feet/165 m) tall, it was also the city's earliest glass curtain wall building. An international committee of ten architects (including the Brazilian Oscar Niemeyer and the Swede Sven Markelius) was assembled by the United Nations Board of Design. Corbusier's scheme '23a', representing France, was chosen as the basis for further design.

Wallace K. Harrison – a powerfully-connected figure close to the Rockefeller family, which donated the site – and Max Abramovitz oversaw the design of the vast office complex for 3,400 employees. Symbolic of technological prowess, international co-operation and monumentality, it has little else in its favour other than the graphic impact it makes on a television screen. Narrow floors make it too cramped for the office spaces and the large expanses of glass cause problems with temperature regulation. Today, the United Nations needs $1 billion to renovate a building plagued by asbestos, lead paint and friable concrete. Nevertheless, it influenced commercial building for years.

The Lever House building, which followed in 1951, took Mies' glass curtain wall and launched a thousand copies all over the world. Architecture could become a process, it seemed to say, one that can be sampled and copied in an instant. The office that produced it, SOM (Skidmore, Owings and Merrill) became the first of many multinational architectural businesses.

Copies of 'Mies' were turned out that were thoughtless, boring and utterly bland. They were purchased more like products than exercises in architecture. After the 1950s, the world would somehow learn to accept the term 'commercial architecture', a euphemism for a joyless, bland, process-driven product that could be reproduced anywhere, at any time. We are still living with the result: acres of shopping malls, offices and public buildings with nothing to recommend them other than the space they enclose and the shelter they provide. Nothing to do with architecture.

Modernism had transformed the city. But was this quite the revolution that Corbusier had wanted? Were concrete, glass and steel – 'honest' enough materials – really enough in themselves? Imitators were everywhere; innovators were few. Along with the Mies-influenced steel and glass office buildings appearing all over New York, Chicago and the rest of the world, modern cities from Singapore to Shanghai were beginning to look – well – exactly the same.

# Frank Lloyd Wright (1867–1959)

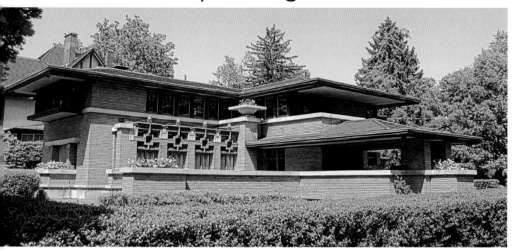

**LEFT** Most of Wright's Prairie homes emphasize the horizontal line. The Meyer May House, built in 1908 in Grand Rapids, Michigan, also has spectacular Arts and Crafts windows

**RIGHT** The Kaufman family loved the waterfall and had suggested the house should face it. Instead, the sandstone and concrete Fallingwater, Pennsylvania, dramatically cantilevered right over it

**FAR RIGHT** FLW remodelled the skylit staircase lobby for Chicago's Rookery Building, with sumptuous Arts and Crafts-inspired detailing

*'The complete architect is master of the elements; earth, fire, light and water. Space, motion and gravitation are his palette; the sun his brush. His concern is the heart of humanity. He of all men, must see into the life of things; know their honour.'*

Frank Lloyd Wright.

Frank Lloyd Wright was one of the architectural world's first celebrities. In fact if it weren't for the plain fact that his buildings, created over a vastly long six-decade career, are those of a total genius, the tabloid quality of his personal life might even have eclipsed his talent.

It was Wright's mother, a teacher, who decided that her son would be an architect. One of his earliest toys was a set of Froebel blocks, a kind of early Lego. The determined Anna Wright is also said to have pasted pictures of the great English cathedrals on her baby's bedroom walls.

This great and idiosyncratic figure would become known for an inspired way of designing that responded instinctively to the landscape. The aesthetics of the East were important to Wright, especially the Japanese concept of *wabi-sabi* – the notion of fleeting beauty that comes from something natural, even imperfect. Wright believed that a house should appear to grow from a landscape, like a tree does from the soil. It should be 'a companion to the horizon'.

His first major impact was on the design of the ordinary domestic house, through commissions he took on when he was 'moonlighting' from his day job. He got the sack, of course, and this lucky reverse propelled him to set up on his own.

His Prairie houses revolutionized domestic architecture. The *Ladies Home Journal* offered its readers the first of them in 1900. FLW guaranteed them a house – including masonry, plumbing, heating boiler, painting and glass – for the tiny sum of $6,970.00. What was so revolutionary? It was his freeform handling of space. The interior revolved around a central core of kitchen and fireplace, with cantilevered outcrops leading off. There were few separate rooms. Garden, forecourts and terraces would also be designed at the same time, in line with the measured, cubic units of the house composition: a return to the Renaissance practice of having a total plan for house and garden. The architect loved working to a detailed level. He would design everything – the cube-shaped furniture, the built-in lighting, sideboards, closets and tables – so the whole house would operate as an organic, living unit. His work was well published and was taught widely in Europe, especially in Holland. The 'Froebel block' cubist element to his work can be traced back to the abstract geometric painting of Piet Mondrian.

Wright's first step with any house would be to work out the best vistas and the best features and landmarks. Then he would make the most of the sunlight in all seasons. Wherever he could, he would join house to landscape, thrusting out balconies or low garden walls. He would use nature – his most famous house is called 'Fallingwater' – to accentuate the feeling of space and freedom. 'As a result,' said *House Beautiful* in 1959, 'his houses seem as big as the outdoors.'

He is credited with inventing the term 'human scale', and his interiors are cosy, calm, reflective places. People could sit comfortably and dream beside his low fireplaces and mantels. By contrast, hallways and corridors, or the centre of the living room, were often raised in proportion to a person's full height. He believed that 'people should belong to the building, just as it should belong to them'.

Today we take open plans for granted. It is hard, therefore, to appreciate just how much Wright shook up the fusty world of the ordinary American house in the early years of the century.

'Boxes beside boxes or inside boxes, called rooms,' he complained, 'are a cellular sequestration that implies ancestors familiar with penal institutions.'

He hated the idea of unused rooms, like damp fusty basements or stuffy parlours. In his influential houses, the interior space was opened up, using short walls or screens to do away with interior walls, while glass frames allowed views in from outside.

A lover of fast cars and the open road, he invented the carport as a cheaper alternative to the 'gaping hole' of a garage. During a career in which he designed more than 600 homes, he created an architecture that despite Mayan, Japanese and vernacular influences was truly American. Eventually, in what he called 'Usonian houses' – modest-cost homes designed to a system – he abolished the separation between kitchen and living room and created a newer, freer lifestyle that stays with us today. The way he organized his living rooms around central brick hearths has become a key motif in IKEA's everyman modern design ethic, as have the built-in, functional, 'workspace' kitchens opening on to dining spaces.

Until he was 42, Wright lived a totally conventional personal life in American suburbia with his wife Catherine and six children – for whom he designed probably the world's most perfect nursery. However, in 1909 he suddenly and abruptly left Catherine and fled to Europe with the wife of a client. Martha Chaney, or 'Mamah', as she was known, was a skilled linguist and translator, unconventional for the times, an independent-spirited woman who earned her own living. On their return they set up home in Wisconsin, in a house called Taliesin. Yet Wright wasn't destined for happiness. Just after serving lunch on 15 August 1914, Wright's cook Julian Carleton, who had quietly gone mad, bolted the doors and windows, poured gasoline around the outside of the house and set it alight.

As the house began to burn, he took a hatchet and attacked and murdered Mamah and her children – 12-year-old John and 9-year-old Martha. Wright rushed home from work, having been told it was just a fire – it was only the waiting reporters who told him the truth. He was too heartbroken to even put up a headstone.

*'All I had left to show for the struggle for freedom of the five years past had now been swept away. Why mark the spot where desolation ended and began?'*

Between 1914 and 1932 Wright's life was a total soap opera: his life was even turned into a novel and then a film. He rebuilt Taliesin and nearly lost it to the bank, then after divorcing Catherine he married, and

**RIGHT** The Johnson Wax building's interior, with its dramatic 'lily' columns, was utterly different from any office that had gone before

**RIGHT** Avant Garde: the Guggenheim New York of 1959. An extraordinary building that has set the tone for all future extensions of the Guggenheim brand

became separated from, a morphine addict named Miriam Noel. He even spent a little time in jail: Miriam was to charge him with desertion and cruelty. In 1927 they finally agreed to divorce terms, with Miriam receiving $6,000 in cash, a $30,000 trust fund and $250 per month for life. His marriage to a third wife, Olgivanna Milanoff, a Bosnian Serb, would be much happier – but all this time his career had been neglected. Wright was forgotten. In a letter to his one-time mentor, the architect's architect, Louis Sullivan, he wrote that he was 'extremely hard up – and not a job in sight in the world'.

But you can't keep a great man down – he wasn't finished yet. In 1939 the nearly-forgotten architect designed one of the most radical commercial buildings ever seen, the Johnson Wax Administration Building in Wisconsin. Its sculpted white concrete columns mushroom upwards in a building that spawned a thousand space-age fantasies. The main work area has a special quality of sparkling light and appears to be held up by 'Lily pad' columns, which do not touch. In fact, the space between them is held together by a membrane of pyrex tubes, filtering the light from a high clerestory window that

wraps around the entire space. This was true humanism in the workspace: hi-tech without the 'machine'.

Cross New York's Central Park to Fifth Avenue and you will find another great white spaceship amid the strait-laced office blocks. The 1959 Guggenheim Museum is a *tour de force,* and utterly different from anything Wright had done before. With its dramatic internal spiral ramp, it is hardly what you expect from an art gallery (where do you put flat, rectangular pictures in a curved building, for one thing?).

It was controversial – there were even complaints that it was an 'attack on art'. But Wright always did what he wanted. And what he wanted was to 'make the building and the painting an uninterrupted, beautiful symphony – such as never existed in the World of Art before'. It's a cause today's architects would recognize – to heighten the aim of the building, not simply reflect it. Wright's Guggenheim is

the father of today's Expressionism, and the stylistic precursor of Frank Gehry's Bilbao Guggenheim.

What did FLW give 20th century America? A reputation as the most progressive nation in the world, one that straddled the commercial sphere as well as the domestic.

As to his legacy to you and me – well, it's hard to pin down, but it has its core in the way he designed domestic spaces that were totally democratic, totally free. During a career in which he designed more than 600 homes, he single-handedly forged an architecture that was truly American.

But he didn't just design houses for the wealthy. Any architect can build a rich house for a rich man, he used to say. But to design a beautiful small house? Now that would really 'test the mettle' of a real architect. His low-cost 'Usonian' houses – homes he individually designed to a system – proved that small houses could indeed be beautiful.

When he died, Frank Lloyd Wright had been building for over 75 years – and had lived for over half the period of the American Republic. In 1991 the American Institute of Architects named him 'the greatest American architect of all time'. Perhaps.

# A NEW EXPRESSIONISM?

There was another way. Frank Lloyd Wright, the grand old man of American architecture, had always forged his own path, especially when it came to remarkable office buildings such as the Johnson Wax Building at Racine, Wisconsin (1936–9). In Wright, Modernism was no bar to tradition, to new materials. He was an iconoclast, in a word. When he produced the Solomon R. Guggenheim Museum, in 1956, New York gasped. More sculpture than architecture, the museum winds up a continuous spatial helix. It is topped by a flat-ribbed glass dome. This was an architecture of idiom, of metaphor. The effect may have been space age, but the inspiration was nature, according to Wright: 'the quiet unbroken wave'.

So could this be the 'new' wave? Two buildings designed the next year hold a special place in the camera lenses of film directors over the world: the TWA Terminal at J.F. Kennedy Airport in New York and the Sydney Opera House.

Eero Saarinen's futuristic TWA building of 1957, with its bird-like roof, is a uniquely sculptural exercise in fluid form. The interior glides between convex and concave, while the great glass spaces let the light flood into the space below. Sadly, the building's interior furniture no longer lives up to the building itself, but if any airport terminal conveys the excitement of travel, this is it. An expressive architecture of emotion – at last.

Thousands of miles away, in Sydney, an international design competition was being launched. Seldom has a building become such a universal landmark as Sydney's much-loved Opera House. Standing out on a tongue of

**RIGHT** The bold sweep of the TWA building, like a bird in flight

**LEFT** The Sydney Opera House. Getting it built was a major feat in itself

land that extends into the harbour, its brilliant white shells – tantalizingly not-quite sails heading off into the harbour – make you think of silver yachts on the waves, of clouds, of journeys to far-off lands. Significantly, it was Saarinen, one of the judges, who insisted that Jørn Utzon's entry be given a chance. He called it 'Genius'.

Utzon, a Dane who had not really worked much away from his own home shores, was a rank outsider and his entry was little more than a series of preliminary drawings. Mies van der Rohe is said to have turned his back when he was introduced to the young architect. It was not an encouraging start.

Working with the engineering practice Ove Arup, Utzon gradually developed a practical way to construct the large shells that

cover the two halls: complex sections of a sphere. Utzon also had spectacular plans for the interior, but sadly things weren't going at all well. Half a century earlier, the citizens of Paris had been suspicious of their Eiffel Tower: Utzon, halfway across the world from his homeland, faced far greater suspicion and distrust. A malicious publicity campaign was launched against him, against a background of some serious political infighting. In mid-1965 he found himself in open conflict with the Australian government. The new Minister of Works, Davis Hughes began questioning both the designs and the escalating cost – initially estimated at Australian $7 million, based on insufficient data. (It skyrocketed to $100 million.) Eventually he stopped payments to Utzon, who was forced to resign as chief

architect in February 1966. Emotionally destroyed, Utzon left the country in secret days later, never to return.

The Opera House didn't eventually open until 1973 so it was a good thing that the design was ahead of its time. The architect was not invited to the opening ceremony: his name wasn't even mentioned. By the time his contribution to Australia was finally recognized in 2003 Utzon's son had to accept an honorary doctorate in his place, as he was too ill to travel. He was awarded architecture's own version of the Nobel Prize, the Pritzker Prize, in the same year. Did he fall victim to a 'lowball' – an unrealistic budget, artificially lowered for political reasons? Either way, Utzon's career was in ruins. He built no more major international buildings: the world's loss.

# ARCHITECTURE AS BEAST

It was Corbusier's 1953 Secretariat Building in Chandigarh, India, that first forced Brutalism on to an unsuspecting world. Architects wanted people to experience space in a new way, and the repeating angles, abstraction and somewhat aggressive monumentality seen in Chandigarh could be adapted to create sculptural shapes that shouted 'modern'.

The dream was a good one – to create a profoundly democratic society. But the very word, Brutalism, first coined by an enthusiastic critic, tells a different story. The actual term comes from a little piece of fate – Corbusier's use of the French term *béton brut*, which simply means raw concrete.

A Brutalist building, at its worst, seems like Soviet-style socialism: grey and faceless. Brutalism's closest stylistic models were to be found in Soviet Russia – the earliest model being Konstantin Melnikov's Rusakov Club of 1927, built for the employees of the Moscow City Soviet. Often constructed in rough poured concrete, like Boston City Hall or the UK's National Theatre, they were criticized for being alien and stark and for not considering the context of their surroundings. Sadly, these criticisms were often valid.

Planners and politicians, who already liked concrete because it was cheap, found this a useful new trend. The style became associated with low-cost shopping centres, rain-stained council offices and dangerous and

**ABOVE** Love it, or hate it? Denys Lasdun's Brutalist National Theatre, London is a series of wide linked terraces that many criticize for being overbearing

depressing car parks. As Brutalism spread over the public sphere, the momentum was building for a backlash.

Modernists had pointed to the talented Louis Sullivan – 'form follows function' – as their godfather in the cause of simplification. Yet Sullivan had always articulated the skin of his structures with delicate and subtle ornament.

Now, with the addition of Brutalism to the vocabulary, Modernism had become monolithic, boring. In plan, or from the air, it might look dynamic and sophisticated. But at its most extreme it had no variation, and little human-level interest at all – like Minoru Yamasaki's World Trade Center. All the worst in drab, heavy-duty buildings like car parks and bus stations – mainly Brutalist – had combined with the worst in city planning to de-humanize urban environments. Modern architects were beginning to get a filthy name. Meanwhile, mainstream Modernism had got so concerned with being rational, so concerned with function (or in some cases, simply making money), that its followers had forgotten about that most fundamental thing of all – beauty. Soulless grey boxes spoke more of an Orwellian nightmare than a Utopian, socialist future. Less is more?

**ABOVE** The startling cantilevered concrete of the Rusakov Club on Stromynka Street, Moscow. Konstantin Melnikov designed a number of these workers' clubs in the 1920s

## Concrete

The idea of using iron-reinforced concrete was first dreamed up by a Parisian, the builder François Coignet in the 1850s. He later designed his own house with roofs and floors reinforced by wrought-iron I-beams. Another builder, François Hennebique would soon develop the idea, particularly for floor construction. He was the first to realize that the iron rods needed to be bent upwards to increase strength near supports. Hennebique travelled to Wales to build Europe's first reinforced concrete building, the elaborately ugly Weaver & Co. Flour Mill in Swansea (1897–8) with Napoleon LeBrun: an engineer/architect collaboration which heralded the skill sets that would be needed in the new age. By the 1950s the crumbling, rain-stained and mildewed Weaver building illustrated the rather ignoble fate awaiting concrete in a wet climate. Historic significance is no defence when it comes to the power of commerce and the building was demolished to make way for an even uglier supermarket.

# THE JOKERS STRIKE BACK

'Less is a bore', said Robert Venturi. And the architectural world took a deep breath. Venturi, an American architect, published his treatise *Learning From Las Vegas* in 1972. It was a celebration of an unselfconscious form of architecture: that of the street, the strip, the mall. Thumbing their noses at the established and numbing architectural orthodoxy, good Postmodernists wanted buildings to communicate their meaning, to say something to the world. They were happy for a building to have wit, like something from the Baroque; they were even happy for the whole building to be a joke.

The buildings of Alison Sky, Michelle Stone and James Wines, who formed a collaborative called SITE (Sculpture in the Environment) in 1970 based out of the Wall Street area of New York, took even the drab architecture of the warehouse and gave it a lift. We love to hate industrial estate commercial architecture, because it's so awful.

In your wildest fantasies, you want to blow the buildings up. So in 1976 SITE built the ultimate shed for Tilt, in Maryland 1976 – one that seems about to self-destruct. This was egalitarian architecture, with a wit and irony everyone could 'understand'. Most importantly, it operates on two levels, the jokey and, from the client's point of view, the functional. Does it look like a still from a disaster movie? Well, why not experience a thrill – and go on in?

It was at this point that the prewar ideals of the new internationalists – honesty,

**BELOW** The artist/architects of Sculpture in the Environment (SITE) questioned the standard 'big box'. James Wines' 1984 Inside/Outside Building, for Best, in Milwaukee

**RIGHT** Philip Johnson, designer of the rigorously minimal Glass House at New Caanan, Connecticut, rejected International Style with the 1984 AT&T Building, Manhattan

**ABOVE** 1995's San Antonio Public Library, Texas, designed by Mexican architect Ricardo Legorreta and others, in 'Enchilada Red'

restraint, simplicity – seemed to cave in. In 1984, Mies' collaborator Philip Johnson did something shocking. He topped the AT&T Building [now Sony] in Manhattan with an ornamental pink granite Neo-Georgian pediment. What on earth was he doing? History was outlawed, yet the master of minimalism had designed a building that looked like an oversized piece of Chippendale. The architectural world reeled. To the devoted, this 'clunky' Postmodern gesture was a bit like showing your underpants in public.

Although Postmodernism was given a bad name in, for example, some of London's Docklands, it was not all dirty linen. Dismissed as lightweight and ignored by most of architecture's current 'big-hitters', as a strand of thinking it hasn't quite gone away. Practices like FAT in the UK still work along these freed-up lines – allowing themselves to have fun.

One example is Frank Gehry's 1986 Venice Beach House, which is littered with ironic ornamental details. Another is Mexican architect Ricardo Legorreta's 1995 library for the city of San Antonio in Texas, which attacks the idea that a library has to be imposing. It has 'enchilada red' walls and overtly comical landscaping touches. People loved it: custom doubled the year the library opened.

Venturi, a pupil of the great formalist Louis Kahn, wasn't against the best in Modernism. He simply wanted to challenge the orthodoxy that had brought a new, cheerless conservatism to architecture, along with a screamingly dull boxy aesthetic.

By this stage, New York's 6th Avenue was a sterile canyon of towering glass skyscrapers, none of which did anything to encapsulate the mood and ethos of the city as well as either the Chrysler Building or the Empire State. Architecture was yearning to wriggle out of the straitjacket.

# PAST PERFECT?

It would have pained the Modernists to find that the language of history was so soon to be revived. When it came to designing the National Museum of Roman Art in Mérida, Spain (1980–5), José Rafael Moneo took the opportunity and went straight back to the classical idiom. Based around a central atrium, this inspired, quiet and somehow unassuming building reinterprets the vaulted naves and aisles of Roman basilicas. Moneo played with perspectives using Roman building techniques, materials, and proportions, along with the Romans' building system of massive masonry-bearing walls filled with concrete.

**M**oneo was covered, though. He was creating a museum about Rome. Any mainstream stirrings in favour of full-blown classicism were going to be controversial with architects who, like the comedian John Cleese, were trying 'not to mention the war', metaphorically speaking. Classicism was discredited and gone. Besides, for decades the football of architecture had been on the pitch of the theorists – who held it in the name of the common man. It was no longer the province of the rich, or of royalty. There was one man who disagreed. Radically.

In 1984, Britain's Prince Charles addressed the Royal Institute of British Architects. Architecture arouses some pretty strong emotions, and the heir to the throne was about to do the unthinkable: make the connection between the death of classicism, and Germany's defeat in 1949.

'You have to give this much to the Luftwaffe,' he said, wine glass in hand. 'When it knocked down our buildings, it didn't replace them with anything more offensive than rubble.'

The quip was in somewhat bad taste, but the Prince was not really joking. The next day, Britain awoke to a tabloid storm: the heir to the throne had touched a very raw nerve.

By the 1980s the friendly values of community, already eroded in the UK since the advent of industrialization, were seriously threatened. Social theorists would blame individualism, consumerism and the cult of the

self. The general public, though, associating most social ills with postwar housing estates, was ready to blame architects. Now that the ancient establishment was on the attack, the general public was right behind it. Architecture had become cold and distant. Architects, it seemed, were haughty aesthetes who didn't care what happened to the people in their buildings. How could it all have gone so wrong?

When Venturi and partner Denise Scott Brown won a competition to design a new extension to London's National Gallery in the city's much-loved Trafalgar Square, the result was a muted, if occasionally mischievous, example of classicism – devised after the previous scheme had been dubbed 'a carbuncle' by the heir to the throne.

There is still a deep suspicion of 'tradition' amongst the architectural

profession. Robert A. Stern, a well respected American Postmodernist and academic, began more recently to call his architectural style 'new traditionalist'. When Stern built a new science centre for a college in Nova Scotia – re-employing the Georgian Classical vocabulary of the rest of the campus – he won a 'Palladio Award', an annual award scheme in the United States.

Stern's Georgian K.C. Irving Environmental Science Centre is finished to a high degree of craftsmanship – hand-moulded red brick, carved-limestone trim, custom-designed mahogany windows made of plantation-grown wood and quarter-sawn white oak on the interior. Admittedly, it is highly conventional, even imitative. It's surprising to find some postings on the award's website are so abusive they have had to be blocked.

**RIGHT** What to do when designing a museum of Roman art? Meridà's Roman ruins have made it a UNESCO World Heritage site

# TECHNOLOGY TAKES THE STAGE

So what was next? It was another spirited attempt to give life to those functional steel and glass boxes – in a word, to decorate. Only this new style would give the eye something radically new to work on: a tough, engineering-led decoration that was a new form of homage to the world of the machine. The new approach was called Hi-Tech.

There was a point at which modern architecture was felt to have 'matured'. In Japan, where Kenzo Tange and Tadao Ando were among the more famous practitioners, Corbusian theory was still a huge influence. Kisho Kurokawa's 1972 Capsule Tower, in Tokyo, part of the so-called 'Metabolist' school, took the idea of mass production to new heights (or lows, depending on your point of view), with individual studio room 'pods', made out of modified sea containers.

Richard Rogers and Renzo Piano's Pompidou Centre in Paris, 1971, was a revelation. It had what was to become a Rogers trademark – exposed service ducts and stairs on the exterior, leaving the interior clean and uncluttered for exhibition displays. The Pompidou was an overnight sensation, although not uncontroversial. Those few French who didn't like it called it 'Bowellism', after the guts of the building. It was a precursor of things to come.

The satirical UK television show *Spitting Image* once depicted Rogers as a grinning puppet, his metaphorical guts spilled out all over the floor. Why? Because Rogers had just designed what will probably be his most famous building, for Lloyd's of London, and like the Pompidou, it was inside out. The services were on the outside – but transformed into a rhythmic, decorative feature. Six towers support the main structure and house the building's service elements: lifts, refuse chutes,

and air-conditioning. The hi-tech building, with an arched transept in homage to Paxton's Crystal Palace, is a hymn in steel and glass, a shiny, ebullient symbol of a traditional organization transformed.

With this building, Rogers also transformed the way that corporations thought about the workplace. Its concentric galleries overlook a central atrium. Rather than enclose people in rows of corridors, Rogers created open-plan offices with acres of glass. Office workers have exciting views out across the city, while glass elevators whizz up and down each of the external stainless steel towers. Even today, the building feels like something out of a science fiction novel. Glamorous and distinctive, Lloyd's is known the world over: the building has become a defining image of the City of London. The Modern movement was rescued – it was out of its rut. Rogers had also done what the early Modernists had only been able to dream of.

**LEFT** Modern living: the Capsule Tower in Tokyo could have its 'pods' added or taken away, according to need

He had made a building that didn't just look like a machine: it functioned like one, and could be adapted like one.

The 1990s, though, was the decade that architecture truly became an art of the machine – and this time the driving technology was the computer, not the internal combustion engine. Computer-aided modelling helped architects create forms by manipulating algorithms in a computer modelling program. The impact of the breakthrough cannot be emphasized enough. To say it gave new impetus to design is to understate, wildly, the impact of CAD, or computer-aided design.

Architectural movements exploded into a kaleidoscope of new 'isms' which, in the speed of their transit, were reminiscent of the pick and mix 'multi-cultural' experiments of the Victorians a century before. As Postmodernism blew itself out and, in Britain, Prince Charles began experimenting with Neoclassicism, creating his own Utopia in the Dorsetshire village of Poundbury, modern architecture came down to a swing between minimalism and maximalism. Classical revivalism was joined by deconstructivism, 'critical regionalism', 'organic' architecture and so-called 'Blobitecture'. How would these divergent themes affect the architecture of the new century? And was the Modern movement well and truly over?

**RIGHT** The Hongkong and Shanghai Bank (HSBC), in Hong Kong, prefabricated by shipbuilders in Glasgow in the UK, with its suspension trusses on the outside

**BELOW RIGHT** Poundbury, the traditionalists' experiment in Dorset, UK. It feels rather contrived; however, it still appears to be a popular place to live

**BELOW** The Pompidou Centre, put together from 1979 by a skilled young team of Renzo Piano, Richard and Sue Rogers, along with structural engineer Edmund Happold

# BRAVE NEW WORLD

*'Everything is becoming science fiction.'*
J.G. Ballard

So architecture has been liberated from ideology
and from rigidly functional Modernism. Although
form is still of course crucial, and in many
architects' buildings, detail is still stripped down to
a minimalist level, decoration is no longer simply
seen as 'bourgeois'. The suffocating anti-history
movement set off by Hitler's colonization of
classicism has been softened, by time itself.
But what direction would the architecture of the
new Millennium take? .

'L'Hemisfèric' of 1998:
an eye emerging from the
water at the centre of
Valencia's City of Arts
and Sciences, designed
by Santiago Calatrava
in collaboration with
Félix Candela

# FRIENDLY BUILDINGS

**T**he refreshing Pompidou Centre (Beaubourg) in Paris, a collaboration between the young Richard Rogers and Renzo Piano, challenged the Modernists' orthodoxy. It was like throwing the baby out with the bath water, then catching it in midair. The architects used the building's technology itself as sheer, exuberant decoration. In doing so, they humanized Le Corbusier's idea of the building as a machine. Above all, they broke the golden Modernist rule that decoration is a

crime. Beaubourg was decorated with its own oxygenated veins: the pipes, ducts and escalators that scale the outside walls.

As to history, Rogers' thrilling Lloyd's building (1978–86) directly 'quoted' Paxton's Crystal Palace of 1851. Soon, Nicholas Grimshaw's complex curved glass roofs at Waterloo Station in London would deliberately evoke the great Victorian engineering heritage. Modernism itself had become historic: today, a sense of history is a valid part of a building's character. One of the

latest New York high-rise apartment buildings is a 'step-back' by the classicist Robert Stern, who was inspired by the great Art Deco scrapers of the 1920s. And with history came more approachable form, as if artists once forced to paint abstract art were suddenly allowed to draw from life. Another New York block, soon to be built in TriBeCa by Dutch architect Ben van Berkel of UNStudio, will have decorative metal 'pleats' that are intended to look like an Issey Miyake dress.

Thanks to computer-aided design, today's architects can create structures they scarcely dreamed of, even 15 years ago. The old-timer Frank Gehry is finally able to create highly complex buildings just like his hand-made models. By the time Rem Koolhaas came on the scene, playing with scale and mixing quality materials with cheap ones, architecture was free – almost – of its crippling Modernist restraints.

The new architecture is an architecture that can be 'read'. It tells stories the public can understand. Frank Gehry's 1997 Guggenheim Museum Bilbao looks *like* something other than a blank block. As a result, it is approachable and endearing and the public loves it. Like Frank Lloyd Wright's original in New York, it is as much a symbol as an art gallery, as much a sculpture as a building. It takes us back to when Erich Mendelsohn created his crouching, Expressionist tower for Albert Einstein at Potsdam – that brief moment before the Nazis drove a splitting wedge into the heart of architecture, creating a schism between classicism and modernism.

Mendelsohn's tower looked like a caged animal ready to spring: Einstein's verdict was that it was 'organic'. Gehry's golden Guggenheim also uses naturalistic metaphors. In an elusive way the image changes from fish to flower to ship, depending on the angle at which you view the building.

The work of the American architect Daniel Libeskind, who will be behind the masterplan of the new World Trade Center, was barely known outside the academic world until the acclaimed Jewish Museum Berlin was built. The zinc exterior is a story of the Holocaust, sliced into dozens of sharp, 'deconstructed' lines and shapes. Libeskind

**LEFT** Inside the Lloyd's Building, the reference to Joseph Paxton's Crystal Palace, built for the Great Exhibition in 1851, is immediately obvious (see pp.174 and 176)

describes the configuration as an exploded Star of David. His Contemporary Jewish Museum in San Francisco is inspired by the Hebrew phrase *L'Chaim* – to life. The organizing principles of the building are the two symbolic Hebrew letters of *chai* (life) – the 'chet' and the 'yud'.

Libeskind, like Gehry, is often described as a 'Deconstructivist' architect. But despite the many descriptions that have been bandied about, the term 'Expressionism' seems to make the most sense when discussing the so-called 'signature' architects like Gehry, Zaha Hadid, Libeskind and Koolhaas (there are many more). A number of modern buildings are almost characters in their own right, with body-like forms that we can all relate to.

One Spanish architect has taken the idea of 'organic' expressionism and turned it into what is almost an art form. Santiago Calatrava's motto is *'natura mater et magistra'*: nature is both mother and teacher. He has said that his architectural hero is Eero Saarinen, and like him Calatrava celebrates the whole idea of movement, with biomorphic designs and acrobatic curves. His TGV station in Lyon (1994), is like a swooping bird, ready to take flight. The stunning L'Hemisfèric planetarium at the City of Arts and Sciences in Valencia rises from the centre of a lake in the form of a giant eye.

Trained in engineering as well as architecture, Calatrava takes the high tech tradition and gives it a surrealist, Gaudí-like touch. Although he is sometimes criticized for introducing an extravagant, almost showmanlike quality into his design, one of his finest works in his homeland of Spain is the calm, unassuming Bodegas Ysios in Laguardia, Álava. With its undulating roof and silvery edges it both exploits and blends in with the surrounding landscape, as the best architecture should.

Another figure who has shot to sudden fame in this era of the 'starchitect' is Zaha Hadid. For years Hadid could never get to build anything for real: she was what the profession calls a 'paper architect'. No more. Hadid is now among the world's most wanted. She too takes up the expressionist/zoomorphic baton from time to time: her designs for the Guggenheim Hermitage Museum in Vilnius, Lithuania, look as if an alien life form has just popped out to sun itself on the river bank.

**ABOVE** Calatrava's structures have critics as well as admirers. But his best work has an emotional resonance that is rare. Here, the ribbed spines of the City of Arts and Sciences

**RIGHT** L'Umbracle, the landscaped garden walk of arches as visitors enter the City of Arts and Sciences. Unlike many architects, the Valencian does hundreds of drawings when designing

# Virtually...

## COMPUTING
Today, software programs allow architects to design structures fast and experiment at will. By using so-called 'open-ended' programs they only have to change one element of a design: the software will automatically modify the entire model. Computer programs can produce intricate designs for classical columns, or even Gothic details. They can design beautifully complex tensile structures, then calculate how they will behave in extreme weather conditions: in high winds, say, or under snow.

And computers are also responsible for the production of the buildings themselves, by creating the cutting patterns for the individual pieces of metal, glass or fabric that are used to make up a complete structure. 3D modelling techniques allow the designer to use a computer to design the surface pattern down to the finest detail before sending it to a manufacturer. This can even be done with stone.

Computer games now simulate entire virtual worlds, fabricated with computer generated imaging. This raises a question: will the fantasy environments created by game designers soon become as influential in architecture as cinema has been?

## REM KOOLHAAS
It is no accident that the 'coolest' architect in the world, Rem Koolhaas, has also worked as a journalist and a scriptwriter. He is uniquely well equipped to deal with the media age and has been able to voice his own PR machine with books like *S,M,L,XL* (part diary, part notebook, it is an awesome 1,376 pages long).

The Dutch architect's work is not without criticism. However, despite his 'star' status he is a genuine theorist and a Harvard professor into the bargain. Koolhaas has designed some of the most challenging, controversial and critically acclaimed ultramodern buildings of the past decade – Seattle Public Library, Casa da Música in Porto, the Dutch Embassy in Berlin. He spent part of his life in Indonesia, and a considerable amount of his current work is in the East. His practice is called the Office for Metropolitan Architecture, or OMA.

**BELOW** Seattle Public Library of 2004, designed by Rem Koolhaas in conjunction with LMN Architects

# THE SHIFT TO THE EAST

Tom Wright was looking for an iconic motif like Sydney Opera House's memorable white spinnakers when the idea suddenly came to him: his building would celebrate another type of sail – the billowing mainsail of a traditional Arabian dhow. Dubai's Burj Al Arab, built by the British firm Atkins, is probably the most surprising building of recent years – the world's tallest hotel, it rises 1053 feet (321 metres) from a man-made island in the Persian Gulf. Wright needed a clear and simple shape that people would remember: a design that would almost be a corporate logo for Dubai.

ABOVE The Burj Al Arab, completed in 1999, rises up from 250 concrete piles penetrating the sea floor to a depth of more than 130 feet (40m), 950 feet (290m) off the Dubai coast

**W**right's 1999 'ship' was one of the first totemic signs of a dramatic shift to the East, both creative and commercial. Suddenly, the minty-fresh glamour of new Western architecture was as popular as the bubbles in champagne. The transformation of Dubai from a sleepy, pearl-diving backwater to a modern metropolis has been one of the major news stories of the turn of the century. A business, economic and development success story, oil-rich Dubai has built on the back of cheap, exploited labour with a speed scarcely seen since the heyday of Victorian Britain.

But Crown Prince Sheikh Mohammed bin Rashid Al Maktoum wasn't stopping with the Burj Al Arab and the world's 10th-tallest commercial buildings, the twin Emirates Towers. Dubai has become a byword for conspicuous consumption. The Mall of the Emirates, opened in 2005, is the largest shopping mall outside North America. The country's indoor ski slopes don't endear it to the environmental lobby: neither do the artificial islands that now extend into the turquoise waters of the Persian Gulf. Dubai's sheikhs have claimed that the Palm Jumeirah, the first of a raft of artificial islands, is 'the eighth wonder of the world'. Indeed, one of the new developments is laid out like a map of the globe – a heady $14bn endeavour consisting of 300 individual islands. The islands go for $7m to $35m each. They might look very pretty from the air but environmentalists worry they disturb and pollute the marine environment, while changing the tidal patterns. It may be that in the long term new habitats will emerge along

the fronds of the 'Palms'. But in the meantime, coral reefs have been buried and nearby beaches are eroding, while a 'protected' marine reserve was handed over to the developers.

The process goes on. At 3 billion square feet (279 million square metres), the amusement park known as Dubailand, complete with a replica of the Eiffel Tower and a 60,000-seat stadium will be three times the size of Manhattan. Its motto is 'The Earth has a new center'. Other Gulf states are following suit: Qatar has launched a spectacular building campaign of its own, as Saudi Arabia and Kuwait rev up to do the same. Abu Dhabi, meanwhile, is looking over its shoulder, hoping to learn from the mistakes of its neighbours. It will be taking a slightly different path – the state has plans to turn its capital into a sort of Arabian Left Bank, with major new cultural venues designed by Jean Nouvel, Zaha Hadid, Frank Gehry and others.

But when it comes to building at speed and scale, it is China that has been struck with construction fever. Only a decade ago this was a land that considered the very term 'architect'

## Burj Al Arab

Jørn Utzon's Opera House, opened in 1973, was such a success that it has become a symbol not just for Sydney but for the whole of the fifth continent – other architects were bound to follow. The V shape of the Burj Al Arab's two 'wings' stretches 1053 feet (321 metres) into the sky to form a vast 'mast'.

Wright cleverly placed a Teflon-coated fibreglass sail in the gap between the wings, which does two things: first, it creates a cathedral-high atrium inside the hotel and, second, the Teflon coating controls the building's temperature. The structure, topped by a helipad for the super-rich who come to stay here, is in reality a technologically complex steel exoskeleton around a reinforced concrete tower. Private butlers are apparently de rigueur at the so-called 'seven-star' hotel, entering Jeeves-like through concealed doors to unpack luggage into drawers hidden from sight.

to be bourgeois. The picture couldn't be more different today.

Ahead of the 2008 Beijing Olympics, architecture was deployed as a heat-seeking missile, diverting the glare of attention away from human rights issues: particularly the Chinese occupation of Tibet. The image makeover and cure-all cost an estimated $40bn.

More than a million workers came to transform the flat, smog-hazed cityscape into an architect's playground. Soon Beijing was home to exciting structures like the giant steel bird's nest that is Jacques Herzog and Pierre de Meuron's Olympic Stadium, Paul Andreu's titanium-egg National Grand Theater as well as Rem Koolhaas' giant-legged China Central Television Headquarters, nicknamed the 'Twisted Doughnut'. If a scheme was ambitious enough, it seems, it got built. The $100m National Aquatics Center – nicknamed 'the Water Cube' – is based on the structure of soap bubbles and glows blue at night. It was designed by the Australian firm PTW along with the China State Construction Engineering Corporation. Most of the major projects, though, have been designed by foreign firms. It's been a surprise to everyone that a small sheikhdom on the Gulf and the world's largest Communist dictatorship have become the twin boiler rooms of experimental architecture.

**RIGHT** Beijing's 'Watercube' incorporates ETFE and research by professors Denis Weaire and Robert Phelan

**BELOW** China's National Grand Theatre (National Centre for the Performing Arts), also known as 'the Egg', Beijing

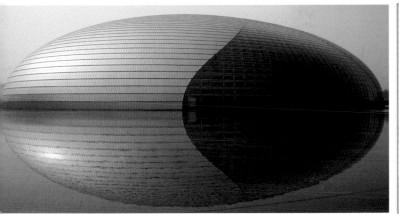

# The Wonderstuff

ETFE. Forget the ridiculous name: ethylene tetrafluoroethylene is the new wonder-material. The iridescent bubbles of Beijing's Water Cube and HdeM's bird's nest both rely on it. To protect spectators from rain and wind, the Olympic Stadium has red ETFE cushions inserted between the 'twigs' of its 'nest'. This is not entirely new (the 'biomes' of Nicholas Grimshaw's famous Eden Project in Cornwall are made of ETFE), but the 750,000-square-foot (70,000 square metres) Water Cube is the largest ETFE project ever. The plastic has high corrosion resistance and a lot of strength, but its flexibility and environmental credentials are the main attraction. Initially developed for use in sailing, the material is 1 per cent of the weight of glass. It also costs a lot less to install – up to 70 per cent less – and transmits more light. It is so slick that dirt, snow, and rain simply slide off – but in any case, Dupont's wonderstuff can bear 400 times its own weight. Just don't walk too close to it with a sharp stick.

# BIGGER, BETTER, TALLER...

The Burj Dubai is the tallest man-made structure on earth, although how long it will stay that way is a moot point. Its final height was kept a close secret, for fear of rivals building higher still: proof positive that the craze to build sky-high is a commercially competitive phenomenon. Globalization is a relentless engine, fed by marketing hubris. Post-9/11, do we really want to keep driving ever higher into the sky? Even in low-rise cities like London, where a comment by Queen Victoria protected the skyline for nearly a century, there are plans for a new wave of skyscrapers. Many argue that this is a vacuous form of macho-driven madness.

**B**ut how to stop it? Right now, in Bogota, Kiev, Moscow, Rangoon and China, a whole globe's-worth of skyscrapers is mushrooming. In Moscow, the skyline has been bulking up like an athlete on steroids. The environmental issues are urgent. The world is already running out of resources, and it will do so even sooner if China and India achieve consumption rates to rival those of America. Skyscrapers, says Singapore architect Ken Yeang, should be thought through as 'green' environments. They should be treated as cities in the sky and mapped in similar ways, looking at use, density, inhabitants and open spaces. In his Tokyo Nara tower (1994), gardens climbed up the building and filtered air quality, temperature and noise. Spiralling floor plans shaded the levels beneath. Over a decade later, building technology is certainly making 'green', energy-producing skyscrapers possible – if at a cost that few architect's clients are prepared to pay.

But there is another cost to consider. In this race to transform world cities into shiny new global megalopolises, much of their true fabric is being ruthlessly erased. The twisted, Atlas-like structure of the Koolhaas cantilevered CCTV building, designed with Arup engineer Cecil Balmond, might suit political China's vision of itself, but what of its people? Beijing's Olympic boom has destroyed whole swathes of the city's traditional *hutong* courtyard houses, forcibly relocating the families living there. It's extraordinary to think that more than a million people have been displaced. Yet as we know from the Modernist and Brutalist experiments, the two things we should not detach from are human scale and a sense of history.

It would be naïve to say this shouldn't happen. It is already happening. In Singapore and urban Hong Kong, land prices are so dear that almost the entire population lives in high-rise apartments. So we have to find better ways of making cities. The recently restored mud-brick Yemeni city of Shibam, most of it built in the 16th century, is being taken as a model for dense urban living. It had 500 defendable 'towers' that protected people from Bedouin attacks, each floor being occupied by a single family. But crucially, each tower was only 5 to 9 storeys high.

Some Italian towns like San Gimignano and Siena follow a similar pattern. Tightly-packed urban spaces, they manage to be beautiful and functional at the same time: this is helped by the loving design detail that exists at ground level.

More than that, the public spaces are practical, refined and designed for people. Their manageable size – and the restrained height of the buildings – stops the spaces becoming wind tunnels, as in Chicago or Canary Wharf. By contrast, the reinforced concrete and steel high-rise developments now marching across the world's cityscapes pose far more serious difficulties – to firefighters, just for starters. As homes, they also pose serious problems. Try getting your shopping up even 20 flights of stairs if a lift breaks down.

The candle-like Chrysler building, the

**LEFT** Aggression or sophistication? The Petronas Towers in Kuala Lumpur, Malaysia were the world's tallest buildings before being overtaken by Taipei 101

**RIGHT** According to architect Renzo Piano, the Shard (left) stands on the London skyline like 'a kind of lighthouse'. He envisaged this 87-storey skyscraper as 'a vertical city, for thousands of people to work in and enjoy'

tallest and most exciting structure of its day for a brief 12 months, was 1,047 feet (319 metres) high. SOM's (Skidmore, Owings and Merrill) Burj Dubai will perhaps rise to 164 storeys – that is, 2,684 feet (818 metres). High; higher; highest. These structures are money machines: logos that market cities or large companies. But the higher they go, the further they get from any human scale. When will this end?

A market economy thrives on novelty. But this is architecture for rich corporations and governments looking to make a nationalist splash. Good civic architecture has different values. The danger is that, as cities compete commercially, the sky will stop feeling like a limit. And in a desperate effort to differentiate one building from the next, 21st century architecture will become ever more manic, centred around more and more extravagant shapes. Idealistic young trainee architects grumble about architecture which doesn't so much try to serve society as bludgeon it into

submission. The good news today is that 'green' design is being taken increasingly seriously, with projects taking shape in cities across Thailand, China, Hong Kong and Singapore. Perhaps in future they will also take on Calatrava's 'nature' mantra, too.

**ABOVE** The Shanghai Tower is the tallest of a group of three super-tall buildings in Shanghai's commercial district. The designers, Gensler, say its curved façade requires 14 percent less glass than a square building of the same total floor area and its spiralling form minimizes wind loads

**LEFT** The Burj Dubai's management aims for their building to be a 'beacon of progress for the whole world'

**ABOVE** An improvement? The rapidly changing Moscow skyline. There are 93 new highrises either under construction or already approved in the city

# Eco Futures

*'In order to transform our cities, we need to move from ego-culture to eco-culture.'*

Rusong Wang, President,
Ecological Society of China

Since the 1960s, environmental pioneers have been warning us that the world will have to change. So-called 'green' awareness has been growing, particularly in 'alternative' America. Efficient energy use, the conservation of resources and new ways of living have all become big issues in architecture. Concrete has a colossal carbon footprint. Brick uses four times more embedded energy than wood; concrete five times; steel around ten times. Aluminium and glass are the most environmentally hungry materials of all.

One response has been to 'downshift': witness the Earthship villages in Taos, New Mexico. The houses follow local historical models, built in adobe (mud) and are simple in the extreme, with walls of used tyres filled with earth and stacked like bricks. But if the future for most of the world is urban, the real challenge is how to make these cities self-sustaining. Can 21st-century technology relieve the pressure on the world's resources? Can we stop polluting the planet? We are gradually moving on in our thinking: the realms of science fiction could soon be reality.

**ABOVE RIGHT** The Co-operative Group HQ in Manchester, England, is the most environmentally friendly building in the world

**RIGHT** Renzo Piano's Jean-Marie Tjibaou Cultural Center in New Caledonia has natural ventilation, taking advantage of ocean wind

**BELOW** Massive vehicles aside, the Earthship communities in Taos, New Mexico are remarkably eco-friendly

# Eco futures: action around the world

• The world's most sustainable skyscraper to date is the Pearl River Tower in Guangzhou, China, designed by SOM. By rotating to the east, the tower takes advantage of the midday sun while the effects of the late-day sun on the larger, southern horizontal exposure are minimized. But getting this right is extremely complicated: in order to reach the tower's ultimate goal of net zero energy successfully, then three power-generating technologies have to be put together: wind, integrated photovoltaics and microturbines.

• The saying is, 'as China goes, so goes the planet'. Leading British engineers Arup are pioneering a true eco-city in Dongtan, which could prove to be a blueprint for new eco-cities round the world. Critics worry that this first experiment is being built next to some sensitive wetlands. Dongtan, however, is being thought of by others as a second Venice, with hydrogen-powered public transport and various green energy sources, including wind turbines, biogas extracted from sewage treatment and a combined heat and power plant that

runs on waste product from local rice mills.

• Abu Dhabi has announced a $15bn five-year initiative to develop clean energy technologies, which it calls 'the most ambitious sustainability project ever launched by a government'. Norman Foster is building a new planned city called Masdar, 11 miles southeast of Abu Dhabi, which will cover 64 million square feet (6 million square metres). Foster looked to ancient walled cities such as Shibam for inspiration. The first phase of the world's

**RIGHT** Dongtan, on an island near Shanghai, is being billed as the world's first Eco-City. Its success or otherwise in this high-polluting country is important: China plans to build about 400 cities in the next 20 years

first zero-carbon, zero-waste city should be complete by 2009. It will be powered by a vast photovoltaic power plant and its food will be grown in the irrigated plantations that will surround it. The new city of Astana, capital of Kazakhstan, is already gridlocked with traffic at rush hour. Perhaps taking note, Masdar will be car-free. Its residents will move around in travel pods running on magnetic tracks.

• Ras al-Khaimah, the furthest north of the UAE's seven emirates, also has plans for a new eco-city. The emirate has commissioned the European 'superstar' Rem Koolhaas, one of Foster's rivals, to design the RAK Gateway. Like Masdar, the RAK Gateway is planned on a grid system, and Koolhaas also takes inspiration from the historic Middle East. Ancient fort cities made sense in the harsh climate and desert winds. The two architects have jostled in public over the 'similarities' between the schemes.

• Living *with* the land rather than just on it is also becoming more important. For instance, in Kampen, Holland there is a need for housing but a shortage of suitable land. MVRDV managed to build new houses on a floodplain by jacking them up on stilts. This also damaged the natural marshlands as little as possible. The Termas Géometricas in Villarrica, Chile are slate-covered hot springs, around which the architect Germán del Sol has constructed a deliberately low-key complex that uses natural materials like local redwood. Roofs are softened by planting and the whole building blends into the landscape.

# REALMS OF FANTASY

In the meantime, we should probably sit back and enjoy the era of the 'starchitect'. The first years of the 21st century have been some of the most entertaining in architectural history.

**ABOVE** The five-star Songjiang Hotel by the British firm Atkins will be fashioned out of a former quarry. Inside, the atrium will incorporate the natural cliff face and its vegetation. Two levels will be underwater, the restaurant facing an aquarium

Today's architects are not afraid to show off their inner Bond. It's a trend that began in America in the 1960s and gained ground with the fibreglass volcanoes and submarine-swallowing ships of *Dr No* and *Dr Strangelove*. Don't be surprised if they soon teleport into a shopping mall near you. The first alien landing was in 2003, in the shape of a remarkable 'blob' of a department store.

Birmingham's Selfridges Building, designed by Jan Kaplicky and Amanda Levete of Future Systems, is like a shimmering blue and silver wave. Although the space-age façade of shiny blue aluminium discs has popped up in the home of some notoriously 'brutal' 1960s public architecture, the Brummies love their new bulbous shopping centre (see p.11).

(see p.11)

# Near Future

## MASS PRODUCTION
Could today's so-called 'signature' architects be in such demand that they will soon run out of the loving care, time and energy that needs to be devoted to a building – never mind the size of their practice? Can an individual like Zaha Hadid really bring her unique creative style to every project if she is designing 20 major buildings at a time, all in different corners of the globe? OMA is now 230 people

strong. Foster & Partners, meanwhile, is a global concern, running hundreds of projects concurrently, from major city planning schemes to bridges and buildings. It has work in 150 cities in 50 countries, and its offices are open 24 hours a day, 7 days a week.

## CRYSTAL ISLAND: THE WORLD'S LARGEST ...
There is a long history of architectural flirtation with crystals. It was the form that fascinated the Expressionists most: the revered French theorist Étienne-Louis

Boullée designed 'crystalline' pyramids. The great restorer Viollet-le-Duc declared the crystal to be nature's perfect model. For the modernist, or the purist, the advantage of crystal is that it conceals nothing. It is perfectly 'honest'.

Most importantly for architects, crystal has extraordinary properties when it comes to light: it can reflect, fragment and magnify that magical commodity. So it's intriguing that Norman Foster should be using this name for the world's largest-ever building, in Russia (see opposite page). An architect's dream...

(see opposite page)

**ABOVE** A computer-generated concept for Koolhaas' Convention and Exhibition Centre RAK Gateway in the Emirate of Ras Al Khaimah, UAE

**ABOVE RIGHT** A crystal for Moscow? This vast complex , 1,476 feet high (450m) speaks of an ambitious and emergent nation with money to spend

Koolhaas' Casa da Música in Porto (2005) has often been described as a meteor colliding with the city. These days his buildings have a movie-like spin. The CCTV building, for instance, is a riff on a *Bladerunner*-like theme of alienation. His latest proposal, dramatically, has gone over to the 'Dark Side', with striking similarities between the RAK Gateway conference centre planned for Ras Al Khaimah, United Arab Emirates, and George Lucas' Death Star in the *Star Wars* trilogy.

Meanwhile the planned Songjiang Hotel near Shanghai, China is pure Ken Adam, the man behind the 1960s Bond sets. The luxury sci-fi hotel is being fashioned by engineering specialists Atkins out of a 100-foot-deep (30 metres) abandoned quarry and will have underwater rooms and indoor waterfalls.

But it is the British architect Norman Foster who is likely to make the biggest changes to the world skyline in the near future. Foster never really renounced Modernism: instead he recast it into a hi-tech aesthetic that has stormed the world. He has a world-class reputation and a record of creating buildings that are both long-lasting and adaptable. In the 1980s he designed the world's (then) most expensive and most technologically clever structure, the HSBC Main Building in Hong Kong.

Foster's practice is producing four out of five of the new 'eco towers' adding to Moscow's rapidly growing skyline. The most astounding proposal is for the staggeringly ambitious 'Crystal Island', which is only 4.5 miles (7.5km) from the Kremlin. It will be, says Foster, a 'city within a building'. The floor surface of Russia's new 27 million square feet (3 million square metres) complex will be four times the size of the Pentagon. Intended to be economical and eco-friendly, the exterior will include solar panels and wind turbines.

Not only will Crystal Island be the world's largest building, it will also be the world's largest naturally ventilated building. The glass tent of the superstructure forms a 'breathing' second skin. Residents, businesses et al. should be shielded from Moscow's extreme weather, summer or winter. So reforming Modernism meets science fiction, then. Never affected by the wind or the rain; insulated – and isolated – from the world. Perhaps this rather scary possibility represents our true architectural future.

# Bibliography

Anon *Reflections on the New Houses of Parliament* (Pamphlet)

Burckhardt, Jacob *The Civilisation of the Renaissance in Italy* (Penguin Classics)

Calloway, Stephen (Ed) *The Elements of Style* (Mitchell Beazley, 1996)

Capitman, Barbara Baer *Deco Delights: Preserving Miami Beach Architecture* (Mount Hope Books, 1988)

Colvin, Howard *Biographical Dictionary of British Architects 1600–1840* (John Murray, 1978)

Corbusier, Le *Toward an architecture* (Francis Lincoln, 2008 translation from 1928 original)

Descharnes, R and Prevost, C *Gaudi The Visionary* (Bracken Books, 1989)

Ettinghausen, Richard and Oleg, Grabar 'The Abbasid Tradition: 750–950', *The Art and Architecture of Islam 650–1250* (Yale UP, 1987)

Frampton, Kenneth *Modern Architecture: A Critical History* (Thames & Hudson, 1982)

Frommel, Christoph Luitpold *The Architecture of the Italian Renaissance* (Thames & Hudson, 2007)

Giaconi, Giovanni *The Villas of Palladio* (Princeton Press, 2003)

Gill, Brendan *Many Masks: A Life of Frank Lloyd Wright* (Ballantine Books, 1988)

Girouard, Mark *The Victorian Country House* (Oxford University Press, 1976)

Glancey, Jonathan *The Story of Architecture* (Dorling Kindersley, 2004)

Handlin, David *American Architecture* (Thames & Hudson, 2004)

Heyer, Paul *Architects on Architecture* (Walker and Company, 1966)

Hoag, John, 'Abbasid Architecture', *Islamic Architecture* (Rizzoli Publications, 1987)

Humpherus, Henry *History, The Watermen's Company*

Jenkyns, Richard *Westminster Abbey* (Profile Books, 2004)

Kostof, Spiro *A History of Architecture* (Oxford University Press, 1985)

Lassner, Jacob, *The Topography of Baghdad in the Early Middle Ages* (Wayne State University Press, 1970)

Lyon, Dominique *Le Corbusier Alive* (Vilo Publishing, 2000)

MacCarthy, Fiona *William Morris: A Life for Our Time* (Faber and Faber, 1995)

Millon, Henry *A Triumph of the Baroque: Architecture in Europe, 1600–1750* (Rizzoli Publications, 2000)

Musson, Jeremy *How to Read a Country House* (Ebury, 2005)

Nicolson, Nigel *The National Trust Book of Great Houses in Britain* (Weidenfeld & Nicolson, 1979)

Norwich, John Julius (Ed) *Great Architecture of the World* (Mitchell Beazley, 1985)

Pevsner, Nikolaus *The Buildings of England* (Pevsner Architectural Guides, The Buildings Books Trust)

Rossi, Corinna *Architecture and Mathematics in Ancient Egypt* (Cambridge University Press, 2004)

Roth, Leland M *Understanding Architecture: Its Elements, History and Meaning* (Westview Press, 1993)

Ruskin, John *Seven Lamps of Architecture* (1857)

Rykwert, Joseph *The Seduction of Place* (Vintage, 2002)

Stern, AM, Gilmartin, G and Mellins, T 'Frontiers of Construction' *Architecture and Urbanism Between The Two World Wars* (New York, 1987)

Summerson, John *Georgian London* (Pelican Books, 1962)

Summerson, John *The Classical Language of Architecture* (Thames & Hudson, 1986)

Tavernor, Robert *Palladio and Palladianism* (Thames & Hudson, 1991)

Vickers, Graham *Key Moments in Architecture* (DeCapo Press, 1998)

Vitruvius *The Ten Books of Architecture* (Cambridge University Press)

Williams, Guy *Augustus Pugin versus Decimus Burton* (Cassell, 1990)

Woodward, Christopher *The Parthenon in Ruins* (Vintage, 2002)

Wright, Frank Lloyd *Genius and the Mobocracy* (Duell, Sloan & Pearce, 1949)

# Index

# Picture Credits